D1576080

18446

THE MYSTERY AND LORE OF MONSTERS

With accounts of some
Giants, Dwarfs and Prodigies

by

C. J. S. THOMPSON, M.B.E.

Corresponding Fellow of the Royal Academy of Medicine (Turin)
Hon. Curator Historical Section of the Museum of
Royal College of Surgeons of England

Stamington Library

BARNES
&NOBLE
BOOKS
NEW YORK

This edition published by Barnes & Noble, Inc.

1994 Barnes & Noble Books

ISBN 1-56619-503-9

Printed and bound in the United States of America

M 9 8 7 6 5 4 3 2 1

CONTENTS

PART I

CHAPTER I

MONSTERS IN TRADITION AND MYTHOLOGY   17

Monsters in tradition—Mythological monsters—Superstitions and beliefs concerning monsters—Legends of monstrous beings —The Arimaspi—The "Gryphons who guarded gold"—"The Anthropophagi and men whose heads do grow beneath their shoulders"—Egyptian monsters—Satyrs—Cyclopean people— The four-eyed man of Cricklade—Men with tails—Men with multiple tongues—Early beliefs in the origin of monsters

CHAPTER II

THE MONSTERS OF BABYLON FOUR THOUSAND YEARS AGO   25

The monsters of ancient Babylon—Monsters as auguries— Divination from monsters—The effect of haloes—Babylonian texts on monsters and their portent—Babylonian descriptions of monsters—Special auguries for Royal personages

CHAPTER III

MONSTERS IN THE EARLY CENTURIES   30

Monsters in Greek and Roman times—Monsters of the early Christian Era—Travellers' stories of monsters—Headless men —The "Biddenden Maids"—Their curious bequest

CHAPTER IV

MONSTERS OF THE SIXTEENTH CENTURY   37

Astronomical phenomena and monsters—The strange monster of Ravenna—Ambroise Paré on the cause of monsters— Parasitic monsters—A child with five horns—Curious monster in an egg—Twins joined by their heads—Female headless monster—A phenomenal prodigy—Three-headed monsters

CHAPTER V

MONSTERS DESCRIBED BY AMBROISE PARÉ IN THE SIXTEENTH CENTURY   49

Early works on monstrosities—Conrad Lycosthenes—A monster of "horrible aspect"—"The terrible child of Craconia"—

The Scottish Brothers—The "three-headed boy of Zarzara"—
"The Secrete Wonders of Nature"—"The Twynne maydes of
Verona"—"A monster from the Tyber"—Monster born in
England in 1552—Extraordinary monstrosities—Twins with
heads united—A headless child—The Swiss monster—A four-
armed monster—Men with six arms—The Hagbourne prodigy
—Man born with one leg

CHAPTER VI

SOME MONSTERS AND PRODIGIES OF THE SEVENTEENTH CENTURY   55

Lazarus-Joannes Baptista Colloredo—James Poro—Man with
a head in his chest—John Valerius—A woman who laid eggs—
A negro with "a twin in his breast"—The monster of Ratisbon
—"A horrible monster"—Horned women

CHAPTER VII

SOME CURIOUS MONSTERS AND PRODIGIES AND THEIR BILLS   63

The "Wonderful child from Austria"—A "Wonder of the
world"—The Dutch twins—Prince Giolo—The man with two
bodies—A strange child with two heads—The High German
woman with no hands and feet—"The eighth great wonder of
the world"—The "child with a bear on his back"—A woman
with two heads, one above the other—The boy with DEUS
MEUS in his eyes

CHAPTER VIII

EXTRAORDINARY MONSTERS AND PRODIGIES   70

Classification and scientific study of monstrosities—The
Hungarian Sisters, Helen-Judith—The monster of Gosmore—
A strange story of a man with two faces, "beautiful girl yet
hideous as a devil"—William Kingston—John Kleyser—
Miss Sarah Biffin—Miss Horton—Marc Cazotte—Extra-
ordinary case of twins joined by their heads

CHAPTER IX

SOME CELEBRATED CONJOINED-TWINS   79

Conjoined-twins—The Siamese Twins—Their visit to London
—Distinct individualities—The "Sassari sisters"—The "Tocci,
brothers"—The Heteradelph

CONTENTS

CHAPTER X

PAGE

THE "TWO-HEADED NIGHTINGALE" AND OTHER NOTABLE TWINS 88

Woman with four legs—Blanche Dumas—The North Carolina twins, Millie-Christine, the "Two-headed Nightingale"—The "Bohemian twins": Rosa-Josepha Blazek—Marie-Rosa Drouin —The "Orissa sisters", Radica-Doadica—Rosalina-Maria— The Brighton twins—The Gibb sisters—The conjoined-twins of Pimlico—Elsie and Marie—Laloo, the Hindu with headless parasitic body

CHAPTER XI

"OF CRAFTY TRICKS AND COZENAGE" 96

Of crafty tricks and cozenage—Fraudulent rogues—The crafty beggar of Anjou—Feigning malformations in the sixteenth century—The wiles of the cozener—The Chinese beggar of Shanghai—An ingenious trickster

CHAPTER XII

WILD MEN OF THE WOODS AND SOME "HORRIBLE MONSTROUS BEASTS" 99

Wild men of the woods and some "horrible monstrous beasts" —A "Horrible Monster"—The Martichora—A man-tiger— The "cruel Unicorn"—A "horrible serpent with seven heads" —A "terrible wild monster killed in Palestine"

CHAPTER XIII

MONSTERS OF THE DEEP 106

Monsters of the deep—The Monk fish—The Bishop fish—A monster sea lion—Mermen and mermaids—A mermaid tamed —The Negro fish—A mermaid comes to London—Great sea-serpents—Monster serpent seen in 1848—A sea monster seen in 1917

CHAPTER XIV

MONSTERS IN ART 119

CHAPTER XV

THE PSYCHOLOGY OF MONSTERS—THE LAW OF MONSTERS 123

PART II

GIANTS, DWARFS AND PRODIGIES

CHAPTER XVI

GIANTS IN MYTHOLOGY—GIANTS IN ANCIENT TIMES   PAGE 129

Giants in mythology—The Gigantes—Polyphemus—Gigantic figures in Egypt and Assyria—Giants of the Bible—Goliath—Giants in ancient Rome—The bones of giants

CHAPTER XVII

GIANTS IN LEGEND AND STORY   134

Gigantic figures in processions—Gog and Magog and their story—Mock-giants on London Bridge—Giants in London pageants—The mock-giants of Chester—Mock-giants in Italy and Spain—Giants in castles—The giants of old stories—Jack the Giant-killer—King Arthur slays a giant—Cornish giants and their stories—Irish giant lore—The story of Fingall—Grana the giantess—"The giant of the Golden vest"

CHAPTER XVIII

GIANTS IN THE SIXTEENTH CENTURY—"THE CHILDE OF HALE"   141

John Middleton, "The Childe of Hale"—A French giant—A Dutch giant and dwarf—The giants of the Tower of London—Queen Elizabeth's giant porter—Walter Parsons, the giant porter of King James I—William Evans, giant porter of King Charles I—Daniel, giant porter of Oliver Cromwell—Anthony Payne, a notable Cornish giant and soldier—A congress of giants and dwarfs

CHAPTER XIX

SOME GIANTS OF THE SEVENTEENTH CENTURY   149

"The monstrous Tartar"—An Irish giantess—"The Living Colossus"—The Saxon giant—"The Miracle of Nature"—A great German giant and his wife—Pepys visits the Dutch giant and "the great Tall woman"—Edward Malone, an Irish giant—"The Indian king"—William Joyce—Some strong men and women

CONTENTS

CHAPTER XX

GIANTS IN THE EIGHTEENTH CENTURY

PAGE
156

The amiability of giants—"The tall Briton"—The King of Prussia and his giant guards—Giant soldiers—Henry Blacker, the Sussex giant—Cajanus, the Swedish giant—A giant on the tight-rope—The "Young Colossus"—Bernardo Gigli, the Italian giant

CHAPTER XXI

SOME FAMOUS IRISH GIANTS OF THE EIGHTEENTH CENTURY   163

Famous Irish giants of the eighteenth century—Cornelius MacGrath—Charles Byrne (O'Brien) Irish giant—How John Hunter obtained his skeleton—Patrick Cotter (O'Brien), Irish giant—Stories of the Irish giants

CHAPTER XXII

SOME GIANTS OF THE NINETEENTH CENTURY   176

"Big Sam"—Chang, the Chinese giant—William Bradley, the Yorkshire giant—Louis Frenz, the French giant—"The long lawyer"—The romance of a giant and giantess—Freeman, the American giant—Murphy, an Irish giant—James Brice, a French giant—The Countess Lodoiska, a Polish giantess—A giant's wedding—Miss Marian, the "Queen of the Amazons"—Jim Tarber, a giant of Texas—Gigantic families

CHAPTER XXIII

EARLY TRADITIONS CONCERNING DWARFS AND PYGMIES   185

Traditions concerning dwarfs and pygmies—Dwarfs "made by the devil"—Dwarfs in Roman times—Dwarf-pets of Emperors—Dwarfs painted by great artists—King Charles IX and his dwarfs—Catherine de' Medici and her dwarfs—Dwarfs at the Russian Court—Dwarfs in the service of nobles—Dwarfs in Turkish Palaces—Tycho Brahe and his dwarf "Zep"

CHAPTER XXIV

DWARFS AT THE ENGLISH COURTS   191

Queen Mary's dwarf, John Jervis—Richard Gibson and Anne Shepherd at the Court of King Charles I—Jeffrey Hudson,

dwarf-page to the King—A dwarf as diplomatist—The dwarf
Bertholde, a king's Prime Minister—Stories of Bertholde and
his will

CHAPTER XXV

SOME DWARFS AND PRODIGIES OF THE SEVENTEENTH CENTURY   199

John Worrenburg, a Swiss dwarf—"The little black prince
and his little horse"—John Grimes—"The Dwarf of the
world"—"The little Scotchman"—A remarkable dwarf—
Barbara Urselin, the "Hairy woman"—John Evelyn's account
of Barbara—Pepys' visit to the "Hairy woman"—"The bold
grimace Spaniard"—"A monstrous female creature"—"The
Suffolk boy with bristles"—"The Changling Child"—"The
little Farey woman"—"Short Jannette and Tall Jacob of
Sneek"—A surprising Persian dwarf—"The little wild man"

CHAPTER XXVI

REMARKABLE DWARFS AND PRODIGIES OF THE EIGHTEENTH
    CENTURY   109

Matthew Buchinger and his accomplishments—Owen Farrell,
a dwarf of strength—John Coan, the Norfolk dwarf—The last
dwarf at an English Court

CHAPTER XXVII

THE "COUNT" BORUWLASKI AND OTHER COURT DWARFS   215

Joseph Boruwlaski, the celebrated Polish dwarf—Boruwlaski
at Court—His travels with the Countess Humiecka—
Boruwlaski and King George IV—His introduction to the
Irish giant—A dwarf's romance—Boruwlaski in England—
Nicholas Feny (Bébé), dwarf of King Stanislaus—The
Skinners and their family—Thomas Allen and "Lady
Morgan, the Windsor Fairy"—A dwarfs' club—"The Corsican
Fairy"

CHAPTER XXVIII

SOME ECCENTRIC AND MUSICAL DWARFS   225

Simon Paap, the Dutch dwarf—Wybrand Lolkes—David
Ritchie and "The Black Dwarf"—He is visited by Sir Walter
Scott—Nannette Stocker and John Hauptman, the musical
dwarfs—Caroline Crachami, the Sicilian dwarf—Leach, the
"Wonderful youth"

CONTENTS

CHAPTER XXIX

PAGE

"General Tom Thumb" and his Career—"Admiral van Tromp" 233

Charles S. Stratton ("General Tom Thumb")—Tom Thumb received by Queen Victoria—Tom Thumb and the Duke of Wellington—Tom Thumb at Windsor Castle—His carriage and pair—His travels in France and Spain—Tom Thumb plays at the Lyceum—Tom Thumb, Commodore Nutt and the Warrens—Jan Hannema ("Admiral van Tromp")—"The Aztecs"—Richebourg, the last dwarf at the French Court

CHAPTER XXX

Dwarfs at Bartholomew Fair. A Curious Gathering 241

Dwarfs at Bartholomew Fair in 1825—Barnum and his Museum—A curious gathering—"General" and Mrs. Small—The Lilliputians—Princess Topaze

Bibliography 245

Index 251

PART I

HUMAN MONSTERS

Conrad von Megenberg, 1499

CHAPTER I

MONSTERS IN TRADITION AND MYTHOLOGY

FROM the earliest period of the world's history abnormal creatures or monstrosities, both human and animal, have existed from time to time and excited the wonder of mankind.

They play a part in traditions and legends of great antiquity that have survived among people of all types of culture, and the stories that clustered round them, are common to civilized and uncivilized races throughout the globe.

They are introduced and described in many of the early mythologies and sometimes represented in artistic forms in primitive sculpture. The births of such creatures were regarded by some nations as presaging disasters and calamities or interpreted as divinations, while by others they were considered as indicative of Divine wrath, a belief that survived in Europe until the end of the sixteenth century.

Extraordinary creatures of human and animal form enter into many of the mythological fables, and monsters possessing two or more heads and beings of gigantic stature, figure in the stories and fairy-tales of nearly every country.

There is little doubt that imagination was responsible for many of the monstrosities attributed to mankind in the early traditions, as there appears to have been a constant tendency to visualize these creatures of belief as human or superhuman, where gigantic strength, wisdom or productiveness was concerned.

Man often represented these to himself by forming images of the beings who possessed them, with multiple or enormous heads, limbs and colossal bodies. On the other hand, it is possible that some of the monstrosities had actual existence. The sight of such strange phenomena would doubtless excite wonder and awe in the minds of those who had seen them, and so the accounts of their existence would be spread far and wide. The superstitions and beliefs that have gathered round monstrous beings arc common to people of various races in the east and west, and it is evident they exercised a profound influence on the mind of man.

The general idea that the birth of monsters, human or animal, portended evil probably arose from the same belief that other physical phenomena, such as comets or meteors, were the precursors of terrible events and disasters. Thus, in the second book of Esdras, included in the Apocrypha,[1] concerning wonders that will happen as signs of the times to come, it is stated: "The sea shall cast out fish and make a noise in the night. There shall be a confusion also in many places and the fire shall be oft sent out again; and the wild beasts shall change their places and *women shall bring forth monsters.*"

Many barbaric races have their legends of monstrous animals, as instanced in the Bun-yip of Australian tribes, which is believed to be a savage water-monster who carries off women, while the dragons of New Guinea are said to swallow youths at initiation. Sometimes, certain distant tribes are believed by others to possess monstrous or abnormal features, and accounts are related of people with only one eye or more than two, others with eyes in their breasts, with enormous ears, with two or more heads or without heads at all. It is quite probable that these stories had some foundation in fact, and that actual human monsters had been seen during the distant travelling of tribes.

Monstrosity of feature is represented in the masks worn on ceremonial occasions by several African tribes and by native races in the islands of the South Seas.

The people of Jabah (Java) were supposed by the Arabs to have heads in their breasts and such monsters are frequently depicted in early Persian manuscripts. Herodotus describes some people who were supposed to live beyond the region inhabited by the Scythians as having goat's feet and some of the men had but one eye, while other tribes were believed by the Libyans to consist of monsters with heads like dogs, or to be headless and with eyes in their breasts. Pliny relates the old tradition that among the

[1] 2 Esdras, chap. v. vers. 7–8.

Scythians inhabiting the country beyond Palus Moeotis, there was a tribe of one-eyed men, and states: "They are called the Arimaspi, a nation remarkable for having but one eye and that placed in the middle of the forehead." These people were supposed to carry on perpetual warfare with the gryphons, who were monsters with wings who guarded the gold that was dug out of the mines.

Milton thus alludes to this legend in *Paradise Lost*:

> "As when a Gryphon through the wilderness
> With winged course, o'er hill or mossy dale,
> Pursues the Arimaspian, who, by stealth,
> Had from his wakeful custody purloin'd
> The guarded gold."
>
> *Book 2.*

The story of the gryphons was probably invented by the gold-seekers in order to deter others from coming near them and interfering with their rich possession, as we find in the legend associated with the cinnamon-trees in Arabia, which were supposed to be guarded by terrible winged snakes and venomous reptiles.

The ancient traditions concerning the Anthropophagi, the headless people with eyes in their breasts, is repeated by Sir John Mandeville, who alludes to the "Iyle where dwell men that have no heads and theyr eyen are in thyr shoulders and theyr mouth is on theyr breaste", and in another isle, he says, are "men that have no head, no eyen and their mouth is in theyr shoulders".

Centuries afterwards, adventurers to the Spanish Main returned with tales of devil-haunted islands peopled with headless men whose eyes were set in their chests.

It was the Anthropophagi, according to Isogonus of Nicaea, who used human skulls as drinking-cups and placed the hairy scalps on their breasts.

Shakespeare thus alludes to them in *Othello*:

> "The Anthropophagi and men whose heads
> Do grow beneath their shoulders."
>
> ACT I, SC. 3.

India and Ethiopia were especially associated with stories of monstrosities, one of which tells of a race of people who were eight feet in height, and of others who had their feet turned backwards, with eight toes on each foot.

Indian art delighted to represent certain deities with many heads and numerous arms, and in Tibet we find both demons and gods often depicted with hideous and monstrous forms.

In ancient Egypt, monstrous creatures were frequently figured on tombs, and the god Ptah-Seker-Asar is represented

MONSTERS FOUND IN GUINANA
Beschryvinge, 1563

as a dwarf, while Bes, another deity, is exemplified as a misshapen and repulsive creature.

Gigantic and monstrous forms were given to the supernatural enemies of the deities, such as those whom Rā was supposed to conquer daily. The Babylonians and Assyrians had representations of monsters in their winged-bulls or lions with human heads, which were often placed at the entrances of buildings to frighten away the spirits of evil. The ancient Maya people of South America probably had their traditions of headless men, judging from a clay figure in the British Museum representing a man with a face in his breast.

Ctesias tells us of a race of people who lived on the

mountains, who had the heads of dogs and who clothed themselves in skins. "They bark instead of speaking, have claws and live by hunting and catching birds." He states also, "in the country called Catharcludi in the mountains of Eastern India, there dwelt the Satyr, an animal of extraordinary swiftness, who had human features and would sometimes run on four feet or walk erect on two".

The tradition concerning the Cyclops is of great antiquity and from an early period there was a belief that certain tribes existed in Scythia, Ethiopia and India, the people of which had but one eye planted in the middle of their foreheads.

Aulus Gellius says that he learned this from very ancient writers, that there was a certain nation who have but one eye in the middle of their foreheads which are called Arimaspi, as stated also by Pliny.

That Cyclopian people or individuals with one eye in the centre of their foreheads were not entirely mythical, we know from the fact that there have been living instances of this phenomenon, although they are rare. Valentini mentions the case of an infant born with one eye in this position in 1884, and Blok records another instance of a new-born child having but one eye and an extremely small mouth, in 1894.

Of people with multiple eyes, the most famous example is that of the "Four-eyed man of Cricklade", of whom Drury gives an account after paying a visit to him.

"So wondrous a thing," he says, "such a *lusus naturae,* such a scorn and spite of nature, I have never seen. This unfortunate had four eyes, placed in pairs, one eye above the other and all four of a dull brown, encircled with red, the pupils enormously large. The vision in each organ appeared to be perfect. He could shut any particular eye, the other three remaining open, or, indeed, as many as he chose, each several eye seeming to be controlled by his will and acting independently of the remainder.

"He could also revolve each eye separately in its orbit, looking backward with one and forward with another, upward with one and downward with another simultaneously.

"He was of a savage, malignant disposition, delighting in ugly tricks, teasing children, torturing helpless animals, uttering profane and blasphemous words and acting altogether like the monster, mental and physical, that he was. He could play the fiddle, though a silly sort, having his notes on the left side, while closing the right pair of eyes. He also sang, but in a rough, screeching voice, not to be listened to without disgust."

A case was reported in 1895 that excited considerable interest at the time, of a child that had been born with its eyes on the top of its head, but further details were not recorded.

The tradition of the existence of a race of people with tails is common in several parts of the world and has persisted for centuries. Both Ptolemy and Ctesias relate stories of tailed-men, and Pliny mentions men of Ceylon who had "long hair tails and were of remarkable swiftness of foot".

Marco Polo states that in the kingdom of Lambri (Sumatra) "there are men with tails; these tails are of a palm in length and have no hair on them".

Aldrovandus, in the sixteenth century, figures a two-headed monster, which he states had "a tail a palme long which ended in a sharp spike", and in the seventeenth century, Dr. William Harvey tells us of "a certain chirurgion, an honest man, who returning from the East-Indies declared, that in the mountains and remote places from the sea of the Island of Borneo, at this day, there is a certain kind of tailed-men of which with some difficulty, for they inhabit the woods, they took a virgin whom he saw with a thick fleshy taile of a span long."

Bartholinus, Falk, Strauss and others describe people with tails, and Struys, a Dutch traveller in the seventeenth century, mentions that in Formosa, when he was there, a wild man was caught on the island who had a tail over a foot long which was covered with red hair like that of a cow.

In Europe, in 1690, one Emanuel König, the son of a

German doctor-of-laws, was possessed of a tail half a span long.

According to an account in the *Lancet* in 1885, a tribe of tailed-Indians were discovered in Paraguay by a number of workmen belonging to Tacura Tuyu. While engaged in cutting grass, they had their mules attacked by some Guayacuyan Indians. The men pursued the attackers, but only succeeded in capturing a boy of eight.

He was taken to the house of Señor Francisco Galeochoa at Posedas and was there discovered to have a tail ten inches long. On interrogation the boy stated, that he had a brother who had a tail as long as his own and that all the tribe had tails.

The Papuans of New Guinea and Niam Niams of Central Africa are reputed to have tails from two to ten inches long, but it is well known to be a custom among many of these native tribes, to don artificial tails made of hairy skin or leaves on certain occasions, which probably accounts for these stories of natural appendages.

Nevertheless, there are many authenticated cases of people with a prolongation of the coccyx to the extent of several inches.

Mention is made in some of the early fables of people with multiple tongues, and Diodorus Siculus alludes to men with double tongues, "with which they could better perform the linguall offices than we do with one."

In the seventeenth century, Hildesius related the story of "the child of a certaine Nobleman who had a double tongue divided according to latitude", and of another, "who had eleven tongues, eleven mouths and two and twenty incomplete lips", but he concludes, "whether this multiplicity of tongues be a meere device of art, we do not know."

Many theories as to the origin and cause of monsters were advanced in ancient times; some attributed them to unnatural unions between different species of animals, common in folk-lore, while according to medieval theology such creatures were believed to be the outcome of the union of supernatural beings with humankind, an idea embodied in the belief concerning the origin of sylphs, fairies and other fantastic beings.

It is evident however from later records, that some of the traditionary monsters owed their origin to a basis of fact, and that actual abnormal or monstrous births may have assisted the formation of many of the old stories which persisted in early times.

CHAPTER II

THE MONSTERS OF BABYLON FOUR THOUSAND YEARS AGO

WE have abundant evidence from the official records of the ancient astrologers of Nineveh and Babylon, which are said to date back to the time of Sargon I, about 2800 B.C., of the importance attributed to monstrous births at that early period.

These interesting documents, in the form of clay tablets inscribed in cuneiform characters, once formed part of the library of Assur-bani-pal, King of Assyria, who flourished from 668 to 626 B.C. Nearly a hundred fragments of these have been recovered containing references to monsters, and the prophetic meanings attributed to them, many of which have been translated by Oppert, Lenormant and R. Campbell Thompson. They tend to show how frequent these monstrosities must have been at least four thousand years ago.

The development of astrology with the casting of horoscopes, led the practitioners of that ancient art to attach the utmost importance to the birth of anything abnormal, either in human beings or animals. The astrologer who could foretell prosperity and good fortune for the nation, and prognosticate disasters or calamities for their enemies, was a man whose words were regarded with reverence and awe. They were inscribed as treasures to be preserved for all time. Nothing was too great or too small to become the subject of an astrological forecast. Every event, from a national calamity, such as famine or disaster to the army, to the appearance of the humblest peasant's last-born child, was seriously considered and proved to be the result of causes which had already been duly recognized.

It was believed that the heavenly bodies influenced the life and destiny of every living thing, so all monstrosities exhibited by new-born infants, were regarded as the result of certain astral positions at the time of birth.

The observation of such abnormalities was taken to be a reflection of the heavens, on which depended all terrestrial things, and from them could be foretold the future with as much certainty as from the planets and stars.

Divination was practised by the Babylonians in various ways, and omens and auguries for good or evil were drawn from the flight of birds, the appearance of the liver, heart and intestines of animals offered as sacrificial victims; so it can be readily understood how monstrosities or malformations in infants or young animals came to be regarded in a similar manner.

Prognostications were even divined from haloes, as illustrated in the following text:

"When a halo surrounds the Moon and Regulus stands within, Women will bear male children."

An augury was also drawn from the birth of a hermaphrodite, as instanced in the text:

"When a hermaphrodite is born, the son of the palace will rule the land (or) the King will capture."

"The prognostics which the Babylonians claimed to draw from monstrous births, in man and animals," says Lenormant, "are worthy of forming a class by themselves," and this may be judged from the following selection taken from the translated texts:

"When a woman gives birth to an infant;—that has the ears of a lion; there will be a powerful King in the country.

"Whose right ear is small; the house of the man (in whose house the birth took place) will be destroyed.

"Whose right ear has a wound below;—and . . . of the man, the house will be destroyed.

"That has two ears on the right side and none on the left; the gods will bring about a stable reign, the country will flourish and it will be a land of repose.

"That has a bird's beak; the country will be peaceful.

"That has no mouth; the mistress of the house will die.

"Whose nostrils are absent; the country will be in affliction, and the house of the man will be ruined.

"That has no nose; affliction will seize upon the country and the master of the house will die.

"That has no right hand; the country will be convulsed by an earthquake.

"That has six toes on each foot; the people of the world will be injured.

"That has no well-marked sex; calamity and affliction will seize upon the land; the master of the house shall have no happiness.

"Whose right foot is absent; his house will be ruined, and there will be abundance in that of the neighbour.

"That has no feet; the canals of the country will be cut (intercepted) and the house ruined.

"That has the right foot in the form of a fish's tail; the booty of the country of the humble will not be . . .

"Whose foot hangs to the tendons of the body; there will be great prosperity in the land.

"That has three feet, two in their normal position (attached to the body) and the third between them; there will be great prosperity in the land.

"That wants the right heel; the country of the Master (King) will be destroyed.

"That has many white hairs on the head; the days of the King will be prolonged.

"That has much . . . on the head; joy shall go to meet the house.

"That has a head on the head; the good augury shall enter at its aspect into the house.

"That has some branches (excrescences) of flesh hanging on the head; there shall be ill-will, the house will perish.

"That has some formed fingers (horns) on the head; the days of the King will be less and the years lengthened (in the duration of his age).

"That has a . . . of a bird on the head; the master of the house shall not prosper.

"That has some teeth already cut; the days of the King will arrive at old age; the country will show itself powerful over strange lands, but the house where the infant is born will be ruined.

"That has on the head the mouth of an old man and that foams; there will be great prosperity in the land, the god B—— will give a magnificent harvest and abundance shall be in the land.

"That has on the head two long and thick ears; there will be tranquillity and the pacification of litigation.

"That has no tongue; the house of the man will be ruined."

The next group refer to monstrosities in animals and auguries to be drawn from them.

"When a sheep gives birth to a lion; the armies of the King shall be powerful and the King shall have no equal.

"If a sow brings forth a pig with eight legs and two tails; the power of the King will be increased.

"When a foetus has eight legs and two tails; the prince of the kingdom will seize power."

From these records it may be gathered that a considerable number of malformations were known to the Babylonians and Assyrians in ancient times, and many of these deformities can be identified with similar abnormalities that are known, from authentic accounts, to have occurred many centuries later.

In a tablet translated by Lenormant, relating to prodigies in royal accouchements it is recorded, that,

"If a Queen gives birth to . . . a male . . . royalty will be reduced to misery.

"To an androgyne (hermaphrodite); royalty will be thrown down.

"An infant whose teeth are already cut; the days of the King will be prolonged.

"Male twins; . . . this will be a good augury for the King.

"A son and daughter at the same time; . . . the land will be enlarged.

"An infant with the face of a lion; the King shall not have a rival.

"An infant with six fingers on the right hand; (the enemy) will oppress.

"An infant with six fingers on the left hand; the enemy will oppress.

"An infant with six toes on the right foot; the enemy will oppress.

"An infant who has six toes on both feet; (the right and the left) the King shall rule the enemies' country."

It is evident from this record that special auguries were drawn from births to Royal personages, and that twins were regarded as portending good-fortune to the King and his country.

It must be remembered, that the art of divining, as practised mainly by the astrologers and priests, was the general belief throughout the country, and from the King to the humblest of his subjects, their aid was sought in all affairs of importance, both to the State and the people.

The common desire to pierce the veil that concealed the future led them not only to consult the stars, but also to draw auguries from dreams, the rustle of the trees, the murmur of streams, the form of lightning, the shapes assumed by flames and smoke and the placid surface of the lakes.

It will be shown later, that these early records compare favourably with the accounts of monsters that have come down to us from writers of the sixteenth and seventeenth centuries, when similar superstitious beliefs still remained associated with the birth of abnormal creatures.

CHAPTER III

MONSTERS IN THE EARLY CENTURIES

THE curious beliefs that gathered round the occurrence of monsters in early times were common also among the ancient Greeks and Romans, and there is ample evidence of this in the mythological stories in which such impossible beings as centaurs, fauns with extremities like goats, and creatures with pectoral eyes, syrens, nereids, double-headed monsters and the other fearsome creatures that play a prominent part in many of their legends and traditions.

Long before the Christian era, Hippocrates, Empedocles and Democritus made several allusions in their writings to abnormal beings who probably existed in their times, while Pliny and Galen, in the second century A.D., give accounts of monsters said to have been seen on land and sea.

Still later, in early Christian and medieval art, we find demons and devils represented in the most sinister and horrible forms, some half-human or half-animal, with exaggerated features, tusks, horns and tails, and others with faces in the stomach, chest and knees.

These fantastic creatures are often represented in the books describing monsters down to the end of the seventeenth century, many of them being but repetitions, depicted with greater freedom of imagination, of those described in earlier times.

Authentic records of monstrous births, until the end of the eleventh century are but few, and only the barest details are given by ancient historians.

In the year 601, a boy with two heads is said to have been born in Rome, and Cicero mentions the birth of a double-headed girl.

Le Beau tells us that in the year 945, two male children were brought from Armenia to Constantinople for exhibition. They were well-formed in every respect and united at the abdomens. They excited great interest and curiosity, but they were removed by order of the authorities, as it was considered at the time that such abnormal creatures presaged evil.

It is stated, however, that at the beginning of the reign of Constantine VII, they returned to the city, after which one of them was taken ill and died. An effort was made to save the life of the other, but he died also three days afterwards.

The case of a child being born with two heads, two chests and four arms but with only a single leg, during the reign of Theodosius, is recorded by Sigbert. According to his account, "the emotions, affections and appetites of this creature were different".

"One head might be crying while the other laughed, or one eating while the other was sleeping. They quarrelled sometimes and occasionally came to blows. They are said to have lived two years, when one died four days before the other."

Roger of Wendover states, that in the year 1062, there existed in lesser Brittany and Normandy, a female monster, consisting of two women with separate bodies, fused into a single lower extremity.

About the year 1225, during the reign of Henry III, Bruchius records "that there was one living with two bodies knit together from the top of their heads to their navells, like two grafts in the trunke of a tree, having two heades, two mouthes, two noses, with their faces faire, well-formed and made in every point requisite in nature and from the navell downwardes, it had but the figure and shape of one only, that is to say, two legs, two thighs, and one nature. When one wept the other laughed, if the one talked, the other held her peace, as the one eat, the other drank. Living thus a long season till one of them died."

The stories related by early travellers like Sir John Mandeville, of a race of people without heads and with eyes in their breasts, is repeated by many historians.

Bulwer says: "St. Augustine makes commemoration of such a nation, and although he there doth not impose a necessity of believing the relations that are made of such kinds of men, he seems to grant, that it is not incredible. Nay, he testifies that he had seen them himself, for he assures us in these words, 'I was now Bishop of Hippo and with certain servants of Christ, I travelled to Aethiopia to preach the Gospel of Christ unto them, and we saw there many men and women having no heads but grosse eyes fixed in their breasts, their other members like unto ours."

The most probable explanation of the story told by Augustine is, that when he was travelling in Aethiopia, he saw some natives of certain nomad tribes near the Nile, who allow their thick, bushy hair to grow until it almost conceals their faces, as they do to-day, and who decorate their chests with designs that might well be taken for eyes and other features.

The earliest record we have in England of conjoined human beings who actually lived, is that of the twin sisters Mary and Eliza Chulkhurst, commonly known as the "Biddenden Maids", who were born at the village of Biddenden, near Staplehurst in Kent, about the year 1100.

Their story is largely founded on popular tradition, but is substantiated to some extent, by the curious bequest which arose from it.

Their parents are believed to have been people in good circumstances in the village, although very little is known of them.

All records agree, that the sisters were joined together at the shoulders and hips, and the impression on the cakes and pictures on the old broadsides describing them, show this method of union and represent the bodies as quite separate beyond these points. They are depicted with four feet and two arms, the right and left respectively, whilst the other arms, left and right, appear to be fused together at the shoulders according to one illustration and a little above the elbow in another.

This mode of union is very unusual in such phenomena, but, as Professor A. R. Simpson suggests, the maids had four separate arms and were in the habit of going about with their contiguous arms round each other's necks,

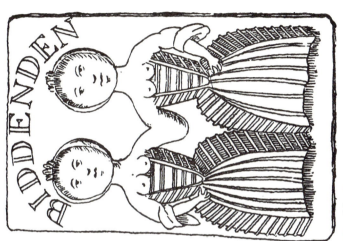

The Biddenden Maids

1. FROM THE IMPRESSION ON THE CAKES   2. FROM A DRAWING BY DUCARELS

which might well give rise to the idea that these limbs were united.

It has been urged, that the date given for the birth of the "Biddenden Maids" is so early as to throw some doubt upon the reality of the occurrence, but it is interesting to recall that in the same year, William Rufus was found dead in the New Forest with the arrow, either of a hunter or assassin, in his breast. The birth of such a monster at the time would have been undoubtedly regarded as of evil-omen and presaging some tragic event.

According to the Anglo-Saxon Chronicle, several prodigies preceded the death of the King, and it is recorded that "at Pentecost, blood was observed gushing from the earth at a certain town of Berkshire even as many asserted who declared that they had seen it. And after this, on the morning of Lammas Day, King William was shot dead." It is possible, therefore, that the date of the birth of the twins may be correct.

Lycosthenes, writing in 1557, mentions, that in the year 1112, "joined-twins were born in England". This statement does not necessarily refer to the "Biddenden Maids", but there is no other record of such a birth having taken place in this country.

The twins are said to have lived to the age of thirty-four years, and when one of them died in 1134, it was proposed to separate them, but the other who remained alive refused, saying: "As we came together, we will also go together, and after about six hours she died also."

They were buried in their native village, and in the church, a stone marked with a diagonal line and situated near the rector's pew, is shown as the place of their interment.

One of the most interesting facts connected with the "Biddenden Maids", however, is the curious bequest they made to their native village, which has ever since kept their memory alive.

They bequeathed to "the church-wardens of the parish of Biddenden and their successors, twenty acres of land, the annual revenue from which was to be spent in the distribution of cakes bearing the impression of their images, to be given away on each Easter Sunday to all strangers in Biddenden, and also 270 quartern loaves, with cheese in proportion, to all the poor in the said parish".

A writer in 1875 states, that "the cost of the Biddenden Maids' cakes with bread and cheese, is defrayed from the proceeds of the twenty acres of land, which yield thirty-five pounds, and is known as the 'Bread and Cheese lands' ".

The cakes, which are simply made of flour and water, are four inches long by two inches wide, and are now much sought after as curiosities. They are given away at the discretion of the churchwardens and are made about three hundred at a time. The bread and cheese, which now amounts to 540 quartern loaves and 470 pounds of cheese, is distributed on land belonging to the charity known as the Old Poorhouse. Formerly, it used to take place in the church immediately after the service in the afternoon, but in consequence of the unseemly disturbances which used to ensue, the practice was discontinued some time ago.

The impressions of the Maids on the present cakes are of a primitive character, and are made by boxwood dies that were cut in 1814. They bear the date of 1100, when Eliza and Mary Chulkhurst are said to have been born, and also their ages at the time of their death.

Hasted, the historian of the county of Kent, appears to cast some doubt on the authenticity of the bequest, and in his work published in 1798, says: "The twenty acres of land called the 'Bread and Cheese land', lying in five pieces, were given by persons unknown, the yearly rents to be distributed among the poor of this parish.

"This is yearly done on Easter Sunday in the afternoon, in 600 cakes, each of which has the figures of two women impressed on them and are given to all such as attend the church, and 270 loaves weighing three and a half pounds a piece, to which latter is added one and a half pounds of cheese, are given to the parishioners only at the same time.

"There is a vulgar tradition in these parts, that the figures on the cakes represent the donors of this gift, being two women, twins, who were joined together in their bodies and lived together so, till they were between twenty and thirty years of age. But this seems to be without foundation. The truth seems to be that it was the gift of two maidens, of the name of Preston, and that the print of the women on the cakes has taken place only within these fifty years, and was made to represent two poor widows as the general objects of a charitable benefaction."

But in spite of Hasted's statement, the popular story of the "Biddenden Maids" is still held by many to be the true one, and while the bequest lasts, they are not likely to be forgotten.

In the broadsides describing them, which have been printed from time to time, the Maids are represented as clad in the costume of the time of Queen Mary, with open bodices, vandycked ruffs and sleeves slashed at the shoulders, and wearing caps.

There have been many examples since of similar conjoined-twins and of the authentic cases on scientific record, ten have been girls, who lived for a number of years, but none of the females are said to have reached the age of the "Biddenden Maids", who, besides being an instance of a rare type, are interesting as occurring at a very early period of our history.

CHAPTER IV

MONSTERS OF THE SIXTEENTH CENTURY

EARLY in the sixteenth century, several works describing monsters and prodigies were printed, some of which were embellished with curious woodcuts supposed to represent many of these abnormal creatures of extraordinary shape and form.

Among the more important are the works of Julius Obsequens in 1508, Conrad Lycosthenes in 1557, and of Licetus, Schenk, Aldrovandus and Ambroise Paré in the sixteenth and seventeenth centuries.

Paré, the famous French surgeon, gives descriptions with illustrations of many of the monstrosities seen in his time, and he was the first to attempt their classification.

Lycosthenes, the author of one of the most interesting of these books, which is entitled *Prodigiorum ac ostentorum chronicon*, was a German philosopher, who was born in Alsace in 1518 and died in Basle in 1557. His real name was Conrad Wolffhart and his complete work, which was printed in Basle in 1557, is illustrated with 1,500 woodcuts of an extraordinary character, made by artists of the German School of that period.

The book consists of a chronology of remarkable events, together with accounts of monsters and prodigies, dating from early times.

Among the descriptions of monsters, he tells us of a man with four eyes, who is said to have been seen in Ethiopia, and another with a long neck like a horse, found in Scythia. He describes, "a great scaly monster with a donkey's head, which is said to have been brought to Rome in 1496, to be shown to Maximilian, and which was also seen by Sebastian Brandt".

Another extraordinary creature he depicts is a monster with an elephant's head, of "horrible aspect, with other heads all over its body, having webbed feet, a long forked-tail and eyes projecting from its stomach". He states, "this was described by Casper Pancer" and was "a precursor of great disturbances and wars".

He mentions two double-headed monsters, who are said to have lived in Bavaria in 1541 and reached the age of twenty years, also a wonderful sea-monster, which had

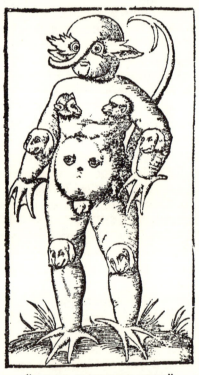

"MONSTER OF HORRIBLE ASPECT"
Lycosthenes, 1557

"a negroe's face and head, which was caught in the sea of Balthico in 1549".

The most marvellous of all, however, appears to have been the "Terrible child", who was "born in Craconia of noble parents, who was indeed most terrible to behold. It had bright fiery eyes, the mouth and nostrils like an oxes.

It had long hornes and a black hairy fur like a doggs, and on its breasts, faces like apes.

"It further had the heads of doggs on both elbows, looking backwards, and at the whirl-bones of each knee, looking forwards.

"It was splay-footed and splay-handed. The feet were like swan's feet and it had a tayle twined upwards, that was crooked backwards about half an ell long.

"It was born and lived four hours, and then spake thus:

" 'Watch, the Lord our God comes!' "

The author naïvely adds, as if fearful that his imagination had carried him too far: "But these are things related onely upon the credit of some particular writer and may, like Popish traditions, be or not be believed."

It is characteristic of this period that monsters, dwarfs, giants and other abnormal beings, came to be patronized, instead of being shunned by monarchs and other notabilities. They were often received at the various Courts of Europe and favoured by the reigning kings and princes.

We have an instance of this in the story of the "Scottish Brothers", who attracted considerable interest in the early part of the sixteenth century, and were brought to the Court of King James IV of Scotland.

They are said to have been born near Glasgow about 1490, and were brought to the notice of the king when he was about eighteen years old. They are mentioned by Buchanan, Drummond, Lindsay and other Scottish historians.

Buchanan says: "About this time (1490) a strange kind of monster was born in Scotland. In the lower part of the body it resembled a male child, differing nothing from the ordinary shape of the human body, but the trunk, and all other members, became double and were distinct both in their use and appearance.

"The king caused it to be carefully brought up and educated; particularly in music, in which it wonderfully excelled.

"It learned different languages, and in their various

inclinations the two bodies appeared to disagree between themselves, sometimes disputing, each preferring different objects and sometimes consulting for the common pleasure of both."

Aikman tells us, that "their faces looked one way. Sitting, they seemed two men, to such who saw not the parts beneath, and standing, it could not be discerned to which of the two bulks above the thighs and legs did appertain."

Lindsay states, that "they learned to sing and to play instruments of music, singing two parts, treble and tenor. They knew Latin, French, Italian, Spanish, Dutch, Danish and Irish."

Drummond remarks how much they differed in opinion, and their "disposals to chide others for disorders in their behaviour and actions".

From another description of the brothers, it appears that they were joined in the upper part of the body, and had four arms and two legs. They would carry on animated conversations with each other and curious debates, on which they sometimes disagreed, and occasionally came to blows.

They lived to the age of twenty-eight years, surviving their royal patron, and died during the regency of John, Duke of Albany. One brother is said to have died before the other, and the survivor only remained alive a few days afterwards, when he also succumbed. This is all that is known of the "Scottish Brothers", who must have been highly intelligent and accomplished, and who owed their fame to the patronage of King James IV of Scotland.

Twins joined by a fusion of the cranial bones are rare, but Geoffroy St. Hilaire records the birth of two girls in 1495, whose heads were thus united while their bodies remained separate. Each child was normal in every respect, but owing to being joined at their foreheads, when one walked forward, the other was compelled to walk backward. Their noses almost touched and their eyes were directed laterally. They lived to be ten years of age.

Bateman says, that in 1501 there was a similar example

of double female twins joined at the forehead, and mentions that in 1855, at a Foundling Hospital in St. Petersburg, there was another case of the same kind then living; the twins, who were also girls, being joined at the heads. They were so united that the nose of one, if prolonged, would strike the ear of the other. Through extra mobility of their necks, they could really lie in a straight line, one sleeping on her side and the other on the back. They had perfectly independent existences.

Bulwer, in his *Artificial Changeling*, states, that at Wittenberg, in 1525, an infant was born without a head, and in Misnia, in 1554, another child was born without a head, "the effigies of the eyes expressed in his breast".

In November 1562, at Villafranca in Vasconia, there is record of the birth of another female child who was headless. Fontanus declares, that he saw it, and informed Johannes Altinus of the prodigy, who afterwards presented it to Ambroise Paré.

Ludovicus Coelius Rhodiginus is reported to have seen two strange monsters in Italy about 1540. One is thus described by Bruchius. He was born at Zarzara in Italy in 1540, and on the "19th day of March, worthie to be considered, for that time Italy was afflicted with the plague and civil wars.

"He had two fair heads, well-proportioned, and two faces joyned one to another and tyed upon the top of the neck, with a proportion marvellous in every way of those partes.

"He had his hair a little long and black, and between these two heads, he had a third head which exceedeth not the length of an ear. And for the rest of his body, it was well-made and proportioned in all things.

"After he had sojourned a certain time in this miserable world he died wherein, as he was made a present to one of the King of Spain's lieutenants governing in that country. He had two livers, two milts, but one heart."

The other monster seen by Rhodiginus was a two-headed woman, who is said to have lived many years. "At such a tyme", says the chronicler, "as Conrad Licosthenes came into the Duchy of Baviere in the year 1541, she was of the age of twenty-six years."

"These two heads", he writeth, "had desire in like to drink, to eat, to sleep, and to talke together, as also did all her other affections.

"Wherefor this mayde went from dore to dore searching for a living, to whom they gave more willingly for the noveltie of so strange a creature and so newe a spectacle."

There is record of a double-headed male monster living

MONSTERS SEEN BY RHODIGINUS
Boaistuau, 1576

in Switzerland in 1538, who at that time had reached the age of thirty.

"Each of the heads possessed a beard, and their two bodies were fused together at the umbilicus into a single lower extremity. They resembled one another in features and face, and were so joined that they could see each other. They had a single wife with whom they are said to have lived in harmony."

This monster was also seen by Rueff, who says, that

"both heads had the same appetite to meat, both sensible of one hunger and their voices were alike. They grew to the perfect stature of a man with his head and shoulders, only double."

Bulwer, who alludes to several curious monsters, states, that in 1552, "there was a masculine infant born with two heads, a double neck and with a body very well compact and agreeing with the other members". This is apparently the same monster that is mentioned by Lycosthenes, who states that in 1553, "in a certain village in Misnia called

MAN WITH TWO HEADS
Lycosthenes, 1557

Zichest, there was an infant born with two heads being absolute in all other members."

"But", continues Bulwer, "we must know above all things, that these apparitions that be contrarie to nature, happen not without the providence of Almighty God, but for the punishing and admonishing of men, these things by just judgment are often permitted, not but that man hath a great hand in these monstrosities.

"At the same day that the Venetians and Genuensians entered into a League, there was born in Italy a monster with four arms and four feet, endowed with but one head, which being baptized lived some time afterwards. Jacob Rueff the chirurgion declares that he saw it."

That the age of credulity and superstition had not passed in the middle of the seventeenth century, is shown by some further remarks of the same writer. He states: "These are hardly to be accounted monsters who have such multiplication of arms, because there are many natives who appear with such Brachiall Redundancy. It is recorded in the acts of Alexander the Great, that in India, there were men endowed with six arms and as many hands, who all their life incur no sickness, which was believed to be another species of men."

We learn also from Bulwer, that "there was a prodigy

TWO-HEADED MONSTER
Lycosthenes, 1557

WOMAN WITH FOUR HANDS
Lycosthenes, 1557

publicly to be seen (at this time, 1653). He was a young man born at Hagbourne within four miles of Abingdon, whose name is John Simons, who was born without arms, hands, thighs, or knees, not in height above three-quarters of an ell from head to foot, and yet from the waist upward, as proportionable a body as any ordinary man wanting his arms.

"He is about twenty years of age, he writeth with his mouth, he threads a needle with his mouth, he tyeth a knot upon thread or hair though it be never so small, with his mouth. He feedeth himself with spoon meat, he shuffles, cuts and deals a pack of cards with his mouth.

"An observing Divine, a friend of mine, told me, that he

saw in Cheapside but a few days before, a child that was born without arms and had two little hands which it could move, standing out of its shoulders. A poore woman had the child in her armes.

"Nature upon such occasions is, that her unsearchable industry as it with great wittinesse appeareth everywhere, yet more eminently in those bodies wherein as t'were unmindfull of her charge or business she hath frustrated

MONSTER TAKEN FROM THE TIBER
Fenton, 1569

of this or that member, which errour, as it were, with some shame-fac'dness she abundantly recompenceth by a munificent liberality."

In a curious book called *Certaine Secrete wonders of Nature*, printed in London in 1569, the author, E. Fenton, describes and depicts some very extraordinary creatures which are chiefly taken from an earlier work by Bruchius.

We give the quaint descriptions accompanying them in his own words.

In his account of conjoined female twins he says: "These maide twynnes, born in the yeare of grace 1475, are knyt together even from their shoulders to their haunches. They were engendered in Italy in the famous Citie of Verona. Their parents were poore and carried them through divers cities to get money of the people.

"In the year of grace 1453, another monster like unto this was brought forth at Rome wyth greate marvell to all the people of the tyme of Pope Alexander the Sixte, who, as Polidorus writeth, prognosticated the evils, hurts and

MONSTER BORN IN ENGLAND IN 1552
Boaistuau, 1576

miseries which should happen and come to passe in the tyme of that Bishoppe."

One of the most fantastic and wonderful creatures he describes, however, is a monster said to have been taken from the Tiber.

He tells us that "In the year 1496, was taken up out of the River Tyber, a monster having the tronke of the bodie of a man, the heade of an Asse, one hande and arme like to a man, and the other of the fashion of an elephante's foote. He also had one of his feete like the foote of an eagle and the other like the hoofe of an oxe. The rest of his bodie with skales.

"He had also growing out behind him, a heade olde and hairie, out of the which came another heade of the forme of a Dragon."

He thus describes another monster born with one leg:

"In the yeare 1548, was born a childe in Almayne which had his heade divided from his body. He had one legge onely, with a crevice or chink where his mouth should be and had no armes at all."

MONSTER SEEN IN 1555
Boaistuau, 1576

He further states that "in the yeare 1552, was born in England, a child whiche had two bodies, two heades and foure hands and yet had one belly. On one syde of the bodye came two perfect leggs and on the other but one, the same having one foote made like two, tyed the one against the other, with ten toes."

He next gives an account of an extraordinary monster that was born in 1554, which he says "had a great masse of flesh in place of a head, and where one of his ears should have been, came out an arme and a hand. He had upon his face writhen haires like to the Moostachoos of a cat. The other arme appeared out of one side.

"He had no form of bodie nor breast, saving a line along the ridge of his backe. There could not be discerned any figure or likenesse of either sex, nor joynts in his armes or leggs. The endes of his handes and feete were soft and somewhat hanging as appeareth by his portrait."

MONSTER SEEN IN 1554
Fenton, 1569

He tells us also of a monster that was born in the year 1555, that had "Two faces, in sorte as the poets sayned the god Janus hadde. He hadde lyke two great pocketts hanging upon his backe. He was one side a male and the other a female."

It is evident that the artist who illustrated this book had a vivid imagination, and drew his portraits from the quaint descriptions given by the author.

CHAPTER V

MONSTERS DESCRIBED BY AMBROISE PARÉ
IN THE SIXTEENTH CENTURY

AMBROISE PARÉ, in his great work on *Chyrurgery*, printed in 1579, devotes a section to the study of monsters, and describes and figures several that came under his notice.

He was the first to attempt classification and thus distinguishes between monsters and prodigies. "We call monsters what things soever are brought forth contrary to the common degree and order of nature. So we term that infant monstrous which is born with one arm or with two heads. But we define prodigies, those things which happen contrary to the whole course of nature."

The belief that the birth of a monster foreshadowed evil and that disasters would follow, was still common in his time. It was also generally believed that certain phenomena of nature, such as an eclipse or the appearance of a comet, exercised an influence on monstrous births.

Thus, Rueff, in 1585, observes, that "in Sicily there happened a great eclipse of the sun and immediately many deformed and double-headed children were born".

Paré relates that "about the time that Pope Julius the second raised up all Italy and the greatest part of Christendom against Louis the twelfth, the King of France, in the year of our Lord 1512 (in which year, upon Easter Day, near Ravenna, was fought that mortal battle in which the Pope's forces were overthrown) a monster was born in Ravenna having a horn upon the crown of his head, and besides, two wings and one foot alone, most like to the feet of birds of prey and in the knee thereof an eye, the rest of the body like a man."

Monsters of this kind with two feet fused into one, were called syrens on account of their resemblance to the creatures of mythology. Several were recorded in ancient times and one is mentioned by Licetus.

With reference to the cause of monsters, Paré remarks:

"There are reckoned up many causes of monsters. The first whereof is the glory of God, that his immense power may be manifested to those who are ignorant of it by the sending of those things which happen contrary to nature; for thus our Saviour Christ answered the Disciples (asking whether he or his parents had offended, who being born blind received his sight from him) that neither he nor his parents had committed any fault so great, but this to have

MAN WITH PARASITIC BODY, SEEN IN 1530
Boaistuau, 1576

happened onely that the glory and Majesty of God should be divulged by that miracle and such great works."

"Another cause is, that God may either punish men's wickedness or show signs of punishment at hand."

He corroborates the story related by Lycosthenes, of the child born with two heads in Bavaria who was carried by her parents from door to door, and also mentioned the case of two girls who were born at Verona in 1475, "with their backs fastened together from the lower part of the shoulders".

There are several early records of monsters having one perfect body complete in every respect, but from it, in the neighbourhood of the navel, some important portion of a second body protruding. Paré describes one and Columbus another in the sixteenth century, while Schenk mentions thirteen examples, Aldrovandus three, and Buxtorf, Reichel and Anderson several others.

Thus Paré says, that in 1530, there was a man of about forty years of age to be seen in Paris who drew great crowds to see him, who carried an additional body without a head, which hung from him.

Bruchius also mentions this monster and says: "He bare the body betwixt his arms with great marvel to the world which hath assembled in great troupes to see him at Valence, and De Coras saw him in Paris." Of this man, Paré observes that, "The second body was perfect in all his members except his head which hanged forth as if he had been grafted there. He carried the other implanted or growing out of him, in his arms, with such admiration to the beholders, that many ran very earnestly to see him."

Paré also tells us, that "at Quiers, a small village some ten miles from Turin, in the year 1578, upon the 17th day of January, an honest matron brought forth a child having five horns, like ram's horns set opposite to one another upon his head. He had also a long piece of flesh, like in some sort to a French hood which women used to wear, hanging down from his forehead by the nape of his neck, almost the length of his back; two other pieces of flesh like the collar of a shirt were wrapped about his neck. The finger-ends of both his hands somewhat resembled a hawk's talons and his knees seemed to be in his hammes. It is said that he gave such a screech that all were so affrighted that they left the house and ran away.

"When the Duke of Saxony heard of it, he commanded it should be brought to him, which performed, one would hardly think what various censures the courtiers gave it."

Another curious monster that he figures, he states was found in the middle and innermost part of an egg. "It had the face of a man but hairs yielding a horrid representation of snakes, the chin had three other snakes stretched forth like a beard.

"It was first seen at Autun at the house of one Bancheron, a lawyer, by a maid breaking many eggs to butter. The white of this egg given to a cat presently killed her.

"Lastly, this monster coming to the hands of the Baron Senecy was brought to King Charles IX, he being then at Metz."

According to Paré, in the year 1546, there was a child

STRANGE MONSTER FOUND IN AN EGG
Paré, 1579

having two heads, two arms and four legs which was brought to him after death. "I dissected it," he states, "and found but one heart by which one may know it was but one infant."

He corroborates the statement that "Renatus Ciretis, the famous surgeon, sent him the Skeleton of twins conjoyned together with one head, in the year 1569".

Some of Paré's descriptions are delightfully quaint. He tells us that "in the village of Bristant, not far from Worms, in 1495, two girls were seen by Munster, perfect and entire in every part of their bodies, but they had their foreheads so joined together that they could not be parted. They lived together ten years, then one dying, it was needful to separate the living from the dead, but she did not long outlive her sister."

Also that in the year 1570, on the 20th of July, at Paris, in the Rue Gravilliers at the sign of the "Bell", two infants were born differing in sex, who were baptized in the Church of Saint-Nicholas-of-the-Fields, one being named Ludovicus and the other Ludovica. Their father was a mason; his

CONJOINED-TWINS
Paré, 1579

name was Peter German, his surname Petit Dieu (little god), his mother's name was Mattea Petronella.

Paré figures and describes another man who had a parasitic head projecting from the epigastric region, who was born in Germany in the year that King Francis I of France entered into league with the Swiss. "He lived to manhood and this lower and as it were inserted head, was nourished as much as the true and upper head." He mentions the headless female monster born in 1562 at Villa-franca, in Gascony, which was given to him by Dr. Altinus, and says, that "this physician gave it to me when

I went about this book, he having received it from Fontanus, the physician of Angolestre, who seriously affirmed he had seen it".

Finally, he gives an account of a remarkable prodigy who was to be seen in Paris in his time. He was a man about forty years of age, "who although he wanted his arms, notwithstanding did indifferently perform all those things which are usually done with the hands, for with the top of his shoulder, head and neck, he would strike an axe or hatchet with as sure and strong blow into a post, as any other man could do with his hands, and he would lash a

MAN WITH PARASITIC BODY
Lycosthenes, 1557

MAN WITH PARASITIC BODY
Lycosthenes, 1557

coachman's whip that he would make it give a great crack by the strong retraction of the air, but he ate, drank, played at cards and suchlike with his feet".

But he came to a sad end, for "at last he was taken for a thief and murderer, was hanged and fastened to a wheel".

Although monsters with three heads are mentioned by various writers of the sixteenth century and some even venture to describe them, few are well authenticated. The most curious example of this type is recorded by Galvagni, who describes a monster with two necks, on one of which was a single head of normal dimensions, and on the other neck, two distinct heads.

CHAPTER VI

SOME MONSTERS AND PRODIGIES OF THE
SEVENTEENTH CENTURY

DURING the seventeenth century more accurate and detailed descriptions of the monsters and prodigies who figured and became famous in that period are available, than of those in former times. One of these historical examples, who came to England in the time of Charles I, was an Italian who bore the names of Lazarus-Joannes Baptista Colloredo. He was born in Genoa in 1617.

He was seen and examined by the famous Thomas Bartholinus, who was professor of anatomy at Copenhagen, and in his *Historiarum Anatomicarum rariorum*, which was printed at Amsterdam in 1654, he has left us a full description of this strange and interesting creature.

"Twice", he says, "I saw with astonishment Lazarus Colloredo, a Genoese, aged about twenty-eight; first at Copenhagen and afterwards at Basle in Switzerland.

"This Lazarus had a small brother born with him, growing out of his breast and adhering to him, if my conjecture is right, by an union of the xiphoides or sword-shaped cartilage with the sternum.

"The little brother had but one, and that the left leg and foot, which hung down; he had two arms, but no more than three fingers on each hand. If pressure was made against his breast, he moved his hands, ears and lips. He received no food or nourishment but through the medium of the body of his greater brother Lazarus.

"As he slept, sweated and stirred, when his greater brother was awake and not in motion and without remarkable perspiration; their vital and animal parts seem to be distinct from each other. They had been both baptized, the greater one being named at the font Lazarus and the lesser John Baptist.

"The head of the little brother was well-formed and covered with hair but his eyes were closed, and his respiration but weak, for when I held a feather to his mouth and nostrils, they gave but little motion. His mouth was ever open and gaping, but I discovered no want of teeth, though no part of him seemed to increase in size except his head, which was much larger than that of his greater brother Lazarus, deformed and with long dangling hair.

"They both of them had beards; that of Lazarus was combed and kept clean, but that of the other neglected.

"Lazarus was of proper stature, comely in person, of morals, humane and courteous, with the polite accomplishments of a courtier.

"He concealed the body of his little brother and preserved it from injury by covering it with his own cloak, so that a stranger to his person would have no suspicion of the monster underneath.

"He was commonly in good spirits, though now and then a little dejected when thinking of his future fate, and as he presaged, the death of his brother."

Colloredo travelled all over Europe and in 1642 visited Scotland. He is credited with having married and with being the father of several children who are said to have been "fully and admirably developed". His portrait, engraved by Hollar and Marshall, represents him in the costume of a courtier of the Stuart period.

Another example of this parasitic type was James Poro, who was born at Genoa in 1686. The independent brother was baptized Matthew. He was brought to London in 1714, where he attracted the attention of Sir Hans Sloane, who commissioned his portrait to be painted.

There is also a record about this time of a West Indian negro slave who was bought by Sir Thomas Grantham and brought to London in the reign of James II. He had a twin brother projecting from his breast. He professed Christianity, and on being baptized claimed his liberty and got his freedom.

We owe several accounts of monsters and prodigies of this period to James Paris, or, as he describes himself, Paris du Plessis, who left a curious manuscript, now preserved in the

British Museum, illustrated with many portraits in colour. He appears to have been greatly interested in all phenomena of the kind, and gives accounts of those he saw personally, some of which are corroborated by other writers.

He mentions a monster, who he says was born a perfect man from head to foot, well-proportioned, from whose right side issued, a little above his hip, a body of a man from the middle upwards.

"Perfectly well-shaped, with hands, arms, and head very much like his brother. It was a male child as was supposed after he was come to the age of a man by its beard, which was of the same colour and thickness as his brother's.

"He could eat and drink with a good appetite. Had very good sight and *could speak as distinctly as his brother*.

"I, James Paris, asked him if he could feel whether he had thighs and leggs in his brother's body, but he said he felt none, nor his brother felt nothing of any motion in his body. Neither showed no signe of life. It had a good colour and two long locks of hair on its head of a black colour and a downy beard.

"It had teeth but we could not see if it had a tongue. Its brother, born sound in all respects, a perfect man of good sense and understanding. Healthy and Strong. Eat and drink very heartily.

"Spoke and writ several languages as Latin, French, Italian, High Dutch and pretty good English.

"He was born about 1678 near Ratisbon in Germany, and was seen by me James Paris in London in the year 1698 in the month of December."

He gives another account of a man with a head growing out of his body, who he says was "Tall and well-shaped. Below his chest came out of his body, a head and neck, with face perfectly shaped, with eyes, nose, mouth and chin, forehead and ears, all well-shaped and alive, but could not speak nor open its eyes, though he had two eyes and did appear that it was as flat as that of another man of the same age and bigness. The whole man held the other up with his right hand."

Among the prodigies he describes, is a boy without legs who is stated to have been born near Vienna about 1699.

"He was about fourteen years of age when I, James Paris, saw him on the 10th of March 1714. He was but one foot and a half high and instead of thighs and legs he had two breasts. He stands and walks and climbs and leaps from the ground upon a table and sits on a corner of it, but three-quarters of an inch broad. He jumps, dances and shows artfull tricks than any other person can do with thighs and legs. He speaks divers different languages as High Dutch, Low Dutch, Sclavonian, French and English.

"He has been seen with admiration and satisfaction by the Emperor and Empress of Germany, Prince Eugene of Savoy, all the Imperial Court as also by the Kings, Queens and Courts of Poland, Prussia, Sweden, Denmark and England." (See page 64.)

A similar prodigy, but a girl, who was named Johanna Megrines, he tells us was born in the County of Waterford in the town of Dungarvan on January 5, 1702. She was without arms or legs.

"She was very thin. Her father carried her upon his back a-begging, till she growing so big and fat, and her father growing old and feeble, could carry her no longer, so she was forced to drag herself upon a leather cushion fastened to her.

"She could dance, skip and lift, very nimbly. She could take up from the ground any piece of money, be it ever so small, also pins, needles and nails, with her stumps."

Another famous prodigy of the time was John Valerius, who was born in Germany in 1667, without hands or arms, and "shews such tricks with his feet that nobody can do with both arms, hands and feet".

Paris says: "He writes very finely with his mouth, right and left foot, without discerning which is the best, in five different languages, and cutts his own pens with his pen-knife. He walks upon his two great toes and stands upon one toe. He lays one foot on his neck and hops upon the other. He stands on the top of a little stool and reaches a glassful of liquor with his mouth from under it, without spilling a drop and drinks it.

"He threads a very fine small needle and sews very prettily, and all actions whatsoever done by others with hands he performs with his feet. He combs a perriwig very well and shaves, dresses and undresses himself.

"He fences with a single rapier and darts a sword with great strength in a deal board at a mark. He beats a drum, charges and fires a pistol or gun and any other fire arm, and shoots at a mark.

"Jumping and vaulting are his masterpieces. He has also several ingenious inventions of glasses. Nobody can do the like. It is impossible to express all he can do.

"He was seen by me, James Paris, the Twelfth of December in 1714."

Valerius came to England in 1698 and remained in London some years. His portrait, showing his different performances with his feet, was engraved and published by himself in Holland with inscriptions in Dutch.

There are several old fabulous stories of women who are said to have laid eggs, and Lycosthenes mentions one such case, but in 1639, there is record of an authenticated instance that, according to the testators, happened in Norway.

It is stated with all seriousness, that in the year 1639, a woman was delivered of two eggs at Sundby, one of which was sent to Olaus Worm the famous naturalist, with "an attestation signed by Ericus Westergard, Rotalph Rakestad and Thor Venes, coadjutors of the pastor in the parish of Niaess".

They certified, that upon "the 20th of May in that year, by the command of the Lord President in Remerige, the lord Paulus Tranius pastor in Niaess, we went to receive an account of the monstrous birth in Sundby by Anna, the daughter of Amundus and wife of Gudbrandas Erlandsonius.

"Upon the 7th day of April she began to grow ill and her neighbours came to her assistance. She brought forth an egg like to that of a hen which was broken by the women present. They found that in it the yolk and white answered directly to a common egg.

"Upon the 18th of April, about noon, she was delivered of another egg, which in figure was nothing different from the former.

"The mother reported this to us and the woman with her confirmed the truth of it.

"Dr. Olaus Worm, the ornament of the University, preserved the egg in his study to be seen of as many as please."

This story is reminiscent of the case of Mary Tofts, "the

WOMAN WHO LAID EGGS
Lycosthenes, 1557

rabbit-breeding woman", who deceived some of the leading physicians in the time of George II by her assertion that she had given birth to a number of living rabbits.

Another curious case of the birth of a monster, which is attested by several physicians and surgeons, is reported from Sluys. The account is given in a document signed and attested by "Doctors of Physick, Surgeons and Apothecaries dwelling in the town, who certify the same at the request of the Lord of Coppensdam and Bonem, Bailiff of the City and jurisdiction of Ardemburg". It states that in "1658, a soldier's wife gave birth at Weerted near Ardemburg to conjoined-twins. They had two heads and two necks and four arms, two whereof were behind clipping about the neck, the one handiest lying on the other. The two other arms hung across downward on each side of the body.

"The body upward was of double breadth, seeming to be that of a double breast and all the other parts were double, yet with the skin covered and lessening downward, appearing to unite at the navel, which was but single, and from thence downward of one body, but had two legs and one splay foot.

"One body was female, the face full and fair, but the other was misshapen, the eyes being where the mouth should be. It had no nose and a mouth under the chin.

"The monster died soon after birth and it was found to have two hearts, two lungs, and one great liver. In the mouth of the female body were found two firm teeth.

"This was attested on the third of December 1658 by

"John Moerman. Doctor of Medicine
"Francis de Raed. Doctor of Medicine
"Ippe Sixtus. Surgeon
"Joseph van der Heeden. Apothecary
"Cornelius de Coninck. Surgeon."

A note adds: "This monster lived but a few days and was anatomized by Mr. Louis de Bills of Ardemburg in the presence of the above."

An extraordinary monster was exhibited in London in 1674, which is described by a contemporary writer as follows:

"On the 25th of January last, one Jane Paterson, living at Dodington in the county of Northumberland, gave birth to a monster having the head, the maine, neck and forefeet exactly like a horse, all the rest of the body directly like a man.

"When born, it looked so dreadfull a manner, that all the women present were struck into such amazement and pannick, that they could not for a great while speak to one another, and were even ready to die with the terrour of it, till at length one of the stoutest of them, a little recovered her senses, and ran and fetcht the School-master of the town, who at first prospect was as much affrighted.

"How she came to have such a child it is impossible to imagine", adds the narrator, "but being *the wife of a jockey* 'tis somewhat the less wonder if she had fixed her thoughts upon a horse."

There are various accounts in the seventeenth century of men and women who are said to have developed horns.

In the Museum of Edinburgh University is preserved a crooked horn several inches long, which was cut from the head of a woman named Elizabeth Love in 1671. She is said to have been fifty years of age at the time and lived for twelve years after the operation.

Another instance of a horned-woman is that of Mary Davis of Great Saughall, near Chester, who when twenty-eight years of age commenced to develop two horns. "After four years she cast them, then grew two more, and about four years later cast these also."

The horns which were upon her head in 1668, were of four years' growth, and a portrait of her is still preserved in the Ashmolean Collection at Oxford.

Another case is thus reported in a newspaper of the eighteenth century: "A few days ago, Mr. Hall, a surgeon in Goswell Street, took a horn from the forepart of a woman's head being in shape and nature like a Ram's. It was about three inches long, which is thought to be as supernatural a production as has been seen."

CHAPTER VII

SOME CURIOUS MONSTERS AND PRODIGIES AND THEIR BILLS

Towards the latter part of the seventeenth century, London appears to have become the Mecca of every variety of monstrosity, from the abnormal in form to the prodigies without limbs who claimed to perform marvels of agility.

On their arrival most of them were first to be seen at their lodgings, but judging from their bills and broadsides, they eventually found their way to West Smithfield and formed part of the attractions of Bartholomew Fair.

Considerable information concerning these people is to be gained from their quaintly worded handbills, some of which are still extant. Such accounts, however, cannot always be regarded as being reliable, as it is probable that many of them were concocted to deceive the credulous, but there are others concerning which there is evidence to prove that their claims were genuine.

In the time of Queen Anne there was to be seen at the "Eagle and Child", a grocer's shop near Shoe Lane in Fleet Street, according to the bill, "A Wonderful Child from Austria who hath been seen by the Emperor and Empress of Germany and the whole Court, by several Kings, Princes and persons of the highest qualities.

"This child was born in Austria and is about fourteen years of age, hath in a manner but half a body, a foot and a half long.

"In the places where the thighs or leggs should be, it hath two breasts in all points like a woman's on which it walks. It climbs or gets from the ground upon a table and sits on a corner of it but three quarters of an inch broad, and shews more artful tricks to the general diversion, satisfaction and admiration of all spectators and speaks several languages."

"VIVAT REGINA"

This evidently refers to the Viennese boy who is described by James Paris in the previous chapter, whom he saw in London in 1714.

Another bill, which is headed "A Wonder of the World", states: "At the Hercules Pillars at Charing Cross is to be seen a girl that was found on a mountain in the West of

To all Gentlemen, Ladies, and other Lovers and Admirers of Curious Rarities, is now to be seen at the Eagle and Child a Grocers-shop next door to the Duke of Marlborough's Head, near Shoe-Lane in Fleet-street.

NOtice is hereby given, that here is arrived from *Hungary* a most wonderful young Man, which hath been seen by the *Emperour* and *Empress* of *Germany*, and their whole Court, by several others *Kings*, *Princes*, and Persons of the Highest Qualities to the Admiration and Satisfaction of all that ever have seen him; and is accounted One of the greatest Wonders of the World.

WONDERFUL CHILD FROM AUSTRIA
Described and seen by James Paris.
From a bill, XVII century

England, where an eminent gentlewoman observing her to be without fingers and toes and without speech, in regard to her distress, ordered her to be brought to her habitation. This gentlewoman for many years was troubled with convulsions of a severe kind, was perfectly cured in a very short time by the girl's stroaking.

"The girl hath like success on Pains that arise from the

spleen, sores and swellings and many other distempers, and what is very remarkable also in her, she never spoke one word in four years and then by prophetic spirit said, the gentlewoman that preserved her would die by two of the clock, which happened accordingly.

"The girl is ingenious and can work at her needle and several other things worth observation.

"Price for seeing her, Sixpence a Piece.

"SHE TOUCHETH GRATIS."

"Stroaking", of which Greatrakes was a famous exponent, was often used in the treatment of certain ailments about this period.

An account of two female children born with their heads joined together at the crowns, at Claems near Bruges, on May 6, 1680, is related in a bill, in the form of a letter written by a merchant of Ostend on May 7th of that year.

He states: "Having for some days resided in this city, I came to understand, that there happened a strange and wonderful birth about an hour and a half or a Dutch mile from this place, in a place called Claems. Yesterday I walked thither in company with several others and found it answerable to the relation I heard, viz; that they are two daughters, well shap'd and perfect in all their members, onely they are joined together at the top of the head and so fast, that it seems to be but one head. Yet, it is apparent, both heads have their perfect faculties and a partition may be easily felt which I felt myself yesterday.

"But yet, several Doctors and Chyrurgeons from Bruges having been there to see whether the children might be parted without danger of death, find no probability.

"The father is called Roelan Voyoen, being by trade a wagon-maker of about twenty-three years of age. The mother's name is Maria Castelmans, about nineteen years old. These were her first-born on the sixth of this month being Ascension Day.

"They are both baptized and the one named Pieternella and the other Barbara. That they are distinct in life, soul, and brains, appears plainly from their actions, which they have both together and sometimes apart. When one sleeps the other is awake, cryes and eats, and they are often times both asleep and both awake, and one asleep and the other awake.

"The heads are so united together, that when that which is awake turns itself, the neck of the other turns also.

"They will never be able to go, sit or stand, for if the one should sit or stand upright, the other must stand on her head with the heels upward. Their face, nose and eyes, are not directly opposite to one another, but somewhat sideways, so as that one looks towards you and the other from you.

"Many people come daily to see them and give three stivers a piece. Their parents are offered a great sum of money for them to be carried about. They told us they did intend, (after the Holy Day so-called) to carry their children to Bruges and it may be from thence to the cities of Holland."

From another bill headed "By His Majesty's authority", we learn that "At the sign of 'Charing Cross' at Charing Cross, there is to be seen a strange and monstrous child with one Body and yet otherwise it hath all the proportions of two children, that is two heads, two noses, two mouths, four eyes, four ears, four arms and four leggs, four hands and four feet.

"The monster is of the female kind. It was born at Fillips Town the twenty-ninth of April, 1699.

"The father of this monster is present where it is to be seen."

In the time of William and Mary, a monster with one head and two distinct bodies, with four arms, hands and legs, was brought to London by Sir Thomas Grantham and was first exhibited at the "Blew-Boar's Head" in Fleet Street. On June 16th he was shown at the "King's Head" near the Maypole in the Strand, where crowds flocked to see him. He was said to have been twenty-one years of age at the time and eventually found his way to Bartholomew Fair, where he proved a great attraction.

A still more extraordinary wonder was exhibited at the "York Minster" by Holborn Bars, a few years later, who is described in a bill, as "A Woman above thirty-five years of age, ALIVE, having two heads, ONE ABOVE THE OTHER, the upper face smooth. She has no fingers nor toes, yet can dress and undress, knit, soe, read, sing and do several sorts of work.

"Very pleasant and merry in her behaviour.

"She hath been shown to the King and all the Royal Family."

Another curious monstrosity was to be seen "Near Hide-Park Corner during the time of May Fair, near the sheep-pens against Mr. Penkethman's booth. He is a Mail Child born with *a Bear growing on his back*, to the great admiration of all spectators."

Such a phenomenon doubtless attracted many visitors.

Another bill printed in the time of George III, informs us, that at "The Rummer", in Three Kings Court, Fleet Street, was to be seen one of the GREATEST CURIOSITIES IN NATURE.

"A Boy and Girl, with two distinct heads and necks and one body, three arms and three legs and feet and one foot with six toes.

"It is allowed by Sir Hans Sloane and several other physicians and other gentlemen who have seen them, to be the greatest curiosity ever seen. They were born in Suffolk on June 25th, 1736."

Among the prodigies exhibited in London and described in a bill about this period, was "A young man about twenty-four years of age who is called 'THE EIGHTH GREAT WONDER OF THE WORLD'", who was to be seen at the "Coach and Horses" at Charing Cross.

"He was born without arms and performs all kinds of martial exercises with his feet. In the first place, he beats the drum and sounds the trumpet at one and the same time. He flourisheth his colours, plays at Back-sword, charges and fires a pistol with great expedition and dexterity. He also plays cards or dice. and can also comb his hair and shave his beard, and does readily pull off his hat and courteously salutes the company.

"Moreover he can thread a needle, embroider, and play upon several sorts of musick, and what is yet more wonderful, write six sorts of very fair hands."

Another phenomenon who is mentioned by several writers of the time, was the boy with "DEUS MEUS" written in his eyes.

According to a bill, he was first exhibited at the sign of the "Golden Lyon", near the Maypole in the Strand, and is described as a "Man child, born at Leford in Freisland having in his right eye these words in Latin, 'DEUS MEUS', that is to say 'My God' in English, and in the left eye the same words in Hebrew characters. He has been seen by most of the Kings and Princes of Europe, being now brought from France, where he was strangely admired by the learn'd and curious."

James Paris, who saw him in London about the year 1718, thus describes him:

"He was a pretty fair-headed boy of about the age of twelve or thirteen years, that had two very fair grey eyes and had extraordinary good sight, and had a circle upon each eye at a little distance from the ball or centre of each eye, whereon there was plain to be read in fair characters, like prints, Deus Meus. As he grew bigger the characters grew larger and more legible."

Prodigies of foreign extraction abounded in London, including the two following curious examples, who claimed to be exhibited by the authority of His Majesty King George I.

One was the "High German woman, that has neither Hands or Feet, yet performs a hundred several things to admiration.

"She sows, threads needle, as quick as any one can with hands, cuts out gloves, writes very well, spins as fine a thread as any woman can do. She charges and discharges either pistol or carbine as quick as any man can do, and makes bone-lace of all sorts. She had the honour of shewing before the King and Queen, and if any person of Quality is desirous of seeing this prodigy of Nature she will wait on them at their own houses."

"Prince Gilolo, a son of the King of Moangis or Gilolo, said to be a fruitful island abounding with rich spices", was another foreign visitor.

According to the bill introducing him "To the citizens of the Great City of London", this unfortunate Prince was wrecked on the coast of Mindanao and with his sister, was made a prisoner by the King of that island.

"The natives had a secret way of staining the body with a pigment prepared from the juice of a certain herb or plant peculiar to that country, which preserved the human body from the hurt of venomous creatures whatsoever.

"This custom they observe, that in some short time after the body is painted, it is carried naked with much ceremony to a spacious room appointed which is filled with all sorts of the most venomous, pernicious creatures that can be found, such as snakes, scorpions, vipers and centipedes.

"Here they decorated the prince with variety of invention with prodigious art and skill. His back with a lively representation of one greater part of the world, upon and betwixt his shoulders and all the other parts, with curious figures and mysterious characters scattered up and down his body."

From the description the "prince" appears to have exhibited some elaborate specimens of the art of the tattooer.

CHAPTER VIII

EXTRAORDINARY MONSTERS AND PRODIGIES

THE systematic study of monstrosities, or abnormal formation of animals, may be said to have begun in the first half of the eighteenth century, when Caspar Friedrich Wolff, by his researches, laid the foundations for a rational science and showed it to possess a more than curious interest for the anatomist and embryologist.

He pointed out that what had formerly been regarded as expressions of the displeasure of the Creator or indicative of evil portent, were explicable by the application of the definite laws of development as set forth by embryology.

Malformations produced by variations in growth or other influences were roughly divided into the following groups:

(1) Single monsters. (2) Dicephalous monsters, with two distinct heads. (3) Pygopagus, with bodies joined almost back to back. (4) Craniopagus, two bodies joined by the heads. (5) Double parasitic monsters in which another body is attached. (6) Tricephalous, with three distinct heads.

At a later period, all human bodies with anything unusual in development not grave enough to be called monsters, were classed as Hemiteratae, but the line between these and monsters is very slight. Such phenomena as mentioned have since been more fully and accurately classified.

It is our intention, however, to refer only to those who have lived and attracted general attention, and to relate some facts of interest connected with them.

The most interesting examples of these abnormal creatures, from several points of view, are the conjoined-twins.

Twins of this description who were known as the "Wasserlinck Sisters", were born at Ardemberg on November 21, 1657, but little is recorded about them beyond that "they had four arms and hands and the left head had a cyclopean eye in the centre".

A better-known example of this type were Helen and

Judith, called "The Hungarian Sisters", who had two distinct bodies that were joined by the os sacrum.

They were born at Szony in Hungary in 1701, and attracted considerable attention throughout Europe in the early part of the eighteenth century.

After being exhibited in Germany, Italy, Poland, France and Holland, they were brought to London by a Hungarian physician in 1708.

During their travels in these countries they were examined by many eminent physiologists, psychologists and anatomists, and later were described before the Royal Society in London.

Pope, besides several minor poets, celebrated their existence in verse, and they are alluded to by Buffon and other celebrated writers of the period.

At the age of twenty, Helen, who had a more attractive appearance than her sister and was also the more active of the two, grew bigger in proportion, but Judith surpassed her in intelligence.

Their emotions, inclinations and appetites were not simultaneous, and although affected in different degrees by their ailments, they both contracted and suffered from measles and small-pox at the same time.

James Paris, who states that he saw them in London on July 12, 1710, when they were about nine years of age, tells us he found them "both merry and well-bred".

"They could read and write and sing very prettily. They could speak three different languages, Hungarian, High Dutch or Low Dutch and French and were learning English."

He further describes them as being "very handsome, very well-shaped in all parts and with beautiful faces.

"Helen was born three hours before her sister Judith. When one stooped, she lifted the other up from the ground and carried her on her back. They could not walk side by side. They loved one another very tenderly.

"Their clothes were fine and neat. They had two bodices, four sleeves and one pettycoat."

The Cardinal-Archbishop of Gran in Hungary, who took a great interest in the twins, fearing that their morals might become corrupted by travelling through so many countries and by being exhibited in such a public manner, redeemed them from the physician who was accompanying them and placed them in the Ursuline Convent at Presburg. He generously paid for their maintenance and education, and they were instructed in religious principles as well as being taught to embroider, do needlework and make lace, which they did with great skill.

On February 8, 1723, when in their twenty-second year, Judith was seized with a convulsive fit, and afterwards remained in a lethargic condition for fifteen days. In that interval, Helen developed a slight fever with frequent fainting attacks, though she retained her speech and was conscious in between them.

She died on February 23rd, and Judith apparently expired at the same moment.

The following lines were written by a Hungarian physician and inscribed on a bronze statuette erected to commemorate their death:

"Two sisters wonderful to behold, who have thus grown as one,
    That nought their bodies can divide, no power beneath the sun.
    Their parents, poor, did send them forth, the world to travel through,
    That this great wonder of the age should not be hid from view."

There is an account of a child who was born at Gosmore, near Hitchen, in Hertfordshire, in 1706, who had "one body, two heads, four arms and hands, four legs and feet with toes and fingers having nails upon them very perfect. The mother's name was Mary Fisher.

"It was born with teeth in each mouth which are plainly visible to all spectators."

Another record states, that "a child about a year and a half old that has three leggs, two off one side and of one equal length. It hath also sixteen toes, six growing on one foot and ten on the other." It was living about the same period.

James Paris gives an account of twin brothers that were

exhibited in London in 1716. He states: "The biggest was born a perfect man, well-proportioned and from his right side issued a little above his hip, a body of a man from the middle upward perfectly shaped with hands, arms and head. He could eat and drink with good appetite, *could speak distinctly* and had very good sight."

A curious question arose on the death of a child with a parasitic body at the Hôtel Dieu in Paris in 1733.

She is described as "a girl of twelve years of age of ordinary stature and fair conformation, except that depending from her left flank was the inferior half of another girl of diminutive proportions, but with a head and features complete. The supernumerary child was immovable and hung so heavily that it had to be supported by the hands or by a sling."

Sensibility was common in the two and an impression applied to the auxiliary body was felt by the other also.

When she was dying, a priest was called in to administer extreme unction, but he could not decide whether he should give it to the girl alone or to the parasitic child as well.

The question arose, were they two separate beings with distinct souls, or one person only? The record does not state the decision arrived at in this particular case, but it was one which gave rise to considerable controversy among the physicians and the clergy of the time.

One of the most extraordinary, as well as pathetic, instances of human deformity is related by Gould, in reference to a young man, who is said to have been heir to one of the oldest peerages in England. "His figure is said to have been remarkable for its grace and his face was that of an Antinous, but upon the back of his head was another face, that of a beautiful girl, lovely as a dream yet hideous as a devil."

The female face was a mere mask, occupying only a small portion of the posterior part of the skull, yet exhibiting every sign of intelligence of a particularly malignant kind.

It would be seen to smile and sneer while the face of the

young man was weeping. The eyes would follow the movements of the spectator and the lips would "gibber without ceasing".

No voice was audible, but the young man averred that he was kept from his rest at night by the hateful whispers of his "devil twin" as he called it, "which never sleeps but talks to me for ever of such things as they only speak of in hell. No imagination can conceive the dreadful temptations it sets before me.

"For some unforgiven wickedness of my forefathers, I am knit to this fiend—for a fiend it surely is.

"I beg and beseech you", he said to his physicians, Drs. Manvers and Treadwell, "to crush it out of human semblance, even if I die for it."

He lived in complete seclusion, refusing the visits even of the members of his own family.

Although a man of fine attainments, a profound scholar and a musician of rare ability, he lived the life of a recluse and never claimed heirship to the title.

In spite of careful watching he managed to procure poison and killed himself at the age of twenty-three.

He left a letter requesting that the "demon face" might be destroyed before his burial "lest it continues its dreadful whisperings in my grave". At his own wish he was interred in "a waste piece of ground without stone or legend to mark the grave".

Many examples of prodigies born without limbs who developed remarkable dexterity, are recorded in the latter part of the eighteenth century.

Among them was William Kingston, who was born without arms or hands, and is thus described by Mr. Walton in a letter to Rev. John Wesley, written on October 14, 1788.

He states: "I went with a friend to visit this man, who highly entertained us at breakfast by putting his half-naked foot upon the table as he sat and carrying his tea and toast between his great and second toe to his mouth, with as much facility as if his foot had been a hand and his toes fingers.

"I put half a sheet of notepaper on the floor with a pen and ink-horn; he threw off his shoes as he sat, took the ink-horn in the toes of his left foot and held the pen in those of his right.

"He then wrote three lines as well as the most ordinary writers and as swiftly.

"He then showed how he shaved himself with a razor in his toes and how he combs his hair. He can dress and undress himself except buttoning his clothes. He feeds himself and can bring both his meat and broth to his mouth by holding the fork and spoon with his toes. He cleans his own shoes, his knives, lights the fire and does almost any other domestic business as well as any other man.

"He is a farmer by occupation and milks his cows with his toes, makes his hencoops, cuts his hay, and binds it up in bundles.

"He goes to the field, catches his horse, saddles and bridles him with his feet and toes. If he has a sheep among his flock that ails anything he can separate it from the rest, drive it into a corner and catch it when nobody else can. He is so strong with his teeth that he can lift ten pecks of beans with them, and can throw a great sledge-hammer as far with his feet as other men can do with their hands.

"In a word, he can nearly do as much without, as others can with their arms."

Another prodigy of this type was John Kleyser, a German, who was born without arms and was seen by James Paris in London. He states that "Kleyser wrote very finely with his mouth and right and left foot, in five different languages. He shaved and combed his hair with his right foot. He could walk upon his two great toes and stand on one toe. He could also lay his foot over his neck and hop upon the other."

Besides the men, there were several women born without arms, hands or legs, who were able to write, draw and sew by means of their lips and showed extraordinary skill. A notable example was Sarah Biffin, who was born at Quantoxhead, near Bridgewater, Somersetshire, in 1784.

She was but thirty-seven inches in height, and although

deprived of arms, hands and legs, by training and per-
severance, she was enabled to use a pen, pencil or paint-
brush by means of her mouth and developed considerable
skill and ability.

She was also clever with her needle in embroidery and
designed and cut out her patterns in paper. She was taught
miniature painting by a Mr. Dukes, with whom she stayed
for sixteen years, and in 1812 was taken round the country
by him on exhibition. She wrote her autograph for visitors,
drew landscapes and painted miniatures on ivory for three
guineas each.

The Earl of Morton became interested in her work, and
through him she received further instruction in painting
from Mr. Craig. Several members of the Royal family
patronized her, and for some time she had a studio in
Leicester Square, to which visitors were admitted to see
her work, on payment of a small fee.

The merit of her work as a miniature-painter was recognized by the Society of Artists, who awarded her a medal
in 1821.

She eventually retired to Liverpool, where she fell into
poverty, but through the exertions of a local philanthropist,
a subscription was raised for her relief with which a small
annuity was purchased. She died in that city on October
2, 1850, at the age of sixty-six years.

Another prodigy of this period was Miss Horton, who is
said to have been an American by birth. She was exhibited
in London and several towns in the provinces about 1793,
and although she was born without any trace of arms, she
had acquired the greatest facility in doing things with her
feet and toes.

"She could lift a pocket-book up with her toes and
unstrap and open it, also fold a sheet of paper properly for
cutting. With a pair of scissors, which she would take from
a case, she would then quickly cut it out for a watch-paper."

She is said to have married and had a family, and went
to reside in Bath, where she died in 1803.

There are also records of similar prodigies in France,

one being described as a girl of great beauty, who was born in Bordeaux without feet or arms. She was able to write letters, draw, knit and load a pistol by means of her mouth and showed skill in playing the piano *with her nose*.

Another example was Marc Cazotte, known as "Pepin", who died in Paris at the age of sixty-two, towards the end of the eighteenth century.

He had no arms or legs, but from very jutting shoulders on each side he had well-formed hands, and two misshapen feet were attached to the flattened part of his trunk. He is said to have been very intelligent and was able to move about with agility.

An extraordinary monstrosity which was born in India in 1783 is described in a letter written by Sir Everard Home to John Hunter, the famous surgeon, on March 25, 1790.

Commenting on how little the early historians are to be depended on and how scanty are the details recorded of such monsters, he states, "to the histories of remarkable deviations from the common course of nature in the formation of the human body, I desire to add the account of one so truly uncommon, that I believe no similar instance is to be found on record.

"This child was born in May 1783 of poor parents at Mandalgent near Bardawan in Bengal, the mother named Nooki being thirty years of age and the father named Hannai, who was a farmer, being thirty-five.

"The body of the child was naturally formed but the head appeared double, there being besides the proper head another of the same size and to appearance almost equally perfect, attached to its upper part.

"This upper head was inverted, so that there seemed to be two separate heads, united together by a firm adhesion between their crowns but without any indentation at their union. The face of the upper head was not that of the lower but had an oblique position, the centre of it being immediately above the right eye.

"When the child was six months old, both of the heads

were covered with black hair in nearly the same quantity. The neck was about two inches long.

"The natural head had nothing uncommon in appearance, the eyes were attentive to objects but the body was emaciated. The parents, who were poor, carried it about the streets in Calcutta as a curiosity to be seen for money.

"Mr. Stark, who resided in Bengal at the time, had a very exact painting made from it while the child was alive by Mr. Smith, a portrait painter then in India. It was then about two years old.

"When the child was roused, the eyes of both heads moved at the same time. Tears flowed from the eyes of the superior head but never from the eyes of the other. When it smiled, the features of the superior head sympathized in this action. It seemed to feel little or no pain when the superior head was pinched.

"When it was a little over the age of two years, the mother went out to fetch some water and upon her return found the child dead from the bite of a cobra da capello.

"From an examination of the internal structure of the double skull there were two brains, and had the child lived to a more advanced age and given men of observation opportunities of attending to the effects of this double brain, its influence upon the intellectual principle must have afforded a curious and useful source of inquiry."

Each head had its own separate vessels and each had an individual sensibility.

Sir Everard Home gave an account of this monster to the Royal Society in 1791, and the double skulls are now preserved in the Museum of the Royal College of Surgeons of England.

It will be noticed from accounts given in the preceding pages, that this was not a solitary instance of twins born with heads fused at the cranium, as several similar cases of an earlier date are on record.

A monster who was born at Leith without head, heart or lungs, was described by Dr. Alexander Munro in 1792, and several similar examples of this type were recorded by Méry and Winslow in Paris at the close of the eighteenth century.

CHAPTER IX

SOME CELEBRATED CONJOINED-TWINS

In the nineteenth century, the study and classification of monstrosities and abnormal creatures to which the name of teratology was given by Geoffroy de St. Hilaire, became recognized as a distinct branch of science. Ballantyne, Hirst and others who added to existing knowledge of the subject, did much to promote its advancement, and a journal was established to record cases of interest.

Among the most interesting and famous examples of conjoined-twins that came into notoriety at this period were the two brothers, Chang and Eng, who were afterwards known throughout the world as the "Siamese twins".

They were born at Maklong, a small village sixty miles from Bangkok, in Siam, about May 1811, their father being of Chinese extraction. His wife's father was also a Chinaman, so they may therefore be said to have been of Chinese blood. Their mother was about thirty-five years of age at the time of their birth and had a family of fourteen children, which included several twins.

It was only with difficulty their lives were saved, as they were very feeble at birth, and when Chowpahyi, the reigning King of Siam, heard of it, in accordance with the superstitious custom of the country and his belief that the existence of such beings portended evil to his kingdom, he wished them to be put to death.

He was, however, at length convinced that they were harmless, and as they were likely to be able to support themselves by labour they were allowed to live.

They were first seen by Mr. Robert Hunter, a British merchant of Bangkok, about 1824, in a fishing-boat on the River Minain. They were naked from the hips upward and very thin, and in the dusk when he saw them he thought they were some strange animal.

Shortly afterwards, he endeavoured to prevail on the Siamese Government to allow them to visit England, but did not at first succeed. However, in March 1829, together with Captain Coffin, they obtained the mother's permission to allow them to leave her, on condition that they would provide for her during their absence. The Government raising no objection, the party left Siam early in April 1829 on board the American vessel *Sachem*, and arrived at Boston in the United States the following August.

On their arrival they at once excited great interest, and were examined and described by Professor J. C. Warren at Harvard University in 1829. They remained in America for two months, and then sailed for England, arriving in London on November 20, 1829.

They were first exhibited at the Egyptian Hall in Piccadilly, where crowds of people flocked to see them.

Mr. G. B. Bolton, M.R.C.S., a well-known surgeon of the time, at the request of their exhibitors was placed in medical charge of the twins, and it is from the account of his observations the following particulars are taken. He states, that when he measured them, they were both of the same height, viz. 5 feet 2 inches, and weighed 180 pounds.

"Their bodies and limbs are well-formed but the spine of Chang, who habitually holds his arm over the shoulder of Eng, is considerably curved laterally, apparently the result of this long-continued habit.

"They resemble the lower-class people of Canton in the colour of their skins and in the forms of their features.

"When in their own country, on rowing a boat, both stood in the stern, each using a one-handed oar.

"When one is lifted up from the ground, allowing the other to hang by the connecting band with his feet raised from the floor, no pain is caused to either, nor is there any middle line where the sense of feeling common to both terminates.

"Their united strength is great, for they can with perfect ease throw down a powerful man, and at Philadelphia they carried without inconvenience, a person weighing over twenty stone for some distance.

"Their agility is remarkable, for they run with great swiftness and elude pursuit. They have the power to bend their bodies in all directions, and often playfully tumble head over heels in bed.

"When playing a game of whist, they prefer not to be partners and rarely play chess with each other.

"They always take their meals together and object to be seen while thus engaged. Neither will eat or drink what the other dislikes, though they occasionally take different sorts of food at the same time, such as meat or fish. When the appetite of one is satisfied, the other is also satisfied. They are cleanly and delicate in their habits and mutually assist each other. They are exceedingly affectionate and docile and grateful for every kindness shown to them.

"It is not often they converse with each other, although their dispositions and tempers agree. Sometimes they engage in different conversations with different persons at the same time upon totally dissimilar subjects, and it is notable, that both are exceedingly fond of music and derive great pleasure from listening to it.

"It does not appear that they ever had a serious quarrel except on one occasion, which occurred, as their mother reported, when they were eight years old.

"While on their passage to America, one of them wished to bathe as was their custom, to which the other objected, the day being cold, and a slight discussion ensued.

"They always fall asleep at the same moment, and it is impossible to wake one without rousing the other.

"One night Mr. Hale went into their bedroom while they were asleep. Eng was restless and tossing about and Chang was screaming.

"He awoke them and inquired what was the matter.

"Eng replied that he was dreaming about his mother, and Chang said that a man was cutting off the long hair from his head. The different dreams appear to have been simultaneous.

"They are remarkably quick in intellect and possess great imitative powers. A person who once visited them at their exhibition in New York, happened to have but one eye, which they at once noticed.

"They inquired of their attendant what he had paid for admission, and on being informed that it was the same as other persons, they remarked that half of it should be returned, as with only one eye he had not the same advantage as the others."

Mr. Bolton declared that these extraordinary individuals were the most remarkable instances on record of perfect and distinctly formed human beings united together, who had attained the age of puberty in a sound bodily health.

He stated that the band of union, when they faced each other, was 1¾ inches on the upper edge and not quite 3 inches at the lower. From above, downwards, it was 3¼ inches, and its greatest thickness was 1⅝ inch. It had no pulsation.

According to a report of their examination in America, the band that united the twins was remarkably strong and had no great sensibility, for they allowed themselves to be pulled by a rope fastened to it without exhibiting uneasiness.

The slightest impulse of one to move in any direction was immediately followed by the other, so that they appeared to be influenced by the same wish. They always faced in one direction and stood nearly side by side, and were not able without inconvenience to face in the opposite direction. Although not placed exactly in a parallel line, they were able to run and leap with surprising activity. They both generally directed their eyes towards the same object, but the perceptions of one were more acute than those of the other. The one who was more intelligent was sometimes more irritable in temper, while the disposition of the other was mild.

There is no part of them which has a common perception excepting the middle of the connecting-cord and a space near it. The pulsations of the hearts of both coincide exactly under ordinary circumstances. The intellectual operations of the two are as perfectly distinct as if they were two persons. They have never been known to lament their union or even to notice its singularity, but were considerate and docile one with another, and usually when they walked, had their arms around the neck of each other.

There is a story that on their arrival in London on their first visit, a dense fog prevailed. They declared it was night and they would go to bed.

A chamber-maid at the hotel where they were staying, tapped their heads and jokingly told them they should be her sweethearts, which caused them much amusement, and at one and the same time they both kissed her.

After visiting the principal cities in Europe, they returned to America, and adopting the name of Bunker, settled down as farmers in North Carolina. At the age of forty-four they married two sisters of English birth, who were aged, respectively, twenty-six and twenty-eight. Domestic troubles, however, soon compelled them to keep the wives at different houses, and they arranged matters by visiting each wife alternately for a week at a time. Chang had a family of ten children and Eng had twelve, all of whom proved healthy and strong.

In 1869, they again made another tour through Europe; it was said with the intention of taking the advice of the most eminent surgeons of Great Britain and France, as to the advisability of being separated. The feasibility of such an operation was discussed in England by Sir William Fergusson, Sir James Young Simpson and Mr. Syme, and by Dr. Nélaton in France, but nothing was decided and they eventually returned and settled down in America.

Their two farms were a mile and a half apart and they then spent three days in each home alternately. While Chang was in his own house for the stipulated period he was entire master, and Eng followed his directions implicitly and could only remonstrate if he did not approve of what was done.

About this time, the physical condition of both began to deteriorate, but it was a pathetic characteristic of the brothers, that they treated each other with affection and forbearance, and bore both trials and ailments with the greatest patience and sympathy.

Later in life, Chang is said to have become addicted to

drinking, and in the winter of 1874 developed bronchitis while in his own house.

"On the evening of January 15th, the twins, in accordance with their arrangement, insisted on leaving Chang's house for Eng's. The weather was very cold and they drove in an open carriage. Chang passed a restless night and finally fell asleep. Near daybreak, Eng called to one of his sons to come and waken Chang, but as soon as the boy reached Chang's side he exclaimed, 'Uncle Chang is dead!'

"Eng at once said, 'Then I am going.'

"He desired Chang's body to be moved closer to him and in a little while requested that his limbs be moved. He remained rational to the end, which came about two hours after he had learned of his brother's death."

Thus ended the Siamese Twins, after having lived sixty-three years and so reached the most advanced age on record of conjoined human beings.

On the 23rd of March, 1829, twin girls, with their bodies united nearly opposite the lungs, were born at Sassari in Sardinia. Their parents were very poor, but they managed to get enough money to bring them to Paris, where they intended to exhibit them and so make a living. They were shown privately, but their public exhibition was prohibited by the authorities.

The one on the right side was baptized Ritta and the other Christina, and they became known as the "Sassari twins".

Their superior extremities were double, but they joined in a common trunk at a point a little below the breasts. The head on the left side was slightly larger than the other, but the four arms were alike in size. The four breasts were all perfect, while the two chests centred into one.

The face of Rita was always sad and melancholy, while that of Christina, who was more vigorous, was of a gay and happy aspect. They had single lower extremities, but the sensations in the upper ones were distinct.

Sometimes the eyes of one head would close in sleep while the other would be awake, but at other times they would both sleep and generally acted independently.

The poverty of the parents appears to have hastened the end of the twins, for they died at the age of five months from want of care or exposure. Rita took ill first and after her death that of the sister soon followed.

An autopsy showed that they had two hearts and separate digestive organs.

The *Examiner*, in commenting on the twins in 1829, says: "Already it is a matter of grave consideration with the spiritualists, whether they had two souls or one; most of them think the twins had two, as sometimes one of the heads cried and the other did not."

Another example of conjoined-twins were the "Tocci brothers", who were born at Locarno in Italy in 1877. They had well-formed heads, perfect arms and thorax to the sixth rib and two legs. The one on the right was christened Giovanni Batista and the other Giacomo.

Their father, who was a working man, was thirty-two years of age, while the mother was but nineteen when they were born, and they looked upon the birth of the extraordinary twins as a godsend. When they were a month old they were taken to Turin for exhibition, where they attracted such attention that the parents were able to live comfortably on the proceeds. Afterwards they were taken on a tour through the principal cities of Italy, Austria, Germany, Switzerland and Great Britain.

When seen at the age of twelve, the boys, in mind and character, are said to have been as two individuals, although their bodies gradually blended into one, beginning on a level with their sixth ribs, so as to form to all outward appearances but one body below the double thorax.

Each twin had power over the corresponding leg on his side but not over the other one, so walking was impossible, but all their emotions and sensations were distinctly individual and independent. The boys were fair-skinned with brown hair, and not of the usual Italian swarthy type.

Giovanni was better formed than his brother, whose foot was deformed and could not be placed flat on the ground. They were thus unable to stand without support, both legs being weak and thin for want of muscular training. Giovanni was also the more intelligent of the two and was able to draw, while his brother had no taste for art, but both had an ear for music and were able to speak a little French and German.

Examination showed that each had two lungs and each had an independent heart located on the left side of the chest.

About 1858, a curious monster was exhibited at Kahn's Museum in Coventry Street, Leicester Square. The person who exhibited it declared that it differed from any other case known and called it "The Heteradelph" and published the following description of the phenomenon: "The child was born in Lancashire in May 1857, both parents being normal people. The name Heteradelph was given to such creatures by Geoffroy St. Hilaire when one body fully developed and perfect had another or part of another adhering to it.

"This example differs from any other in the fact that the appended child is perfectly developed, with the exception of the upper extremities, and is much larger than usual.

"The boy is perfect in all parts, well-developed and in good health.

"Attached to it at the chest is another child, also male, united most curiously with its fellow, the lower part of its body quite perfect, the arms in a rudimentary condition and the head entirely absent, one head and neck serving for both.

"Here are two bodies placed exactly opposite to one another, connected at the sterna and the viscera of the trunk, apparently perfectly distinct. It was the third child of a normal family and, although several cases are on record, very rarely has life been preserved."

Among the notable prodigies of the early part of the nineteenth century who developed artistic talent was Discornet, who became celebrated as a painter. He was born at Lille on January 10, 1806.

He had no arms, but the rest of his body was well-formed with exception of the feet. This deformity, however, which made a space between the great toe and its neighbour, was much larger than ordinary and the toes much more mobile, so that he was able to hold a pencil or brush.

He executed a picture nearly four metres high, representing Mary Magdalene at the feet of Christ after the Resurrection, which was purchased by the Government and presented to the city of his birth.

In the records of the Société d'Anthropologie de Paris, there is an account of a young man without arms, who was able to play the violin with his feet and could also perform on the cornet. He could take a handkerchief from his pocket and blow his nose, make a cigarette, light it and place it in his mouth. Also, by the aid of his toes, he could play cards, drink from a glass and eat with a fork.

Another prodigy who became a skilful acrobat, was Harvey Leach, known as "Hervio Nono", whose skeleton is preserved in the museum of University College, London. He was one of the most remarkable gymnasts of his time.

He had extraordinary power and agility, and besides being a skilful rider either standing or sitting, he could walk and leap partly with his feet and partly with his hands. His lower limbs were so short that, erect, he could touch the floor with his fingers. His left lower limb between the hip and heel measured but sixteen inches, while the right, between the same points, measured nine inches.

Another man without arms or legs, who was known in France as "l'homme Tronc", was exhibited at the Paris Exposition in 1886.

He enjoyed excellent health and could eat, drink and converse with intelligence.

One of his chief occupations was that of making small tables and chairs, by nailing together pieces of wood which had been previously cut for him. He could take a nail in his mouth, plant it in the wood and drive it in very adroitly. He was also able to thread a needle with his mouth, and could take up a glass of water when given to him and drink it without spilling any of the liquid. He was wheeled about the grounds of the Exposition in a small perambulator.

CHAPTER X

THE "TWO-HEADED NIGHTINGALE" AND OTHER NOTABLE TWINS

In more recent times there have been several other examples of conjoined-twins and similar teratologic phenomena, some of which are within recollection.

Among these were the North Carolina twins, Millie and Christine, better known as the "Two-headed Nightingale".

CONJOINED-TWINS
Boaistuau, 1576

They were born on July 11, 1851, their parents being negroes or half-breeds who had settled in Columbus County, North Carolina. Like the "Hungarian Sisters", their bodies were joined together in the lumbar region, but not back to back.

They were first brought to Europe in 1873, and after being exhibited in Paris, toured through England, where they attracted a considerable amount of attention.

They were dark in colour, with black curly hair, and were both intelligent and of pleasing appearance, though slightly undersized.

Christine was physically stronger than Millie, and could bend and lift up her sister by the bond of union, but the latter had the stronger will and was the dominating spirit. They walked and ran without difficulty and danced with apparent ease and grace.

One from long habit yielded instantly to the other's movements, thus preserving the necessary harmony.

When one moved her leg the other knew of it, although she could not say which leg had been moved.

They ate separately, had distinct thoughts and were able to converse with two people at the same time, while each sister had her own likes and dislikes.

When the writer saw and conversed with them during their second visit to England in 1885, they talked as distinct persons and expressed their own individual opinions on different matters. Their voices varied, that of one sister being lower pitched than the other. They sang duets for soprano and contralto, accompanying themselves on guitars which they had learnt to play with considerable skill and charm. After they had again toured through Europe they returned to America and settled there.

Another interesting example of similar type were Rosa and Josepha Blazek, who were born at Skerychova in Bohemia on January 20, 1878.

Their mother was twenty-two years of age at the time of their birth, and during their childhood the twins were both healthy and vigorous. Their bodies were almost separate and joined only by a broad bony union at the sacrum and lower part of the spinal column.

Rosa was the stronger of the two, and when she ran or walked forward, she drew her sister with her, who otherwise would have had to have reversed her steps.

They were exhibited in Paris as the "Bohemian Twins" and were brought to London in 1891.

Rosa was a pretty and intelligent child, active and restless, but Josepha was of a quieter temperament, preferring to rest the greater part of the day.

Mentally the girls greatly differed, and while Rosa was quick and conversed well, Josepha was slow and did not care to talk. They had separate minds and independent thoughts, and one could sleep while the other was awake. Their appetites were quite different, as instanced in the preference of one for beer as a beverage, while the other liked wine. Rosa was very fond of salads, while her sister detested them. Neither thirst nor hunger was simultaneous and when one was hungry she would eat a meal alone.

Though the same blood circulated through the two bodies, it was notable that if one felt ill the other did not necessarily feel the same. One might be feeling quite well, while the other was ailing, but if medicine or a drug was given to one, it reacted on both. At the age of thirty-two they entered a hospital at Prague, where Rosa became the mother of a boy.

According to a story published in 1910, the father of the child fell in love with Rosa and they were to have been married but the parents forbade it. The curious question then arose as to how the twin-sister Josepha was affected by the occurrence.

Concerning the suggested marriage, it was declared that the twins were legally but one, or if they were two persons and had the union taken place, might not the bridegroom be charged with bigamy?

However, as the marriage did not take place, these difficult questions were not referred to the Courts for a decision.

Two other later examples of conjoined-twins were Marie and Rosa Drouin, who were born at Montreal in 1878, and Rosalina and Maria, who were born in Cachoeiro de Stapemerin in South America in 1899.

The former girls had a single trunk, which commenced at the lower part of the thorax of each. Marie was of fair complexion and more strongly developed than her sister.

Their pulsations and respiratory movements were not synchronous; sensations of hunger and thirst were not experienced at the same time, and one might be asleep while the other was crying.

Rosalina and Maria, the South American twins, were joined at the breasts, almost front to front, yet they could not see each other. They had two arms and four legs, all well-formed. With them also their tastes and appetites were quite separate.

There have been but few instances of conjoined-twins having been successfully separated by an operation. One of these was the "Orissa sisters", Radica and Doadica, who were exhibited in London in 1893.

At their birth in India, the inhabitants of the village where their parents lived, instigated by Brahmins, consigned the whole family to prison on the supposition that the twins were the incarnation of the devil.

When one of them later developed tubercular disease, they were separated by a French surgeon and Radica for a time survived.

There are several other examples of conjoined-twins, said to be still living, of whom mentioned may be made. Of these, Violet and Daisy Hilton were born at Brighton in 1909 and were described by Dr. Rooth.

Their mother was tall and well-built and both girls were well-formed and of average size. They were nursed by a foster-mother, who had some trouble in rearing them during the first few months of infancy. During an attack of bronchitis, while one child was distressed and fretful, the other seemed to be quite undisturbed by her sister's misfortune. Both twins were vaccinated and they were registered as two separate individuals.

They led, to some extent, independent lives and sometimes while one slept, the other played. Their uniting band was fleshy, cartilaginous and very firm, and at birth the children were almost attached back to back. At the age of two and a half years, however, there was much freer movement. The band became more flexible and allowed the girls to turn and almost face each other, so that they could fight or play with one another.

At this age, both children are said to have been bright and intelligent, the elder one especially, who could talk as much as any child of her age.

They left England at the age of three years, and after being exhibited in various Continental countries were taken to the United States, where, according to a recent account, they settled in Texas.

The "Gibb Sisters", Mary and Margaret, were born at Holyoke, Massachusetts, U.S.A., in 1912. Both their parents are said to have been normal, as also a younger sister. Both girls, who are now eighteen, have been trained to sing, play and dance, and have appeared on the variety stage in America.

As recently as September 1927, twin girls, joined together for about nine inches and facing each other, but otherwise perfectly formed, were born at Pimlico. One being very weak and sickly, they were taken to St. Thomas's Hospital, and were there christened by the chaplain, one being named Mary and the other Ann, but they did not long survive.

A more curious phenomenon were the twins born at Derby on December 10, 1927. They were joined together, head-to-head, their legs pointing away from each other, so that their bodies formed a straight line. They were brought to Guy's Hospital on December 22nd of that year and died less than a fortnight afterwards. They were baptized and called Elsie and Marie.

Both the children could cry, but one would sleep while the other was awake. The nurses had great difficulty in feeding them as they lay on their backs, and it took three to hold the children when placed on their sides.

If they had survived they would have been unable to sit or stand upright, for if one sat up, the other would be resting on her head with her feet in the air.

An attempt was made to separate them in the hope of saving the life of the larger and more vigorous of the two, but they succumbed.

Sir Bernard Spilsbury, who gave evidence at the inquest, attributed death to shock and said he should call them conjoined-twins.

"They were two individuals in the sense that the essential organs were complete and separate, and were in theory capable of a separate existence. The brains, although separate in themselves, lay in contact with each other."

A Hindu youth called Laloo, to whom a parasitic body was attached, was well-known in Europe and America in the latter part of the last century. He was born at Oovonin, Oudh, India, about 1874, and was first described in the *Indian Medical Gazette* (July 1886) as a fairly well-grown Mohammedan boy of twelve years of age and, with the exception of his deformity, was perfectly formed in every respect. He was the second of four children, all of whom, with his exception, were normal.

The headless parasitic body was well-formed in the upper and lower extremities and was attached to the boy's epigastric region by short fleshy pedicles. It had two arms and legs, fairly developed, but the forearms and hands were deformed and on the left hand the thumb was wanting.

It was incapable of active motion and no pulse could be felt, but sensation was acute in the accessory limbs and the boy could localize the place touched. Perspiration and elevation of temperature seemed to occur simultaneously in both.

He was first brought to England in 1891, and after visiting the principal cities he went to the United States, where he was engaged by Barnum and toured with his show.

Dr. Dickenson, of St. Louis, U.S.A., states that in 1880 he saw a child of five years of age who was being exhibited in that city, "who was an amalgamation of two children. From the body of an otherwise perfectly formed child, was a supernumerary head protruding from a broad base attached to the lower lumbar and sacral region.

"It was covered with hair about four or five inches long, and showed the rudiments of an eye, nose, mouth and chin."

Monstrosities with duplication of the lower extremities have been recorded at various times from the fourth century, but there are several examples that have been described in recent years.

In 1830, a male child with four legs was shown to the Académie des Sciences in Paris, but the supernumerary legs were immovable, and again in 1838 Bardsley described a boy who was born with one head, four arms and four legs.

In 1869, there was an account given of a female child named Louise L——, who was born in France and who lived to maturity. She was known as "La Dame à quatre jambes", on account of having two supernumerary legs attached to her body in the pelvic region. She could localize sensations except in her feet. She married and within three years had two well-formed children.

Another remarkable example, which is said to have been the most perfect of its kind, was that of an American lady who was described by Wells in 1888. She was born in 1868 with four legs, all of which were symmetric, but the inner limbs were smaller than the others. Duplicity began just above the waist, and below, everything was double. She grew up into a very beautiful woman and married in her nineteenth year. She was alive and healthy in 1892. She walked without difficulty with her two outer limbs and appeared to be normal to the ordinary observer.

A similar example, but with one auxiliary leg, making three in all, was recorded in France, when a child called Blanche Dumas was born in 1860.

Duplication of faces is of rare occurrence, but in 1827, there is an account of a female child who was born at Taunton with two distinct and perfectly formed faces. The mother, whose name was Elizabeth Verrien, was the wife of a carpenter.

There is a growing feeling that the public exhibition of the unfortunate human beings who may be called monsters should be prohibited by law.

It is certainly against all ideas of humanity, that they should become the appanages of travelling circuses and shows in order to pander to the morbid and curious, or to appear on the stages of variety theatres.

It has been urged, however, that it is generally a necessity for them to earn a living. In most cases they have been born of parents in poor circumstances, who have only been too glad to have them exploited by showmen as a means of making money.

Many of these cases are sad and pitiful enough for obvious reasons, but trading on deformity should not be permitted. In common humanity they should be placed in suitable homes or institutions and cared for by the State.

CHAPTER XI

"OF CRAFTY TRICKS AND COZENAGE"

AT all periods in the history of monsters, there have been the cunning ever ready to prey on the credulity and pity of others by practising various means of deception.

In ancient times the maimed, the halt and the blind frequented the gates of the cities to excite compassion and collect alms from those who passed by, and among them no doubt fraudulent rogues were to be found who, by feigning some deformity, were easily able to make a living.

A writer of the sixteenth century refers to the subtle devices of these "begging companions" and cautions the benevolent against the "craft and cozenage of such men".

Ambroise Paré tells us, that when he was at Anjou in 1525, there stood a crafty beggar at the church door, "who tying and hiding his own arm behind his back", showed instead thereof, one cut from the body of one that was hanged, and this he propped up and bound to his breast, and so laid it open, to show as if it had been all inflamed, so to move such as passed by into greater commiseration of him.

"The cozenage lay hid, every one giving him money, until at length his counterfeit arm not being securely fastened, fell to the ground, many seeing and observing it; he being apprehended and layed in prison by the appointment of the magistrate, was whipped through the town with his false arm hanging before him and so banished."

Of other frauds he says: "Some of them there are who besmear their faces with soot, layed in water, to seem to have a jaundice.

"Some there be, who not content to have mangled and filthily exulcerated their limbs with caustic herbs and other cauteries, or to have made their bodies more swollen or else lean, with medicated drinks, or have deformed themselves some other way, but from good and honest citizens who have charitably relieved them, they have stolen children, have broken or dislocated their arms and legs, have cut out their tongues, have depressed their chests or whole breast that with these as their own children begging up and down the country they may get the more relief, pitifully complaining that they came by this mischance by thunder or lightning or some other strange accident.

"Such as feign themselves dumb, draw back and double their tongues in their mouths. Such as fall down counterfeiting the falling sickness, bind straightly both their wrists with plates of iron, tumble or roll themselves in the mire, sprinkle and defile their faces with beasts' blood and shake their limbs and whole body.

"Lastly, by putting soap into their mouths, they foam at the mouth like those that have falling sickness. Others, some with flour, make a kind of glue, wherewith they besmear their whole bodies as if they had leprosy.

"This art of counterfeiting and cheating begging is by no means new," concludes Paré, "for long ago it flourished in Asia and even in the time of Hippocrates."

Thus it will be seen that the wiles of the cozener have survived the centuries, for the trick of putting soap in the mouth to simulate the effects of an epileptic fit, is still sometimes practised by fraudulent rascals.

Fabricius Hildanus says, that in the year 1593 at Paris, there was an infant about fifteen or eighteen months old, which had the skin of its head so extended that it exceeded the magnitude of any infant that was ever seen. "This child's parents did carry it about from town to town to show and thereby exceedingly enrich themselves.

"At length there was a great concourse of people, and the Parisian magistrate, being a very discreet man, suspecting it be some base deceit did cast the parents into prison. And being examined they confessed their barbarous and impious crime, saying they had cut the skin of the infant's head by making a little hole about the crown to the very muscles and by that very hole (putting in a reed between the skin and the muscles) had blown into it, and by degrees, within some months (by continually puffing into it) the skin of the infant's head was extended to that altitude and that they did expose it to all here and about France to get money thereby.

"They made the hole so neatly that drawing out the reed, with wax or some such material, they could easily close the same.

"When they had fully found out this horrid, savage inhumanity for certain, they put both the parents to death."

Such were some of the deceits practised by fraudulent rogues in times gone by.

Some years ago, a Chinaman excited much pity in the streets of Shanghai and gathered alms from the passers-by, by exposing to view the mutilated stumps of his legs, while the feet that belonged to them were slung round his neck.

One, day, when scrambling out of the way of a policeman who had ordered him off, he was knocked down by a carriage and taken to hospital. When questioned how he had lost his feet, he admitted that he had performed the amputations himself, starting about a year previously. He had commenced by fastening cords round his ankles, drawing them as tightly as he could bear, and then increased the pressure every two or three days.

At the end of six weeks he was able entirely to remove his feet, by partly snapping and partly cutting the dry bone, and so successfully feigned the appearance of them having been severed by an accident. The pair of feet are now preserved in the Museum of the Royal College of Surgeons.

A still more recent "cozener" was unmasked at St. Louis, in the United States, in 1890. This ingenious individual was accredited with earning his living by breaking, or pretending to break, his leg, in order to sue for damages for the supposed injury. He had but one leg and was accustomed to go about on crutches.

He would look for a defective place on the footpath, stick his crutch into it and fall screaming to the ground, declaring that he had broken his leg. He would then sue the authorities of the city for damages and was several times successful, until the fraud was discovered.

CHAPTER XII

WILD MEN OF THE WOODS AND SOME "HORRIBLE MONSTROUS BEASTS"

STORIES of the finding of wild men and women covered with hair, who were discovered in woods or on mountains, are told by several early writers. Aldrovandus describes several of these creatures, amongst whom were a man with

A WILD HAIRY-MAN
Sluper, 1572

his son and daughters who were brought from the Canary Islands, all covered with hair, and first shown in Bologna.

Fabulous tales of "horrible monstrous beasts of frightful aspect" are also numerous. Such an one is described by

STRANGE MONSTERS ON LAND AND SEA

Conrad von Megenberg, 1499

George Fabricius, who says, that "in the territory of the Bishop of Salceburgh in a forest called Fannesbergh, there was a certaine four-footed beast of a yellowish, carnation colour, but so wilde, that he would never be drawn to looke upon any man, hiding himself in the darkest places and beeing watched diligently, would not be provoked to come forth so much as to eate his meate.

"The hinder legs were much unlike the former and also much longer. It was taken about the year of the Lord, one thousand, five hundred and thirty."

Ctesias describes an Indian animal called martichora, who had three rows of teeth in each jaw. "It is as large and rough as a lion and has similar feet, but its ears and face are like those of a man.

"Its eyes are grey and its body red. It has a tail like a land scorpion in which there is a sting. It darts forth the spines with which it is covered instead of hair, and it utters a noise resembling the united sound of a pipe and a trumpet. It is not less swift of foot than a stag, and is wild and devours men."

Pliny describes a similar monster, but declares it had azure eyes and was of the colour of blood and could imitate human speech. It had no gums in either of its jaws and the teeth were one continuous piece of bone.

Topsell says: "I take this beast to be the same which Avicen calleth Marion. Although India be full of divers ravening beastes yet none of them are stiled with a title of 'andropophagi', that is to say 'men-eaters', except onely this 'mantichora'."

Du Bartas, in his *First Week or the Birth of the World*, thus alludes to this strange animal:

> "Then th' Unicorn, th' Hyaena tearing tombs,
> Swift Mantichor, and Nubian Cephus comes;
> Of which last three, each hath (as heer they stand)
> Man's voice, man's visage, man-like foot and hand."

A man-tiger, said to have been brought from the East Indies, was exhibited at the sign of "The George" against the steps of Upper Moor-Fields, in the time of Queen Anne.

According to the bill, "This strange and wonderful creature was of several colours. From the head downwards it resembled a man.

"Its foreparts clear and its hinder parts all hairy. Having a long head of hair and teeth, two or three inches long.

"It takes a glass of ale in his hand like a Christian, drinks it, and also plays at quarterstaff."

The unicorn also had a reputation as a "monster of terror", for Solinus states, "the cruellast is the Unicorn, a

"HORRIBLE SERPENT WITH SEVEN HEADS"
Boaistuau, 1576

monster that belloweth horriblie, bodyed like a horse, footed like an Eliphant, tayled like a Swyne, and headed like a Stagge.

"His horne sticketh out of the middle of hys forehead, of a wonderful brightness about foure foote long, so sharp, that whatever he pusheth at, he striketh it through easily.

"He is never caught alive; kylled he may be, but taken he cannot bee."

Fenton, in 1569, gives an account, together with a picture, of a "horrible serpent with seven heades that was sent out of Turkey to Venice embalmed, which long after was made a present to Francis de Valoys, the French King, by whom for the rareness of it, it was valued at 6,000 ducats.

"I think", he says, "nature hath never brought out a form any thing more marvellous amongst the monsters that ever were, for besides the fearfull figure of this serpent, there is yet a further consideration and regarde touchyng the faces, which both in view and judgment seem more human than brutal."

"TERRIBLE MONSTER WITH HUMAN HEAD FOUND IN THE FOREST OF HAUBERG"

Boaistuau, 1576

For ferocity, however, none of these creatures can compare with the "Terrible wild monster" that is said to have been killed in the neighbourhood of Jerusalem, on November 15, 1725, whose depredations are described in a manuscript now preserved in the British Museum.

The account states, that "fourteen miles from Jerusalem towards the Forest Mountain, has been noted for a great many days a strange devastion of men, cattle, horses and other animals passing that way, half eaten, without ever being able to find out the cause of so great a calamity; till a man travelling that way, saw another who went before him assaulted by a monstrous animal, who with her talons, parted him in two. Seeing this, full of feare, he fled to the neighbouring town where he related his adventure.

"The inhabitants of the towns and villages near by were summoned to kill the beast, and provided with all sorts of arms, proceeded to the place where she lay, but finding themselves unable to do him any mischief, they advised the Bashaw, who sent a regiment of Infantry and another of Cavalry to this expedition.

"They waited not long before the horrid monster appeared.

"Their horses frighted at the sight of the monster and not able to withstand her fury, for the most part flung their riders to the ground.

"Amongst these was a soldier, against whose horse the beast coming threw him down, so that despairing of his life and happening to have a launce, ran it with so good fortune down her throat that killed her.

"Great damage this monster did, for in one months time there was killed by her forty-nine persons, besides those killed in the fight. This monstrous animal was of the bigness of a horse, but had a head and teeth like a lyon and two horns like a bull.

"At the end of the nose there came out a beak like an eagle's and ye ears hung down like an Elephants, each eighteen inches long.

"It had four duggs like a cow, nine inches in length and its breast was defended by a skin as strong as a Lyon's.

"On the feet were very long claws and strong as a griffins.

"The Tail was knotted like a Basalisk's and four feet and a half long, with a sting at ye end.

"From the shoulder bone and along the back down to its feet, grew spurs like a cock's, only larger. It had wings like a serpent and all the body cover'd with scales like Mother of Pearl, but joined so close and thick one upon another, that they were impregnable.

"The origin of this beast is thought to be thus:

"An independent Prince of Tartary wanting to take vengence of some people who had deny'd obedience to him, he by a stratagem got 'em together on a mountain, where in his sight he had 'em all murdered by opening their veins. The blood in which was involved so many exasperated spirits, being congealed betwixt the Rocks and mixt with the Earth, fermenting by little and little, produc'd this monstrous animal, for carrying with itself the passions of the spirits of so many bodies it may be call'd a sign of ye greatest cruelty, for it did not kill men and beasts to eat their bodies but only to drink their blood, and then left them torn in pieces in the fields."

One does not know which to admire most, the fertile imagination of the writer displayed in his description of this "terrible wild monster", or the ingenious account of its origin.

CHAPTER XIII

MONSTERS OF THE DEEP

THE sea has ever been the home of mystery, and strange and marvellous are the creatures that have been described throughout the ages as denizens of the great waters.

"Of the wondrous nature of some marine things", says Paré, "which of this sort there are many, especially in the

THE MONK FISH
Sluper, 1572

seas whose secret corners and receptacles are not pervious to men."

Curious sea-monsters bearing resemblance to human beings are described by several early writers.

Thus: "In our time", says Rondeletius, writing in the sixteenth century, "in Norway was a monster taken in a tempestuous sea, the which as many saw it, presently termed a Monk by reason of the shape."

Gesner also tells us, that "in the year 1531 there was

seen a sea-monster in the habit of a Bishop covered with scales".

He further states, that "not long before the death of Pope Paul the third, in the midst of the Tyrrhene Sea, a monster was taken and presented to the successor of this Paul. It was in shape and bigness like a Lion, but all scaly and the voice was like a man's voice. It was brought to Rome to the great admiration of all men, but it lived not long there,

THE BISHOP FISH
Sluper, 1572

being destitute of its own natural place and nourishment as it is reported by Philip Forrest."

Another sea monster is described as having "the face of a man and also the figure thereof. The head looked very ghastly, having two horns, prick ears, and arms not much unlike a man, but in the other parts was like a fish. It was taken in the Illyrian Sea as it came ashore out of the water to catch a little boy, for being hurt by stones cast by fishermen that saw it, it returned a while after to the shore from whence it fled and there died."

Traditions concerning creatures half-human and half-fish in form have existed for thousands of years, and the Babylonian deity Ea or Oannes, the Fish-god, is represented on seals and in sculpture, as being in this shape over 2000 years B.C.

He is usually depicted as having a bearded head with a crown and a body like a man, but from the waist downwards he has the shape of a fish covered with scales and a tail.

According to Berossus, Oannes appeared out of the Erythrian Sea (Persian Gulf) and taught the Babylonians the use of letters, arts and sciences. He had a human voice and possessed great learning.

The human-fish legend again appears in Hindu mythology

THE NEGRO FISH
Lycosthenes, 1557

and later in the early Greek stories of the tritons and mermaids, which were believed also by the Romans.

Such traditions are found among races all over the world, and accounts of mermen and mermaids having been seen, come from the east and west.

One of the old Dutch colonial chaplains named Valentyn states, that in 1663, "a lieutenant in the army and some soldiers saw mermen swimming in the sea near the beach at Amboyna. They had long and flowing hair of a colour between green and grey, and one is said to have been captured and given to the Governor."

He also tells the story of a mermaid that was "driven through a breach in a dyke at Edam in Holland, and was afterwards taken alive in the lake of Parmen, whence she was taken to Haarlem. Here she was cared for by a kindly Dutchwoman, who taught her spinning and other house-wifely callings, and she eventually became a Roman Catholic!

With reference to the Bishop and Monk fishes depicted in the works of Gesner and Aldrovandus, Sluper also mentions an extraordinary fish with the head of a negro.

THE FISH-BOY
From a bill of the XVII century

Du Bartas writes concerning these creatures:

> "Yea Men and Mayds, and which I more admire,
> The mytred Bishop and the cowled Fryer;
> Whereof examples (but a few years since)
> Were shown the Norways and Polonian Prince."

In 1684, a merman or fish-boy is said to have been born at Beiseiglia in Italy. He was brought to London and shown at the house of Mr. Barton, a milliner, next door to "His Royal Highness" Coffee-house at Charing Cross.

The father's name was Peter Anthony Consiglio and the mother's Elizabeth Nastasia. According to their account, "when born, the boy was quite covered with the scales of fishes, having nevertheless a beautiful and comely neck and face with no unseemly colour.

"His head is adorned with curious flaxen hair and from the neck down to the sole of the foot, he is all over blackish and hairy intermixt with spots of several sorts and colours like the scales of a fish.

"He is of human stature and tender-limbed. The bottoms of his feet are white and so are the insides of his hands, like unto the shells of a sea-tortoise. He is about ten years of age and is named Barnardin.

"His mother admiring him, kept him secretly, so that it was not publick in the country, she in the meantime often dipping and washing him all over in water, thinking and hoping thereby the scales would fall off. But Almighty God was pleased that he should retain them thereby to show the world.

"No sooner than the old scales and shells drop off, but presently others come instead of them.

"He hath a very sharp eye. He speaketh three several languages viz. Italian, French and the Low Dutch. He hath been seen by the Kings of England and France and also by the Sworn Physicians of my Lords, the States of Holland, who declared, that never hath been seen so Prodigious a birth."

A merman or sea-monster was exhibited in London in the time of Queen Anne, which is said to have been taken on the coast of Denmark.

According to the bill, "The whole creature was very large and weighed (according to computation) at least Fifty Tuns and was Seventy feet in length. His upper part resembled a man, but from the middle downwards he was a fish."

Another curious creature exhibited in London, was a boy named Francis Lambert, who was shown at Laxton's Rooms, in New Bond Street, in 1820. He is described in his bill as "a new species of Man".

He was born in Suffolk, and was said to be covered with scales with the exception of his face and the soles of his feet and the palms of his hands. "These scales were hard and firm and nearly half-an-inch long. He had been seen with interest by Sir Robert Walpole and other distinguished persons."

Much curiosity was aroused in London in 1822 by the announcement in the *London Literary Gazette* of the capture of a mermaid on the coast of Japan.

The story was reproduced from a letter written by the Rev. M. Phillip, representative of the London Missionary Society at Cape Town, which was published in the *Philanthropic Gazette* of July 31, 1822.

He states: "I have to-day seen a mermaid now exhibiting in this town. I have always treated the existence of this creature as fabulous, but my scepticism is now removed. As it is probable no description of this extraordinary creature has reached England, the following particulars respecting it may gratify your curiosity and amuse you.

"The head is almost the size of that of a baboon. It is thinly covered with black hair, hanging down and not inclined to frizzle.

"On the upper lip and on the chin are a few hairs. The cheek bones are prominent, the forehead low, but except in this particular, the features are much better proportioned and bear a more decided resemblance to the human countenance than any of the baboon tribes.

"From the position of the arms, I can have no doubt, that it has clavicles, an appendage belonging to the human body which baboons are without!

"The canine teeth resemble those of a full-grown dog; all the others those of a human subject. The length of the animal is three feet. From the point where the human figure ceases, it resembles a fish of the salmon species and is covered with scales all over. It has six fins and a tail.

"The proprietor of this extraordinary animal is Captain Eades of Boston in the United States. From him I have learned, it was caught somewhere in the north of China by a fisherman who sold it for a trifle, after which it was brought to Batavia. Here it was purchased by Captain Eades for 5,000 Spanish dollars.

"Captain Eades is a passenger on board the American ship *Lion* now in Table Bay, and he leaves this port in about a fortnight and the *Lion* visits the Thomas, so it will probably be soon exhibited in London."

This announcement from so reliable a source, caused considerable interest among scientific men and the public generally, and the visit of the mermaid to the metropolis was eagerly looked forward to.

One day early in September, the *Lion* came up the Thames and Captain Eades, accompanied by the mermaid, duly came ashore, but as the Customs authorities were apparently in some doubt if she could be passed without paying duty, she was ignominiously deposited in the East India baggage warehouse.

Meanwhile, Captain Eades made an application to Sir Everard Home, who was at that time President of the Royal College of Surgeons, requesting him to examine it.

Sir Everard wrote to Mr. William Clift, then Conservator of the Hunterian Museum, asking him to go and see the specimen and report the result to him.

Accordingly, on Saturday, September 21st, Mr. Clift took his way to the Dock warehouse to be introduced to the mermaid, and he has left the following account of his visit.

He tells us that he found it "locked in a tin case, very carefully wrapped in soft materials and surrounded by a silken mattress to protect it from injury.

"Captain Eades permitted me to examine it very minutely, and I immediately saw it was a *palpable imposition* and soon made out the manner in which it had been prepared.

"The cranium appears evidently to belong to an ouranoutang of full growth, the teeth and probably the jaws, do not belong to the cranium, but from the size and length of the canine teeth, they appear to be those of a large baboon.

"The scalp is thinly and partially covered with dark-coloured hair, which is glossy like that of an ouran-outang. The skin covering the face has a singularly loose and shrivelled appearance and on a very close inspection, it appears to have been artificially joined to the skin of the head across the eyes and upper part of the nose.

"The projections in lieu of ears, are composed of folds of the same piece of skin of which the face is formed.

"The eyes appear to have been distended by some means, so as to have kept very nearly the natural form, and there is a faint appearance as though the cornea had been painted to represent the pupil and iris. The object has been so contrived as to leave no appearance to a cursory observer of its having been opened, but simply dried, and there are two small holes on the forehead, through which a string has been passed for its suspension while drying.

"The nails of the ouran-outang being very short and their peculiar appearance well known, these have been removed and their places supplied, or else covered with pieces, either of horn or quill, but from their opaque, whitish appearance, probably the latter, but of whatever substance they are formed, they have not the character of nails.

"The mammae appear to have had some slight stuffing from within, and immediately below them is a deep fold, in order to hide the junction with that which forms the lower or posterior part of the figure. This consists of the entire body of a fish, apparently of the salmon genus, separated from the head immediately behind the branchiae and the pectoral fins and brought immediately below the situation of the ensiform cartilage of the ouran-outang.

"On the posterior part of the body of the fish, the skin has been preserved as high as possible towards the head, so as to terminate in a point of very thin skin, which is placed between the scapula of the ouran-outang, and has been pressed down very closely upon the spinous processes of the dorsal vertebrae while drying.

"The place of junction, and for a little distance on each side of it, has been smeared over with some ochry substance, but the whole figure has acquired a brown mummy-like appearance from drying which prevents this from being readily perceived.

"But, if anything were wanting to convince me that the anterior and posterior parts of the figure have been separate from each other, there is a hoop of some firm substance, similar to paper or pasteboard, which distends the body of the fish nearly all the way from the pectoral to the anal fins, but below or behind this part, the body has shrunk in from the want of the same support, leaving a distinct edge all round.

"The fins appear to correspond exactly in number and situation with those of the salmon, but if they did not, it would only have proved how very practicable a thing it was for so ingenious an artist as the person who prepared it, whether Chinese or European, to have added some by way of embellishment, as well as the tuft of black hair, which has been inserted into and projects from each nostril.

"This object", concludes Mr. Clift, "such as it is, measures about two feet ten inches in length, and was first exhibited in London at the Turf Coffee-house in St. James's Street at the corner of Jermyn Street on Tuesday, October 15, 1822. Admittance, one shilling."

He adds a further note to his report, that he "saw it again with Sir William Blizard on November 28th."

A contemporary writer states, that from "three to four hundred people paid daily one shilling each for the indulgence of their credulity."

An echo of this exhibition appears in the *Morning Herald* of November 21, 1822, in which it is reported that in the Court of Chancery, "Mr. Hart applied for his Lordship's injunction to restrain a Mr. Eles (Eades) from removing a certain mermaid or dried specimen from the room in which it was now exhibiting in St. James's Street, and from selling or disposing of it."

It appears that a Mr. Stephen Ellery claimed to have a joint interest in the mermaid in 1817, and was part-owner of a vessel which was commanded by Captain Eades. A cargo was obtained from Batavia and the ship sailed for Europe, and it was declared that the Captain had obtained the money to buy the mermaid by selling the vessel and cargo, seven-eighths of which belonged to Mr. Ellery.

On the Captain's arrival in London, he had taken a room for the exhibition of this mermaid and retained the profits for his own use. He threatened that if any claim was made he would remove the mermaid.

The Lord Chancellor said, that "whether, man, woman or mermaid," if the right to the property was clearly made out, it was the duty of the Court to protect it. He asked whether the plaintiff swore positively to his belief that it was purchased with his money. Mr. Hart said it was so sworn, and that he believed this purchase was the motive of defendant's return to England.

The Lord Chancellor then pronounced the injunction, and that is the last we hear of the mermaid and its story.

What became of it? Who can tell? Perhaps it is still treasured in some American Museum as a specimen of that mysterious denizen of the sea.

Legends of monstrous and gigantic sea-serpents go back at least four thousand years, and such creatures are depicted in Assyrian sculptures in the Royal Palace at Khorsabad, in the carvings illustrating the voyage of Sargon to Cyprus.

Mention is also made of great serpents of the sea in the Sagas, and Aristotle alludes to a gigantic sea-monster that attacked and capsized the galleys off the Libyan coast.

Another early reference to such a monster is made in a "Narrative of the North-East Frosty Seas, declared by the Duke of Mosconia, his Ambassadors to a learned gentleman of Italy named Galeatius Butrigarius".

It is as follows: "In the Lake called Mos and the Island of Hoffusen, appeareth a strange monster, which is a serpent of huge bigness and as to all other places of the world, blazing stars do portend alternation, so doth this to Norway.

"It was seen of late in the year of Christ 1522, appearing far above the water, rowling like a great pillar and was by conjecture far off esteemed to be fifty cubits in length."

Olaus Magnus describes a sea-monster that was "two hundred feet in length and twenty feet round, having a mane two feet long, being covered with scales and having fiery eyes. It disturbed ships, and raising itself up like a mast, sometimes snapped some of the men from the deck and devoured them."

In the sixteenth century, the appearance of such monsters was believed to portend disasters, calamities and war.

The story of another sea-monster is thus related by Hans Egede in his *Full and Particular Relation of my Voyage to Greenland* in the year 1734. He says:

"On the 6th of July 1734, when off the south coast of Greenland, a sea-monster appeared to us whose head when raised was on a level with our main-top. Its snout was very long and sharp and it blew water about like a whale. It had large broad jaws, its body was covered with scales, its skin was rough and uneven, but in other respects it was as a serpent, and when it dived its tail, which was raised in the air, appeared to be a whole ship's length from its body."

There are many other stories of the appearance of a great sea-serpent in the eighteenth century, and some of the observers even had a shot at it.

In an account of one, related by Knud Leems in 1767, it is said to have been "forty paces long, equalling in size the head of a whale in the form of a serpent. This monster had a maned neck resembling a horse, a back of a grey colour and a belly inclining to white."

Sir Arthur de Capell Brooke collected all the stories of the kind he could gather during his voyage to the North Cape in 1849.

He states, that "thirty persons saw the great monster of Otersoen in July 1849, which is described as being of a greyish colour. It moved with a loud crackling noise and emitted a strong odour."

Judging from the numerous narratives concerning sea-serpents, these monsters appear to have frequented certain Norwegian fjords and narrow seas, and were rarely seen in the open sea.

They are stated to have been seen on our coasts, at Loch Durch, in the Sound of Mull, off Cape Wrath and in the Mull of Kintyre.

The Rev. John McRae gives a detailed account in the *Zoologist* (May, 1873) of a great sea-serpent that appeared on the western coast of Scotland in August 1872.

He states that "it looked at least sixty feet long and had a black head and made a rushing noise when passing through the water".

In 1848, a monster serpent was seen by the Captain and officers of H.M.S. *Daedalus*, while on a voyage from the Cape to St. Helena. In an official report made to the Admiralty on October 11, 1848, it is described as an "enormous serpent with head and shoulders kept about four feet constantly above the surface of the sea and as nearly as we could approximate, by comparing it with the length of our main topsail-yard, would show in the water, there was at the very least sixty feet of the animal à fleur d'eau, no proportion of which was in our perception used in propelling it through the water.

"The diameter of the serpent was about fifteen or sixteen inches behind the head, which was without any doubt that of a snake and it was never during the twenty minutes it continued in sight of our glasses, once below the surface of the water; its colour a dark brown with yellowish white about the throat. It had no fins, but something like the mane of horse or rather a bunch of sea-weed washed about its back.

"It was seen by the quarter-master, the boatswain's mate, and the man at the wheel in addition to myself and officers.

(*Signed*) PETER M'QUHOE, *Captain*.

To Admiral Sir W. H. Gage, G.C.B.,
    Devonport."

A similar monster appears to have been seen by the mate of the American brig *Daphne*, who boarded the *Mary Ann* of Glasgow on October 19, 1848, and declared to the Master of that vessel, James Henderson, that he had seen an extraordinary monstrous animal from the deck of his ship "which had the appearance of a huge serpent or snake with a dragon's head.

"Directly it was seen, one of the deck guns was brought to bear on it and fired, when it immediately raised its head in the air and plunged violently with its body."

A volume might be filled with the many stories that have been related of these elusive monsters of the deep. Two more recent accounts need only be mentioned, as proving that some great snake-like monsters probably exist in the sea and still remain a mystery, of which nothing is known beyond the descriptions recorded by credible eye-witnesses.

On June 6, 1877, according to Lieutenant Haynes, a great sea-serpent was seen from the deck of the Royal Yacht *Osborne* when off Cape Vito, Sicily. It was observed by the Captain and several of the officers, and is described as extending about thirty feet above the surface of the water, having a head about six feet thick. Its shoulder was about fifteen feet across and it had flappers, each of which was about fifteen feet in length.

A still more recent story is related by Captain F. W. Dean, R.N., who states that when in command of H.M.S. *Hilary* during the War, when off Iceland in 1917, he saw "a sea-monster with a cow-like head on a neck about twenty-eight feet long".

CHAPTER XIV

MONSTERS IN ART

THE influence of monsters on the imagination of man and their effect on the human mind, is amply illustrated in sculpture and the decorative arts throughout the ages.

The subject is a vast one and can only just be touched upon here. From early times we find deities represented in human form, but with the heads of animals, or with the bodies of beasts with human heads, and various other fabulous and fantastic creatures were employed as symbols for the decoration of pottery or lamps and other objects of utility.

Monsters are also represented in the art of primitive tribes, as instanced in the winged-creatures with human heads with faces in their bodies, and other figures of monstrous aspect, depicted on the totem poles by the Indians of British Columbia and Alaska. Some of the Polynesian deities are represented with half-human and half-animal figures, and among the gods in the Marquesas, rough stone images with enormous misshapen limbs and bodies are to be found.

The ancient Egyptians represented Thoth, one of their greatest deities, with a human body and the head of a hawk, and many of their other deities, such as Anubis, Bes, Bast and Taurt, are depicted with the heads, limbs or bodies of animals. The mysterious and inscrutable Sphinx has the body of a lion with a human head.

The Assyrians had their great winged-bulls with human heads, and curious animals with horns and wings, men with four wings, animals with human heads and fish-like bodies. Monstrous birds with long necks and legs, are also often figured on their seals and cylinders.

In early Greek art, various monstrous forms and such mythological creatures as centaurs, griffins, goat-headed men and fabulous birds are frequently depicted in sculpture and on pottery.

Hecate is represented as a triple-headed monster in a bronze statuette, and the two-headed Janus in marble; the winged-sphinx with the head of a female on an animal's body is also found on sculptured reliefs.

Fauns and nereids were often painted on their vases and rhytons, while Amphitrite, with the upper part of the body in the form of a man and the lower extremities like a fish, is frequently represented in statuary.

During the Roman period, such monsters introduced into decoration became more naturalistic. The sea-horse and the griffin were often figured in marble, stone and bronze, and the winged-sphinx and satyrs entered into many of the decorative schemes for the bases of their altars.

In early Christian art, the use of monstrous forms was chiefly symbolic, and fantastic animals formed a feature also in early Byzantine sculpture and decoration. Animals with human heads were introduced into stone reliefs and the illuminated miniatures that illustrated manuscripts. In one example of the tenth century, St. John is depicted with the head of a tortoise, St. Luke with the head of a fox and St. Mark as a lion.

Fantastic and curious creatures are often to be seen sculptured in stone about the cathedrals, abbeys and churches of the thirteenth and fourteenth centuries, where the monastic sculptors and carvers gave free play to their imagination. The most grotesque and fabulous monsters are sometimes represented as gargoyles and on the misericords. Among them are to be found human and animal faces contorted with pain or obviously suffering from certain diseases; others take the form of devils and demons, people with deformities, dwarfs performing acrobatic feats, diabolical heads and hideous masks.

From the Middle Ages, monsters in the form of grotesque creatures have played a prominent part in heraldry and we find dragons, griffins, minotaurs, wyverns, unicorns, mermaids, birds like the liver and the phoenix, as well as many other fabulous creatures, employed in the blazoning of arms and used as crests.

The influence of monsters was also reflected in the decoration of armour in the fifteenth century, and dragons and the heads of other frightful creatures, were sometimes represented on Italian helmets and burgonettes.

They were employed in the decoration of sword-hilts and semi-human figures also formed part of the decoration of many beautiful specimens of the metal-worker's art. Masters, such as Benvenuto Cellini, introduced tritons and fantastic fish into several of their designs on cups, ornaments and jewellery which they wrought with such exquisite skill in the precious metals.

In Italian art, in marble, wood and mosaic, monstrous creatures frequently entered into the schemes of decoration. In some of the famous fountains of Rome, mermen, mermaids, nereids and sea-horses are represented disporting themselves and play a prominent part.

Human bodies with the legs of animals and monsters with horns, were often employed in the decorative designs of the Flemish and German woodcarvers of the sixteenth century, and fabulous birds and animals were introduced into some of the famous panels carved by the brothers Flores of Antwerp.

Lucas van Leiden included several fantastic creatures with human heads and the legs of goats in his designs, while Albert Dürer's beautiful conception of a Sea Venus riding on the back of a dolphin is well-known.

Among the woodcarvings of the Renaissance period in Chartres Cathedral, some extraordinary monsters with human heads are represented, and in early stained-glass, fabulous animals and birds often enter into the designs and colour-schemes.

In furniture, the woodcarvers frequently found expression for their imagination in the decoration of interiors, and curious caryatides and grotesque masks played a prominent part in carvings on cabinets, cupboards and table-legs in the sixteenth and seventeenth centuries.

Rubens sometimes introduced monsters into his allegorical

compositions, as exemplified in his fine conception of the winged Pegasus.

Some extraordinary monsters are represented in the carvings of Sambin in the time of Charles IX, which take the form of fantastic caryatides, armless men and women and triple-headed figures with bodies of human shape.

In tapestries, monsters of various kinds were introduced into the decorative designs, and satyrs, centaurs and human-headed animals are frequently represented. This is especially notable in French fabrics of the eighteenth century, as instanced in the winged-lions of Lameire and in the allegorical compositions in the Gobelin tapestries.

Clodion executed some curious designs in which dancing fauns formed a motive, and Fragonard introduced a whole family of these fabulous creatures in a marble relief. Very beautiful also were some of the decorative designs of Simon Vouet in the time of Louis XIV, in which human butterflies, with satyrs and griffins holding garlands, form the principal feature.

Some curious fantastic animals are carved in stone on the Château de Pierrefonds by Fremiet, who represents winged-bulls, grotesque birds having the heads of eagles, with spurred legs clad in mail. He also depicts strange conceptions of lions with dragons' tails, and a creature with the head of a pelican with short wings.

These are but a few of the many instances of monsters that were introduced into decorative art. Examples might be multiplied indefinitely, but those mentioned are sufficient to show the extraordinary and lasting influence they have exercised over the imagination of man.

CHAPTER XV

THE PSYCHOLOGY OF MONSTERS—THE LAW OF MONSTERS

THE study of the psychology of monsters is both difficult and complex, but in the cases of conjoined-twins and duplex monstrosities it is a subject of considerable interest.

The *New English Dictionary* defines the meaning of the word "monster" as (1)Something extraordinary or unnatural. A prodigy. (2) An imaginary animal, centaur, sphinx, or heraldic griffin, wyvern, part brute and part human. (3) An animal or plant deviating in one or more of its parts from the normal type.

None of these definitions can be regarded as satisfactory, and what is called a human monster is something more than a deviation from the normal type.

A mere deformity in any part of the body does not constitute a monster in law, provided he or she has human shape, and as to the question of separate individualities, each case must be considered and judged by the peculiarities attending it.

In former times, if a monster were found to possess two hearts it was deemed to be two human beings, and at a later period a test of monstrosity was based on the viability of offspring.

Smellie, the famous obstetrician, in 1754, stated that "when two children are distinct they are called twins and monsters when they are joined together".

In considering some of the types of monsters of which we have authentic particulars it is evident, that there was a dual personality in most of the cases of conjoined-twins.

The bodies of the Scottish brothers, the earliest example of which we have details, were fused into one at the trunk. They had two heads and four arms, but only two legs. They evidently had a dual personality, as we are told that sometimes they disagreed and disputed, and occasionally even came to blows. They preferred different things, though sometimes they came to an agreement for a common object. They carried on animated conversations with each other and sang with two different voices, and acted apparently in every way as two individuals.

In the case recorded by Ambroise Paré in 1546, of a monster having two heads, two arms and four legs, he states he found, on dissection, it had but one heart, and therefore concluded it was but one infant.

We gather from the description of the "Hungarian twins" that their emotions, inclinations and appetites were not simultaneous, and that they were affected by ailments in different degrees. They had two distinct bodies that were attached by the os sacrum.

The "South Carolina twins" also had independent thoughts and each sister had her own likes and dislikes. They talked as distinct personalities, sang in different voices and each had her own individual opinion on various subjects.

We find similar characteristics recorded in the cases of the "Blazek sisters" and the "Drouin twins", each of which had independent minds and thoughts. They had different ideas and appetites, and one might be ill while the other was unaffected.

Of the same type were the "Brighton twins", who were born, in 1909, joined almost back to back by a cartilaginous band. The upper parts of their bodies were normal, and they were baptized, vaccinated and registered as two distinct individuals.

These cases cannot but be regarded as distinct individualities and looked upon as two human beings, although they may have been vitally connected with each other. Although distinct as regards certain essential organs, in each case, the death of one was soon followed by the decease of the other.

With respect to duplex monsters or those in which a subsidiary part is nourished by the autosite or principal organism, the question of individuality is more difficult and complex.

In most of these cases, as far as can be ascertained, the parasitic body growing from the otherwise perfect one, is dependent upon its autosite for life and nourishment. In most of the recorded examples it was imperfectly developed, although, as in the case of Colloredo, it may have a separate head and upper extremities. It may even have had a separate heart and lungs, as some are said to have had, but the parasite can hardly be regarded as having a distinct existence. The autosite, or what may be called the parent body, is the controlling power, and the parasite could not exist without it. There is no evidence of separate thoughts, independent reason or will-power as in the cases of conjoined-twins, therefore it is difficult to regard them as distinct individuals.

The earliest example of this type of which we have a detailed description is that of Lazarus-Joannes Baptista Colloredo, who was born in 1617. Bartholinus, the anatomist, tells us that although Lazarus was a perfectly formed man, the parasite attached to him had but one leg and two arms. If pressure was made against its breast it caused its hands, ears and lips to move. Their vital and animal parts seemed to be distinct from each other, but it received no nourishment except through the medium of the body of Lazarus. The head of Baptista was larger than that of his brother. The Church, however, regarded them as distinct and separate persons, and they were baptized by different names.

In the remarkable case recorded by James Paris in 1716, in which the parasite issued from the right side of the autosite, he states: "It was perfectly well-shaped with limbs, arms and had a beard like the parent body." Further: "It could eat and drink with good appetite, had good sight and *could speak as distinctly* as its brother, but its sensations could not be felt by him." If this account is correct, the parasite appears to have been a distinct personality.

In the cases of double-headed monsters, few seem to have survived sufficiently long to form an opinion as to individuality. The opinions of authorities vary as to what constitutes such and where the line can be drawn that divides a single from a double individuality, and the psychological conditions that may be regarded as deciding the question.

The general rule followed in most countries is to consider every monster with two equally developed heads as two human beings, and every monster with a single head as one.

St. Hilaire ascribes the origin of this rule to the custom of performing the rite of baptism in all Christian countries upon each head.

With reference to the question as to how far one is responsible for the act of the other, he records a case decided in Paris in the XVIIth century in relation to a double-headed monster that killed a man by stabbing him. "The monster was condemned to death, but was not executed on account of the innocence of one of its component halves."

The law of England gives no precise definition of a monster, but according to Lord Chief Justice Coke, it is a being "which hath not human shape of mankind".

The legal question relates only to external shape and not to internal conformation.

There is a very ancient rule in the law of England, that "a monster not having the shape of mankind, but in any part evidently bearing the resemblance of the brute creation, has no heritable blood and cannot be heir to any land, even though it be brought forth in marriage; but although it hath deformity in any part of its body yet if it has human shape, it may be heir."

The Roman law agrees with our own in excluding such births from successions, yet accounts them, however, children in some respects, where the parents, or at least the father, could reap any advantage thereby, esteeming them the misfortune rather than the fault of that parent.

"But our law will not admit a birth of this kind to be such an issue as shall entitle the husband to be tenant by the courtesy, because it is not capable of inheriting.

"Therefore, if there appears no other heir than such a prodigious birth, the land shall escheat to the lord."[1]

[1] *The Laws of England.* Broom and Hadley.

PART II

GIANTS, DWARFS AND PRODIGIES

CHAPTER XVI

GIANTS IN MYTHOLOGY—GIANTS IN ANCIENT TIMES

In almost every race and people throughout the globe, traditions and legends are to be found of monstrous and gigantic beings who were supposed to live in caves, forests or mountains, to the terror of normal human beings.

In mythology, we have such creatures as the Titans, who are described as of gigantic stature and enormous strength, who carried on wars against the gods. From them sprang the Gigantes, beings of fearful aspect with terrible faces and the tails of dragons, and others with fifty heads, a hundred arms and serpents in place of legs. Hercules, the embodiment of physical strength, who is supposed to have been seven feet in height, who slew the giant Alcyoneus, was prominent in the wars against the Gigantes and eventually, with the aid of Zeus, crushed them to death under mountains or killed them with clubs.

Polyphemus, the traditionary Cyclops, too, was credited with gigantic stature and enormous strength. Homer describes him with,

> "A form enormous; far unlike the race
> Of human birth, in stature or in face
> As some lone mountain's monstrous growth he stood,
> Crown'd with rough thickets and a nodding wood."

He dwelt in his cave on the coast of Sicily and lived on human flesh. He sought for victims with his mighty club, which Homer thus describes:

> "The monster's club within the cave I spy'd,
> A tree of stateliest growth, and yet undryéd,
> Green from the wood; of height and bulk so vast,
> The largest ship might claim it for a mast."

The legend of Polyphemus, in one form or another, survived in fairy-tales and stories until after the Middle Ages, and other early writers perpetuated the marvels wrought by the giant heroes of Greek mythology.

The huge images of deities, like the immense figures still to be seen at Karnak and Luxor in Egypt, and in the ruins of Memnon, show, that even the early civilized races possessed a faith in giantology and a reverence for the colossal.

It is probable that these and other ancient representations of enormous human forms were the corporeal shapes perpetuated in stone, which served to aid and continue the early belief in giants.

In the Bible, there are several allusions to races of great stature and people of abnormal height.

The first mentioned are the Nephilim, referred to in Genesis.[1] "There were giants in the earth in those days; and also after that, when the sons of God came in unto the daughters of men which were of old, men of renown."

Then there were the Rephaim, referred to also in Genesis,[2] who were defeated by Chedorlaomer and allied kings at Ashteroth, and the Emims, who dwelt in the wilderness of Moab, "a people great, and many, and tall as the Anakims; which also were accounted giants as the Anakims".[3]

The land of Ammon "also was accounted a land of giants; giants dwelt therein in old time; and the Ammonites call them Zamzummims, a people great and many and tall as the Anakims".

Og, King of Bashan, was the last of the race of these giants, as it is stated in the Book of Joshua.[4] "All the Kingdom of Og in Bashan, which reigned in Ashtaroth and in Edrei, who remained of the remnant of the giants; for these did Moses smite and cast them out."

It is probable that Og, whose story survived in many Eastern legends, was about nine feet in height, although in some accounts he is said to have been much taller, and according to a statement in the Targum, he was "several miles" in height.

We read later in the Second Book of Samuel[5] how the giants joined the Philistines and fought against the Hebrews,

[1] Chap. vi, ver. 4.   [2] Chap. xiv, ver. 5.   [3] Deut. ii, vers. 10–11.
[4] Chap. xii, ver. 12.   [5] Chap. xxi, vers. 15–22.

and that "there was a battle in Gath, where was a man of great stature, that had on every hand six fingers, and on every foot six toes, four and twenty in number, and he also was born a giant. And when he defied Israel, Jonathan the son of Shimeah the brother of David slew him."

Goliath, whom David slew and whom the Philistines regarded as their champion, is said to have measured 6 cubits and a span, or about 9 feet 9 inches high. His coat of mail weighed 5,000 shekels of brass, computed to be about 208 pounds, and from the accounts of him in the Book of Samuel and that given by Josephus, he must have been a man of abnormal strength as well as of gigantic stature.

That there was another race of giants who dwelt at Hebron, and who excited the wonder and alarm of the spies sent by Moses into Canaan, is evidenced from the allusions in the Books of Joshua and Numbers. They are variously described as the sons of Anak or Anakim, and the descendants of Anak. They were "men of great stature", they said. "And there we saw the giants, the sons of Anak which come of the giants; and we were in our own sight as grasshoppers, and so we were in their sight."[1]

They are described in Deuteronomy [2] as "A people great and tall, the children of the Anakims, whom thou knowest and of whom thou hast heard say, Who can stand before the children of Anak?"

Hannah More, in *David and Goliath*, thus describes the giant as of Anak's race:

> "This man of war, this champion of Philistia,
> Is of the sons of Anak's giant race;
> Goliath is his name. His fearful stature,
> Unparallel'd in Israel, measures more
> Than twice three cubits. On his towering head
> A helm of burnished brass the giant wears,
> So ponderous, it would crush the stoutest man
> In all our hosts."

Both the ancient Greeks and Romans had a common belief

[1] Numbers, chap. xiii, vers. 32–33. [2] Chap. ix, ver. 2.

in giants, and we find them represented in their sculpture and on pottery. Gigantic stature was often given to their heroes, and the body of Orestes, found at Tegea, is said to have been over 10 feet in length. Gabbaras the giant, who, according to Pliny, was brought to Rome by the Emperor Claudius Caesar from Arabia, is said to have been 9 feet 9 inches in height, and the remains of Idusio and Secundilla, found in the reign of Augustus Caesar in the Sallustian Gardens, of which they were supposed to have been the custodians, are estimated as having been 10 feet 3 inches in height.

Herodotus states, that the sandals of Perseus measured the equivalent of 3 feet, and Josephus mentions a giant called Eleazar, who was among the hostages sent by the King of Persia to Rome, who was nearly eleven feet in height.

An allusion to Eleazar is also made by Vitellius, who says, that when "Darius, son of Artabanes, was sent as a hostage to Rome, he took with him, with divers presents, a man 7 cubits (or 10 feet 2 inches) high, a Jew named Eleazar, who was called a giant by reason of his greatness."

Antonius, who was born in Syria in the reign of Theodosius, is said to have been 5 cubits and a handbreadth or 7 feet 7 inches high. According to Nicophorus he died at the age of twenty-five.

The Emperor Maximilian is said to have been a man of gigantic stature and of enormous strength. He is supposed to have been between 8 and 9 feet in height, and his shoe was a foot longer than that of any other man. He generally ate 40 pounds' weight of meat and drank 6 gallons of wine every day, and he is said to have been able to draw a wagon which two oxen could not move.

The Emperor Jovianus, too, is reputed to have been a man of abnormal height, and Charlemagne, who likewise was of more than ordinary stature, had a giant named Aenotherus in his army, who "threw down whole battalions as he would have mowed grass".

Ferragus, the monster supposed to have been slain by Roland, the nephew of Charlemagne, was said to have been nearly 11 feet high, and another giant who lived in the twelfth century, during the reign of King Eugene II of Scotland, is declared to have been 11 feet 6 inches in height.

From time to time, bones of gigantic size have been excavated in various parts of Europe, such as instanced in the story of the remains of the giant Theutobochus Rex, which are said to have been disinterred in France in 1613. This skeleton is said to have measured 25 feet long, the jaws having teeth as large as those of an ox; but most of these stories lack verification and it is probable, that many of the bones were those of some huge animal.

Another story is recorded by Jacob Lemaire, who states, that on December 17, 1615, he found, at Port Desire, several graves covered with stones and beneath them, the skeletons of men which measured between 10 and 11 feet; while Riolan, the anatomist, tells us, that at one time, in the neighbourhood of St. Germain, was to be seen the tomb of the giant Isoret, who was reputed to have been 20 feet in height.

There are many tales told by early travellers of people of gigantic stature, such as that related by Magellan, who declared that some of the natives he saw in Patagonia measured 5 cubits high, and also by Turner, who states that on the River Plata, near the Brazilian coast, he observed "naked savages who appeared to be 12 feet high"; but few of such statements have been verified, and there is no evidence of races of gigantic size inhabiting the South American continent.

CHAPTER XVII

GIANTS IN LEGEND AND STORY

GIANTS have ever appealed to popular imagination and from ancient times have been associated with the foundation of various cities. Their stories are still perpetuated by huge figures, which at certain times take part in public processions in several towns and cities on the Continent. In the Low Countries, notably in Antwerp, Ath and Douai, some of these gigantic figures, about 25 feet in height, are carried through the streets on certain holidays or feast days, much to the delight of the inhabitants.

A curious exhibition of some of these giants, which had been lent by various towns in Belgium, was recently held in Brussels. Most of the gigantic figures in basket or wickerwork were dressed in quaint and ancient costumes, surmounted with enormous hats, and were from 20 to 30 feet high. Thus arrayed, in two ranks, they formed an extraordinary spectacle.

London, too, is not without its giants, and the burly figures of Gog and Magog are still prominent in the Guildhall, although probably few people now remember their story.

As told by Geoffrey of Monmouth, it appears that after the destruction of Troy, Brutus gathered a band of Trojans and sailed in search of adventures. Together with Corinaeus, a man of gigantic stature and great strength, they landed in Albion and conquered the country.

Brutus then divided the land between his followers and Corinaeus, one portion being called Britain and the other Cornwall, which he gave to the giant.

One day later, when Brutus was holding a festival on the Cornish coast, a company of giants made their appearance. The Trojans fell upon them with such fury, that eventually all but one named Geomagot or Gogmagog, who was the biggest and strongest of them all, were slain. He was 12 cubits in height and could pull up trees by their roots with the greatest ease. It was decided that Corinaeus, who was thought by the Trojans to be equally strong, should engage him in a great wrestling match. The combatants closed with one another, but the giant broke three of Corinaeus's ribs, which so enraged him that he carried Gogmagog to a high rock and threw him into the sea.

The figures therefore represent Corinaeus and Gogmagog, the names Gog and Magog being a later adaptation, which eventually became applied to the two figures which took part in the city's pageants.

Giants formed part of many of the pageants in old London, and when King Henry V entered the city in triumph in 1415, after the victory of Agincourt, a giant and a giantess stood at the Southwark entrance of London Bridge to receive him, the male bearing the keys of the city gate.

When King Henry VI made his triumphal entry in 1432, at the same place, he was greeted by a great giant who carried an enormous sword, and by his side the following inscription was displayed:

"All those that be enemies to the king
I shall them clothe with confusion."

When Philip and Mary entered London in 1554, huge figures of the city giants, in the shape of Gogmagog and Corinaeus, were placed on London Bridge bearing words of greeting, and they also took part in the reception of Queen Elizabeth at Temple Bar upon her coronation in 1558.

On the coronation of James II, in 1685, images of the giants, filled with combustibles, were placed on a raft on the Thames and exploded during the celebrations.

In those days, the figures of the giants were made of wicker-work or paste-board, so that with men inside them they could perambulate the streets and take part in processions such as the Lord Mayor's Show, but in 1708 these were done away with and replaced by the more permanent figures, carved in wood, of about 14 feet in height, which still stand in the Guildhall.

Though popularly known as Gog and Magog, the oldest

figure is said to represent Gog and the younger one Corinaeus.

Alluding to the midsummer pageants in London, Puttenham, writing in 1589, says: "To make the people wonder, are set forth great and uglie gyants, marching as if they were alive and armed at all points, but within they are stuffed full of browne paper and tow, which the shrewd boyes under peering, do quite fully discover and turne to greate derision."

Several cities in the provinces also had their giants, and we learn from an ordinance of the Corporation of Chester in 1564, "the pageant for the setting of the watch on St. John's eve was directed to consist of, among other things, four giants according to ancient custom".

In 1599, the Mayor caused the giants used in the Midsummer Show "to be broken and not to goe the devil in his feathers", but two years later the giants were restored to their former place.

There is a record that in the time of Charles II, the citizens of Chester replaced the giants which had been destroyed in the period of the Commonwealth, and the estimated cost of "four great giants" was five pounds each, and of four men to carry them, two shillings and sixpence a-piece. The materials for making the giants were "deal board, nails, paste-board, scale-board, paper, buckram, size-cloth, and old sheets for their bodies; sleeves and shirts, which were coloured; also tinsel, gold and silver-leaf and different sorts of colours. A pair of old sheets covered the father and other giant and three yards of buckram were provided for the mother's and daughter's hoods."

There is a curious note added to the charges stating that "one shilling and fourpence is charged for arsenic to put in the paste to save them from being eaten by rats".

Both in Italy and Spain, there are accounts of great giants that took part in civic processions during certain festivals.

In Padua, the procession held at the feast of St. Anthony was formerly preceded by "giants moved by men hidden within their bodies", and in Valencia, in the early part of the nineteenth century, eight statues of giants of prodigious height always took part in the processions.

"Their heads were made of pasteboard and of enormous size, frizzed and dressed in the fashion of the time. They were dressed in coats or robes and men covered with drapery falling to the ground, carried them at the head of the procession, making them dance, caper and bow to the people."

There was a foundation for their support, and a house belonging to them where they were kept. Two benefices were founded in their honour, and it was the duty of the ecclesiastics who possessed them to look after the giants and their ornaments, together with their costumes.

From ancient times giants have also typified protection and strength, and even their representations in wood or paste-board were set up in many castles and great houses, as symbols of courage and power. They sometimes took the form of great savages or barbarians, armed with clubs, such as the giant said to have welcomed Queen Elizabeth on her return from the hunt to Kenilworth Castle. He is described as carrying "an oaken plant plucked up by the roots in his hand, himself all foregrown in moss and ivy".

Laneham states that also "over the first gate of the Castle, stood six gigantic figures, eight feet high, and by this dumb-show it was meant that in the daies of King Arthur men were of that stature, so that the Castle of Kenelworth should seem still to be kept by King Arthur's heirs and their servants".

The giant who plays such an important part in the old nursery story of Jack the Giant-Killer, which has delighted youngsters for centuries, is supposed to have had his origin in Thor or the giant Skrimmer in the Edda of Snorro, but there are many versions of the story.

In one which has ever been popular, the giant is a Welshman whose castle was in Flintshire and he had two heads, so he was a monster as well as a giant.

This story, no doubt, was handed down by word of

mouth for generations and is said to have been first printed about 1711. The words put into the mouth of the giant when he discovers Jack—

> "Fe fi fo fum,
> I smell the blood of an English man"

—are similar to those spoken by a giantess in an ancient Mohammedan tale called Sunebal and the Ogress, and the legend itself may be traced in various forms back to the early part of the Christian Era.

Romance has woven many stories about the life of King Arthur, who is not only said to have been a man of great stature and bravery, but also a slayer of giants.

John de Wavrin, in his *Chronicles of Great Britain*, written between 1445 and 1455, tells the story that while Arthur "was sojourning in his tents on the sea-shore of Britain, tidings came to him that a giant of wonderful size had come into the country from Spain and carried off Helen, whom he had taken to the top of St. Michael's Mount in Cornwall. Numerous knights had followed him in order to rescue the maiden, but they had all been worsted in the fights and hurled down the mountain or eaten by the giant.

Arthur determined to fight the monster and ascended the Mount, where he found the giant warming himself by the fire and eating men whole. On seeing Arthur, he aimed a mighty blow at him with his great iron club, but he warded it off with his shield, and in return struck at the giant's head with his sword and wounded him.

In the combat which ensued, Arthur proved the victor and killed the giant, cut off his head and rescued the maiden.

There are many other stories of giants in Cornwall, a county which abounds in legendary lore, and is still the home of fairies and the "spriggans", who are believed to be the ghosts of giants who guard hidden wealth.

Besides the giants of Trecrobben, who were wont to toss huge pieces of rock about when playing their games, there was the giant of Trebiggan, who is said to have "dined every day on children, whom he fried on a flat rock outside his cave. His arms were so long that he could snatch sailors from the ships which passed the Land's End!"

Then there was Holiburn of the Cairn, who killed a young countryman by patting him on the head in mere good humour. Bolster, the giant who lived on St. Agnes's Beacon Hill, who was able to stretch his legs six miles apart, and the giant Wrath, who used to lie in wait in his cave on the coast near Portwreath, and wading out to sea, would tie boats to his girdle and take their occupants back to his cave and devour them.

Ireland was also rich in giant lore and even in later times produced some men of great stature.

Prominent among the Irish giants was Fingall, who, according to tradition, was converted by St. Patrick to Christianity.

There is a story, that while he was young, Fingall fell into the hands of another giant and was compelled to serve him for seven years, during which time the giant was fishing for a salmon, which had the property of giving to the person who ate the first piece of it, the gift of prophecy. At length, when the seven years had passed, the giant caught the fish and gave it to Fingall to roast, threatening him with instant destruction if he allowed anything to happen to it.

Fingall hung the fish before the fire by a string, but forgot to turn it, so that a blister arose on the side of it. Frightened at the consequences of his carelessness, he tried to press down the blister with his thumb, which he thus burnt, and the pain caused him to put the thumb in his mouth. A portion of the fish happened to have stuck to his thumb and he immediately received the knowledge for which the giant had long toiled in vain.

Knowing that his master would kill him if he remained, he fled, but was soon pursued by the irate giant.

"Whenever Fingall was in danger of being caught, his thumb pained him, and on putting it into his mouth he always obtained knowledge how to evade his pursuer. At last he succeeded in blinding the giant and ever after, when in difficulty or danger, on putting his thumb in his mouth, he was informed how he might escape."

The story of the rock of Carrigogunnel is associated with the Irish giantess Grana. She was a terrible old woman who lived on the rock and desolated the surrounding country. Every night she lit a candle in order to lure victims to destruction, while she lay in wait in her cavern on the Rock of the Candle.

At length, a brave man called Regan crept up one night and extinguished the fatal light, which so enraged the giantess, that she tore up a huge piece of the rock and flung it after him, but it fell harmless and she was never seen again.

The stone, however, remains; "it is far taller than the tallest man, the power of forty men could not move it and deeply imprinted on it are still to be seen the marks of the hag's fingers".

Another Welsh giant of renown was Benlli, who is said to have lived at Mold in Flintshire, and the hill on which he collected his warriors is still called Moel Benlli. He is supposed to have lived about the year 500 and was called the "giant of the Golden Vest". In 1833, when making some new roads, a tumulus was disturbed in which were found some bones of large size, a skull of abnormal proportions and a Lorica or gold vest. From ancient documents it was believed to be the grave of Benlli, as the field in which it was found near Mold, had been known from time immemorial as the "Field of the Goblin".

The Golden Vest, which is now preserved in the British Museum, is of leather, cased with thin, fine gold of beautiful workmanship, and there is a local tradition that on the site of the tumulus on certain nights, the ghost of a man of gigantic stature may be seen wearing a breastplate or vest of gold.

CHAPTER XVIII

GIANTS IN THE SIXTEENTH CENTURY—"THE CHILDE
OF HALE"

LEAVING the realms of tradition and coming to a period
when more reliable records are available of people of
gigantic stature, probably the tallest man of whom we have
some authentic account in England was John Middleton,
who was known as the "Childe of Hale".

He was born at the little village of Hale near the banks
of the Mersey in Lancashire in 1578, and afterwards became
renowned for his extraordinary strength and great stature.

According to a local tradition, until after his boyhood he
was of ordinary height, but one evening he went down to the
beach and slept the night and returned to his home in the
morning a youth of gigantic size. He continued to grow
until he reached the height of 9 feet 3 inches, and his fame
soon became known beyond the county.

It is stated that Sir Gilbert Ireland, who was sheriff
of Lancashire in 1620, took him to London and introduced
him to King James I, and on his return to his native place,
his portrait was painted in the costume that he wore at
Court. This picture is still preserved at Brasenose College,
Oxford.

He is said to have stayed at Oxford on his way to London,
and on visiting Brasenose, the outline of his hand was traced
in the plaster on a wall of the college to commemorate him.

According to Dr. Plot, the portrait was placed in the
college before 1686, for he states in his *Staffordshire*, "John
Middleton, commonly called 'The Childe of Hale', whose
hand from the carpus to the end of the middle finger was
seventeen inches long, his palm eight inches and a half
broad, and his whole height nine foot three inches, wanting
but six inches of the height of Goliath, if that in Brasenose
College Library (drawn at length, as 'tis said, in his just
proportions) be a true piece of him".

Middleton died at the age of forty-five in his native place, and was buried in the churchyard of the village of Hale. A large stone about twelve feet long which covers his grave is inscribed as follows: "HERE LYETH THE BODIE OF JOHN MIDDLETON THE CHILDE. NINE FEET THREE. BORNE 1578. DYEDE 1623."

In the early part of the last century the grave was opened, and it is said some bones of great size were found, but, unfortunately, no measurements appear to have been taken of them.

Cassanio gives an account of a man of great stature who lived at Bordeaux, where he was seen by Francis I of France between 1515 and 1547, who, struck by his height, commanded that he should become one of his guards. The giant joined the King's suite and became an archer of the guards, and is said to have been of so great a stature that a man of ordinary size could walk upright between his legs when they were astride.

There is also an account of another giant warrior who belonged to the Archduke Ferdinand's bodyguard. He was called Aymon and was said to have been 11 feet in height, but he did not live much beyond his fortieth year. A wooden image of this giant was preserved in the Castle of Ambras in the Tyrol.

Stow records in his *Chronicle*, that "In the yeare 1581 there were to be seen in London two Dutchmen of strange statures, the one in height seven foot and seven inches, in breadth betwixt the shoulders, three quarters of a yard and an inch, the compasse of his breast one yard and halfe and two inches and about the wast one yard, quarter and one inch, the length of his arme to the hand a full yard; a comely man of person, but lame on his legges (for he had broken them with lifting of a barrel of beere).

"The other was in height but three foote, had never a good foote nor any knee at all and yet could he daunce a galliard; he hadde no arme but a stumpe to the elbow or little more on the right side, on the which singing, hee would daunce a cup and after, tosse it above three or four times and every time receive the same on the sayde stumpe.

"He would shoote an arrow neere to the marke, flourish with a rapier, throw a bowle, beate with a hammer, hew with an axe, sound a trumpet and drinke every day ten quarts of best beere, if he could get it.

"I myselfe, on the 17 of July, saw the lesser man sitting on the same bench, and having on his head a hat with a feather, was yet the lower. Also the taller man standing on his feet, the lesser (with his hat and feather on his head) went upright between his legs and touched him not."

It is related by Harrison Ainsworth, in his romance *The Tower of London*, that the great arched doorway was guarded by three gigantic warders, brothers, who claimed descent from Henry VIII. On account of their height they were called Og, Gog and Magog. All the giants were nearly 8 feet high, though Magog exceeded the others by an inch. "Og the eldest of the trio is said to have been the image of King Hal. By their side with an immense halberd in his hand stood a diminutive dwarf, not two feet high, dressed in the costume of a page. Kit, as he was called, who had a malicious and ill-favoured countenance with a shock of yellow hair, was in constant attendance on the giants." According to the story, he had been found when an infant one morning on Og's doorstep. He adopted the tiny foundling, who eventually became a plaything for himself and his brothers.

From the sixteenth century, giants appear to have been in demand by Royal personages as porters and to act as janitors at the doors of their palaces or castles.

Queen Elizabeth's giant porter, whose portrait in Spanish costume by Zucchero is still to be seen at Hampton Court Palace, is said to have been 7 feet 6 inches in height, but little is known of him beyond that he was said to have come from the Low Countries.

King James I also had a giant porter in the person of Walter Parsons, who was born in Staffordshire.

Fuller tells us, that as a boy Parsons was apprenticed to a smith, but he grew so tall in stature, that "a hole was made for him in the ground to stand therein up to the knees, so as to make him adequate with his fellow workman. "Seeing as gates generally are higher than the rest of the building", he continues, "so it was sightly that the porter should be taller than other persons. He was proportionable in all parts and had strength equal to height, valour to his strength, temper to his valour; so that he disdained to do an injury to any single person. He would make nothing to take two of the tallest yeomen of the Guard (like the gizard and liver) under his arms at once and order them as he pleased."

His height is stated to have been from 7 feet 2 inches to 7 feet 7 inches.

After the death of James I, he remained as porter to Charles I, and is said to have died about 1628.

In the account of Parsons given by Plot, it is stated that when he walked in the streets of London, "if affronted by a man of ordinary stature, he only took him up by the waistband of his breeches and hung him upon one of the hooks in the shambles, to be ridicul'd by the people and so went his way.

"A true measure of his hand yet remaineth upon a piece of wainscot at Bentley Hall, by which it appears, that from the carpus to the end of the middle finger it was eleven inches long and the palm six inches broad."

Parsons was succeeded in his office as janitor by William Evans, who was born in Monmouthshire and exceeded his predecessor in height by about two inches.

Fuller says that he was "full two yards and a half in length, but far beneath Parsons in an equal proportion of body; for he was not only what the Latines call compernis, knocking his knees together, and going out squalling with his feet, but also haulted a little; yet made he shift to dance in an antimask at court, where he drew little Jeffrey the dwarf out of his pocket, first to the wonder then to the laughter of the beholders".

There is still to be seen over the entrance to a court in Newgate Street, a stone tablet carved in relief, with representations of "The King's Porter and Dwarf". The giant is garbed in a long gown with hanging sleeves and holds his staff of office, while his companion, Jeffrey, the dwarf, who was only 3 feet 9 inches in height, wears a loose cloak. Evans is said to have died about 1635.

Before leaving the Royal giants, mention should be made of Oliver Cromwell's giant porter named Daniel, who is said to have been 7 feet 6 inches high. His height is recorded

WILLIAM EVANS, THE KING'S PORTER, AND JEFFREY HUDSON THE DWARF

From a stone relief in Bullhead Court, Newgate Street, E.C.

by a large O on the back of the terrace at Windsor Castle, almost under the window of the gallery.

Daniel was a religious fanatic, who frequently preached, and is said to have had the gift of prophecy. One of his greatest treasures was a large Bible that was given to him by Nell Gwynne.

Leslie states, that "people often went to hear Daniel preach and they would sit many hours under his windows with great signs of devotion.

"His brain eventually became affected and he was sent to Bedlam."

It is said, that "Oliver's porter had an amanuensis in Bedlam who used to transcribe what he dictated. Though Oliver's porter was crazed his misfortune never made him forget that he was a Christian."

Much has been written about Antony Payne, the Cornish giant, who became the faithful henchman of Sir Bevil Grenville of Stowe. His father occupied the manor-house of Stratton and both of his parents were of normal stature.

As a boy he was of unusual size and grew rapidly in height and strength. He excelled in games of all kinds and yet his mental faculties increased with his growth.

At the age of twenty-one he measured 7 feet 2 inches without his shoes, and afterwards grew another 2 inches, but in spite of his height he was "wide-chested, ample-limbed and symmetrical in figure."

He entered the service of Sir Bevil and became leader of his sports. He would disembowel and flay the slain deer and carry the carcases on his shoulders to the hall. It is said that it took the hides of three full-grown deer to make him a jerkin.

There is a story told that one Christmas Eve, a boy with an ass was sent into the woods to collect logs, and as he loitered, Antony went to fetch him and brought home the animal, logs and all, on his back. On another occasion "he walked from Kilkhampton to Stowe with a bacon-hog weighing three hundredweight on his shoulders, because a taunting butcher doubted his strength for the feat."

When the Civil Wars broke out, Sir Bevil espoused the King's cause and Antony accompanied him as his squire or bodyguard. When news came later that the Parliamentary troops were marching on Stowe, Antony and a picked body of men went out to meet them.

An engagement took place and after the fight Antony arranged to bury the dead on the battlefield. He had large trenches dug, each to hold ten bodies side by side, and there, he and his followers carried the slain.

After Payne had carried nine and laid them in one of the trenches, he was carrying in another under his arm, when the supposed dead man cried out, "Surely you wouldn't bury me, Mr. Payne, before I'm dead?"

"I tell thee, man", replied Payne, "our trench was dug for ten and there's nine in it already; you must take your place."

"But I bean't dead, I say, I haven't done living yet. Be massyful, Mr. Payne; don't ye hurry a poor fellow into the earth before his time."

"I won't hurry thee; I mean to put thee down quietly and cover thee up, and then thee canst die at thy leisure", cheerfully responded the giant.

Payne, however, who enjoyed the situation, carried the wounded man carefully to his own cottage and looked after him.

Sir Bevil was killed in the same year at the battle of Lansdowne, in which the Royalists were defeated. Payne was at his side when he fell, and mounting young John Grenville, the heir, who was barely sixteen, on his father's horse, led the troop again into the fight.

When Charles II came to the throne, John Grenville was appointed governor of Plymouth garrison and Payne went with him and was made halberdier of the guns.

The King became greatly interested in the giant and commanded his portrait to be painted by Sir Godfrey Kneller, which for many years hung in the great gallery at Stowe.

This picture, which went through many vicissitudes, represented Payne as halberdier of the guns, standing with one hand resting on a cannon and the other holding his halberd. A large gallon flask which occupies a place in the foreground is said to have been the one which held Antony's allowance of wine.

The portrait forms the frontispiece to Gilbert's *History of Cornwall*, Vol. II.

Payne lived to a good old age, and when he retired from the Army returned to live in his native place and died at

Stratton. After his death it was found impossible to remove his body from the house, either by the door or the stairs, so the joists had to be cut and the floor lowered to enable the giant to be taken to Stratton churchyard, where he was buried.

A curious assembly of giants and dwarfs gathered from Germany, to gratify a whim of the Empress of Austria, took place in Vienna in the seventeenth century.

According to Guy Patin, it was necessary that all attending the gathering should be housed in one extensive building. Instead of the giants terrifying the dwarfs, as was feared by the promoters, the latter teased and insulted and even robbed the giants to such an extent, that they "complained with tears in their eyes of their diminutive persecutors, and as a consequence, sentinels had to be stationed in the building to protect the big creatures from the little".

CHAPTER XIX

SOME GIANTS OF THE SEVENTEENTH CENTURY

A NUMBER of giants and prodigies were exhibited in London in the seventeenth century, and James Paris du Plessis, in his *Short History of Human Prodigies, Dwarfs, etc.*, records several that he actually saw. Among them was a "Monstrous Tartar" who came from Hungary, who was to be seen at "Ye Globe in the ould Baily in February 1664.

"He was taken prisoner by Count Serini and was a creature of extraordinary strength and valour, who having spent all his arrows in fight against the Christian, was taken alive and so continues being carefully kept in those parts."

He also tells us of a "Monstrous hairy woman of about thirty years of age" whom he saw in London. He describes her as having "a very handsome face. Black hair on her head. Her body was uniparted, and all her right side was from the shoulder to her knees, all hairy. The leg and hand of a fine smooth white colour, without hair, but the other halfe side of her was a pure white, soft, smooth and white skin, but all over bestowed with moles of a reddish colour, with a few hairs on each of them, from the shoulder down to the knee, her hand and foot as them on the other side and so behind alike as before."

He further mentions "a giantess who was seven feet high without her shoes, who was born in the Isle of Portrush, not far from the wonderful Causeway in the most northern part of Ireland". She was twenty-three years old when he saw her first in London in 1696. Her head was very well-shaped and she was very well-proportioned and had a very handsome face.

"In the year 1701", he continues, "she was at Montpelier in Languedoch in France at the time of the Fair, where I seen her again shown for money as she had been before in London.

"I not knowing she was the same I had seen five years before in London, and though I was something disguised by wearing a perriwig, she remembered me very well and told me where she had seen me."

Some of the old bills which are still extant, tell us of other famous giants of the time. Thus at "The Lottery-office, next door to the Green-Man at Charing Cross", was to be seen "THE LIVING COLOSSUS" or Wonderful Giant from Sweden.

"He is near a foot taller than the late famous Saxon or any person yet seen in Europe" (see p. 159).

The Saxon giant mentioned was probably Maximilian Christopher Miller, who was born at Leipzig in 1674, and who came to London after travelling through several of the countries of Europe. He was 7 feet 8 inches in height and, according to his bill, was to be seen at "The Two Blue Posts and Rummer, near Charing Cross."

"A giant born in Saxony almost eight foot in height and every way proportionable; the like has not been seen in any part of the world for many years. He has had the honour to show himself to most princes in Europe, particularly to his late majesty the King of France, who presented him with a noble scymiter and a silver mace."

Another bill of Miller's states: "This is to give notice to all gentlemen, ladies and others. That there is just arrived from France and is to be seen at 'The Fan' over against Devereux-court, without Temple Bar, a Giant, born in Saxony almost eight foot in height.

"He is to be seen from ten in the morning till eight at night, without any loss of time, his stay in this place being but short, he designing to go for Holland."

There are several portraits of Miller, including an engraving by Boitard done from life in 1733, and Hogarth represents him as the giant on the show-cloth, in his picture of Southwark Fair.

He attracted considerable attention in London, especially on account of the costumes he affected.

At the age of fifty-nine he stood nearly 8 feet high, and his head and face were huge in size. His hand measured 12 inches and one of his fingers was 9 inches long.

He usually wore in public, a Hungarian tunic and a velvet cap with a large plume of feathers. When on exhibition, he carried a gilt sceptre in his right hand, and his left hand rested on the hilt of an immense, richly mounted scimitar, and thus he paraded up and down his apartment with great dignity and state. He died in London after reaching the age of sixty years.

An Irish giant, who is described as "THE MIRACLE OF NATURE", was exhibited in London in 1684.

His bill states: "Being so much admired Young man, aged nineteen years last June 1684, he was born in Ireland of such a Prodigious Height and Bigness and every way proportionable, the like hath not been seen since the memory of man.

"He hath been several times shown at Court and His Majesty was pleased to walk under his arm, and he is grown very much since. He can now reach ten and a half feet. Fathomes near eight feet. Spans fifteen inches, and is believed to be as big as one of the Gyants in the Guild-Hall."

Molyneux gives this giant's name as Edmond Malone, and Wood states, that he was seen at the "Blew Bore" in Oxford in 1681.

Plot also refers to him in 1686, and says: "The hand of Edmund Maloon a youth of nineteen years old, born at Port Leicester in Ireland, for his extraordinary stature shown here publickly in Oxford in 1684, which though from the carpus to the end of the middle finger it were twelve inches long, yet the palm was no more than five inches broad." William Musgrave also gives an account of Malone which he says was communicated to him by Dr. Plot, in which his height is given as 7 feet 6 inches. He was probably the same giant who is described as "The Miracle of Nature", and was exhibited at Southwark Fair in 1684 and was shown to Charles II.

In a later bill, apparently printed about 1692, we find he was at Bartholomew Fair, and is described as "Miracula Naturae", being "that admired Gyant-like young man aged twenty-three years last June, born in Ireland.

"He was shown to his late and present majesty and several of the nobility at court five years ago; and his late majesty was pleased to walk under his arm and he has grown very much since. And it is generally thought that if he lives three years more and grows as he has done, he will be much bigger than any of those gyants we read of in story, for he now reaches with his hand three yards and a half, spans fifteen inches and is the admiration of all that sees him.

"He is to be seen at Cow Lane end in Bartholomew Fair where his picture hangs out. Vivat Rex."

We learn from another bill in 1678, that "At the Golden-Lyon near the Hospital gate in Smithfield was to be seen for 2d. the tall black called THE INDIAN KING, who was betrayed on board an English Interloper and barbarously abused on board of that ship by one Waters and his men and put in irons.

"From thence carried to Jamaica and sold there as a slave and now redeemed by a merchant in London. The like hath not been seen before in England."

Another giant who claimed to have been over eight feet in height, was to be seen at the "Golden Ball", in Great Suffolk Street, near Charing Cross.

"This gentleman lately arrived from Holland was the tallest person that ever was seen here before, between 7 and 8 (feet) and 20 years of age. He was the son of a clergyman and was born in Swedish Finland.

"N.B. He is to be seen for two shillings and sixpence each person, at the house aforesaid."

About the same time, at "Mr. Francis Strut's, Perfumer, at the Civet Cat over against Exeter-Exchange in the Strand", was to be seen a "Tall Woman of seven foot and three inches high. Weighs 415 pounds, who has had the honour to be shown before seven Kings in Europe."

According to a bill printed about 1664, a great German giant and his wife paid a visit to London and were to be seen at "The Swan", near Charing Cross. "His stature is nine feet and a half in height and the span of his hand a cubit compleat. He goes from place to place with his wife, who is but of an ordinary stature and takes money for the shew of her husband."

Pepys, who always delighted in the curious, records his visit to this giant in his *Diary*, on August 15, 1664, thus:

"Was at Charing Cross and there saw the great Dutchman that is come over, under whose arm I went with my hat on, and could not reach higher than his eye-browes with the tip of my finger. He is a comely and well-made man, and his wife, a very little but pretty comely Dutch woman. It is true he wears pretty high-heeled shoes but not very high, and do generally wear a turban which makes him show yet taller than really he is." The giant described himself as being a German.

On January 4, 1668-9, Pepys also paid a visit to a giantess. He says: "W. Hewer and I went and saw the great tall woman that is to be seen, who is but twenty-one years old and I do easily stand under her arms."

He was evidently so pleased with the giantess that on February 8th, he took his wife to see her, and says: "To my wife, and in our way home, did show her the tall woman in Holborne, which I have seen before and I measured her, and she is without shoes, just six feet five inches high and they say not above twenty-one years old."

Evelyn also mentions the Dutch giantess, and on January 29th records in his *Diary*: "I went to see a tall gigantic woman who measur'd 6 feet 10 inches high at 21 years old, born in the Low Countries."

Men of abnormal strength have at all times excited popular admiration and been objects of general interest.

In the past, the heroes of Greek mythology like Hercules were regarded as the embodiment of physical strength and bravery, and the story of Samson of Biblical history, and the literature of the Middle Ages, abounds with traditions of men who have exhibited abnormal feats of strength.

One of the most remarkable prodigies of the late seventeenth century was William Joyce, who was not only a man of gigantic stature but also of great strength.

He was exhibited before King William at Kensington Palace on November 15, 1699, and the account of his amazing exploits shown before His Majesty is related as follows:

"The wonderful and amazing strength of Mr. William Joyce, the Kentish man. His Majesty King William had a desire to see him and on Wednesday last he was introduced before his Majesty at Kensington.

"Asked how much he was capable of lifting, he reply'd 'Above a tun weight', whereupon a solid piece of lead was prepared according to his desire and being weighed, it contained a tun and fourteen and a half pounds. Notwithstanding which he lifted it up from the ground to the admiration of his Majesty and his nobles who were eye-witnesses thereof.

"After which, his Majesty commanded a rope of incredible thickness to be brought and fastened about his middle, and the other end to an extraordinary strong horse, at which time he told his Majesty that the horse could not move him; upon which to try the experiment, the said horse was whip't in order to pull him out of his place, but notwithstanding all his strength, Mr. Joyce stood as immovable as an oak tree. Whereupon, seeing his Majesty and others of the nobility to be seemingly astonished at this strange action, he there upon declared that he could by meer strength break the same rope in two. Whereupon tying the same to two postes he twitch'd it in pieces seemingly as easie as another man does a piece of pack-thread and not only so, but afterwards putting his armes about one of the said postes, which was of extraordinary magnitude, he at one violent pull broke it down.

"At which strange performance his Majesty was mightily well pleased, and it is said has ordered him a considerable gratuity besides an honourable entertainment for both him and his acquaintances.

"Mr. Joyce is further said, to have pulled up a tree of near a yard and a half in circumference by the roots, at Hamstead, on Tuesday last, in the open view of hundreds of people, it being modestly computed to weigh nearly 2,000 weight."

In later times there was Thomas Topham, who could lift three hogsheads full of water, weighing 1,386 pounds, and Tom Johnson, another strong man, who was a Thames riverside porter, who could carry four sacks of corn weighing 1,400 pounds.

In recent years there have been men like Sebastian Miller, another Samson, Louis Cyr and Sandow, all of whom have exhibited remarkable physical development and abnormal strength.

The feminine sex also have had their exponents of great muscular power. Notable among them were Madame Elise, who could lift eight men and support a seven-hundred-pound dumb-bell, with a person hanging on each end across her shoulders; also Miss Darnett, known as the "Singing strong lady". She could support a platform on which stood a piano and a pianist who played while the strong lady sang a song.

CHAPTER XX

GIANTS IN THE EIGHTEENTH CENTURY

CONTRARY to the general idea, giants have usually been found to be persons of mild and quiet dispositions, and not by any means the blustering and bellicose individuals they are often represented to be in romance and story. As a rule, their order of intelligence is low and they are naturally clumsy and slow in their movements. Judging from their histories, they were often characterized by mental and bodily weakness, and seldom have had strength or courage commensurate with their physical proportions.

Their great stature is generally due to excessive growth of the lower extremities, the size of the head and body being usually about the same as that of a boy or man of the same age.

There is a close association of acromegaly with giantism, and as Marie observed, "acromegaly is giantism of the adult; giantism is acromegaly of adolescence."

Virey remarks: "Tall men are generally much more weak and slow than short men, for all exertions both of body and mind."

"If men of high stature are preferred for their fine appearance in the body-guard of princes, and in the service of eminent persons, they are certainly neither the most robust nor the most active; but they are docile, candid and naïve, little prone to conspire for evil, and faithful even to the worst master.

"In war, they are more fitted for defence than attack; whereas, an impetuous and brusque action suits better for short and vivacious men.

"Tall men are mostly tame and insipid, like watery vegetables; insomuch that we seldom hear of a very tall man becoming a very great man. Little men manifest a character more firm and decided than those lofty and soft-bodied people, whom we can lead more easily, both morally and physically."

A number of remarkable giants came into notoriety in the early part of the eighteenth century, and among them was the young Welshman known as the "Tall Briton", who was exhibited in London in the time of William and Mary and Queen Anne at the beginning of the eighteenth century.

He is said to have been born on a mountain near Llanrwst in North Wales, and to be "the tallest youth that ever was shown in the kingdom". According to his bill, "from the age of sixteen he had travelled abroad and been shown before all the foreign kings and princes in Christendom, and is now lately come into England and had the honour to have been shown before her present Majesty of Great Brittain and her Royal consort the Prince. He is to be seen by any one single person from 9 in the morning till 10 at night. Vivat Regina."

About this period, a demand appears to have arisen for men of exceptional height as professional soldiers. The King of Prussia was the first to form a regiment of gigantic guards which afterwards became famous throughout Europe. For fifty years this regiment was stationed at Potsdam and Foster makes the curious observation that, "the present inhabitants of that place are of very high stature, which is more especially striking in the numerous gigantic figures of women. This certainly is owing to the connexions and inter-marriages of those tall men with the females of the town."

An account was published on June 17, 1732, of a review of the regiment at Berlin, when his Royal Highness the Prince presented to his father, the King of Prussia, a man twenty years of age, 7 feet 6 inches high and extremely well-proportioned. He was the tallest man in the regiment.

In the *Daily Post* for August 1, 1733, there is a paragraph stating that "about the middle of July, an Irishman named Fitzgerald who was seven feet high and a lieutenant in the King of Prussia's Guards, came to London." A few weeks following came the statement that, "the King of Prussia having been informed that there was a soldier of extraordinary stature in the service of the King of France, in the regiment of dragoons of Baufremont, caused an application to be made to the captain of the company in which this soldier was, desiring him to send the giant for enlistment in the Prussian regiment of Grand Grenadiers. The captain having obtained the necessary permission from the King of France, caused the soldier to be handsomely clothed and equipped and sent him to Berlin, where he was very kindly received by the King, who gave him a pension of one thousand livres tournois and a thousand louis-d'ors to his captain."

Voltaire says, that "King Frederick William armed with a huge sergeant's cane marched forth every day to review his regiment of giants. The men who stood in the first rank were none of them less than seven feet high, and he sent to purchase them from the farthest parts of Europe to the borders of Asia."

On one occasion, it is said, the King invited the English, French and Spanish ambassadors to be present at a review of his gigantic guards and asked the three foreign representatives whether an equal number of their countrymen would engage with his monster soldiers. The French and Spanish ambassadors replied in the negative, but the Englishman said that, though he could not assert that an equal number of his countrymen would beat them, he could affirm that half the number would try.

The Duke of Brunswick-Hanover had a guardsman who is said to have been 8 feet 6 inches in height, and the Duke of Würtemberg had one who measured 7 feet 6 inches.

James Paris mentions several giants whom he saw in London in the early eighteenth century. One he describes as being twenty-five years of age when he saw him, on May 12, 1716. "He was seven feet five inches high and every way proportionable; he was born in Saxony and had travelled all over Europe. The King of the Romans presented him with a suit of armour proportionate to his size. He was seen by George I, the Queen, the Prince of Wales, the rest of the Royal Family and the Court, at Windsor. He was so strong that he could hold a ten-pound weight at arm's length for twelve minutes."

This was probably the Saxon giant alluded to previously, who was at the "Two Blue Posts and Rummer", and was presented by the King of France with a scimitar and a silver mace. Paris also mentions an Irishman born near Dublin, who was "seven feet eleven inches high without his shoes or anything on his head. Each of his shoes weighed three pounds two ounces and for a wager in my presence, I saw one of the shoes measured, which was a foot and three inches long and ten inches wide."

One of the most famous English giants of this period was Henry Blacker, who was born at Cuckfield in Sussex in 1724.

He came to London in 1751, when he was twenty-seven years of age, and attracted considerable interest.

He was 7 feet 4 inches in height and well-proportioned.

His exhibition is thus announced in the *Daily Advertiser* of December 8, 1752: "This is to acquaint the curious, that Mr. Blacker, the 'Modern Colossus' or 'Wonderful Giant', who has given universal satisfaction, is to be seen in a commodious room in Half-Moon Court joining Ludgate. This phenomenon in nature hath already had the honour of being inspected by great numbers of the nobility and gentry, by many of the Royal Society, and several gentlemen and ladies who are lovers of natural curiosities; who allow him to be of stupendous height and affirm him to be the best proportioned of his size they ever saw.

"He is to be seen by any number of persons, from nine in the morning till nine at night, without loss of time.

"Note. *Lost*, last Tuesday night between Norton Falgate and Ludgate, *a boot*. Whoever has found it and will bring it to the above Mr. Blacker shall receive three shillings reward."

He was visited several times by William, Duke of Cumberland, who was himself a very tall man, and in an engraving of Blacker by Carpenter, the Duke is represented among the spectators.

About the same period Daniel Cajanus, who is called the "Swedish Giant", was exhibited in London. His height is variously given and by some was stated to be 7 feet

8 inches (Rhenish) and by others as 8 feet 4 inches (Swedish).

His bill announces, that "This is to acquaint gentlemen and ladies, that that prodigy of nature, the 'Living Colossus' or 'Wonderful Giant' from Sweden, is now to be seen at the Lottery Office, next door to the 'Green Man', Charing Cross. It is humbly presumed that of all the natural curiosities which have been exhibited to the publick, nothing has appeared for many ages so extraordinary in its way as this surprising gentleman. He is nearly a foot taller than the late famous Saxon or any person ever yet seen in Europe, large in proportion; and all who have hitherto seen him declare, notwithstanding the prodigious accounts they had heard, that he far exceeds any idea they had fram'd of him."

According to an advertisement in the *Daily Advertiser*: "The 'Living Colossus' or 'Wonderful Giant' (who has been these five weeks very dangerously ill of a fever, which has occasioned a report of his death) is now so well recovered as to be able to shew himself to all ladies and gentlemen, who will be pleased to honour him with their company at the same place, at the sign of the 'Mansion House and French Horn', between the Poultry and the Royal Exchange, at the usual price of sixpence each person, from the hour of nine in the morning till eight at night. This is really the same giant as has been shown to great numbers of the nobility and gentry, notwithstanding the petty insinuations of some people (upon hearing of this recovery) to the contrary."

Dr. Bryan Robinson records that Cajanus's pulse-rate was fifty-two and it is stated, that the last on which his shoes were made was $14\frac{1}{2}$ inches long.

He died at Haarlem on February 28, 1749, and his coffin measured 9 feet 7 inches in length. A marble stone on a pillar at the porch of the Brouwer's chapel in the great church at Haarlem records his height.

A giant who performed on the tight rope attracted considerable attention in London in 1745. Although but fifteen years of age, he is said to have been 7 feet high, and was a native of Hurtfield in Sussex.

He is announced first as being on exhibition at the sign of the "French Horn and Mansion House", opposite the Mansion House, on February 23, 1745. Later in the same year he appeared at the New Wells in Clerkenwell, a popular open-air resort at that time.

According to a newspaper account of this place of amusement, where he evidently proved an attraction, "The undertakers of the New Wells near the London Spaw, beg leave to assure the town, since thronging audiences have been pleased to encourage their endeavours, they intend to double their pains and hope for a continuance of favour. The god of wine and deity of wit have long gone hand-in-hand and to keep them both alive the best way is to blend them, therefore for the reception of the curious, they have provided the best of both their productions; and as varieties in nature are as pleasing as those of art, the greatest that can now be shown is every evening to be seen at the Wells, viz. a Young Colossus, who, though not sixteen, is seven feet four inches high, has drawn more company this season than was ever known before and must convince the world, that the ancient race of Britons is not extinct, but that we may yet hope to see a race of giant-like heroes.

"The Wonderful Young Giant will perform on the rope this present Saturday at the New Wells, near the London Spaw, Clerkenwell."

An advertisement in the *Daily Advertiser* of March 4, 1751, appears to refer to the same youth. It reads: "The modern living Colossus or wonderful giant is to be seen at Mr. Squire's, peruke-maker, facing the Mews-walk, within two doors of the Panopticon, Charing Cross, from ten in the morning till eight at night, at 1s. each person. This wonder in nature is thought by those who have already privately seen him, to be the tallest of the human species in Europe, large in proportion, and much superior in straightness to any one ever exhibited to publick view of an uncommon size; in short he may be justly stil'd a phenomenon in nature."

In 1755, an Italian giant named Bernardo Gigli, who is said to have been 8 feet in height, arrived in London and took up his lodgings at the bottom of the Haymarket, next to the Prince Orange Coffee-house.

The following year his exhibition was thus announced:

"The Italian Giant named Bernardo Gigli. A Giant indeed! who, tho' but nineteen years of age, is eight feet high and of admirable symmetry, is to be seen from ten in the morning till eight at night, at a commodious apartment the bottom of Pall-mall, near the Haymarket."

A later advertisement states, that "The Italian giant who has been beheld with astonishment as well in England as in most parts of Europe, will be exhibited during the time of Southwark Fair at 6d. each person, after which he will immediately set out for Ireland."

A portrait of Gigli at the age of nineteen years was engraved by Fougeron, after Millington.

CHAPTER XXI

SOME FAMOUS IRISH GIANTS OF THE EIGHTEENTH
CENTURY

IRELAND produced some famous giants in the eighteenth
century, and notable among them was Cornelius MacGrath,
who was born at Tipperary in 1736.

His parents were people of ordinary stature and none of
the family except Cornelius was of abnormal height. At the
age of sixteen, he measured 6 feet 8¾ inches, and on visiting
Cork in 1752, he was followed by crowds of people as he
walked the streets who were attracted by his great size.

When fifteen, he is said to have been seized with violent
pains in his limbs and in the space of twelve months grew
nearly twenty-one inches.

The Bishop of Cloyne, Dr. Berkeley, took an interest in
him, and kept him in his house until he recovered the use
of his limbs and regained his health. His hand at that time,
is said to have been as large as a good-sized shoulder of
mutton and the last of his shoes, which he carried with him,
measured fifteen inches. His appetite was very moderate and
he drank very little but cider, which he took with his meals.

He came to England in 1753, and was first exhibited at
Bristol. His arrival in London is thus announced in the
Daily Advertiser for January 31, 1753: "Just arrived in this
city from Ireland, the youth lately mentioned in the
newspapers as the most extraordinary production of nature.
He is allowed by the nobility and gentry, who daily resort
to see him, to have the most stupendous and gigantic form
(although a boy) and is the only representation in the
world of the ancient and magnificent giants of that kingdom.
He is seven feet three inches in height without shoes. His
wrist measures a quarter of a yard and an inch.

"He greatly surpasses Cajanus the Swede in the just
proportion of his limbs, and is the truest and best-propor-
tioned figure ever seen. He was sixteen years of age the
10th of March last, and is to be seen at the 'Peacock' at

Charing Cross, from eight in the morning till ten at night."

There was a story circulated at the time which is repeated by Geoffroy St. Hilaire ,that while living with the Bishop of Cloyne, Dr. Berkeley put him under a course of diet in order to increase his stature with the idea of producing a giant, and his experiment proved successful. There appear to be no grounds whatever for such a story, and there is little doubt that the good bishop looked after the boy for a time purely out of charity and until he had regained the full use of his limbs.

After leaving London he went to Paris and toured through many of the principal cities in Europe. While in Florence, he attracted the attention of Bianchi, the celebrated naturalist, who wrote a pamphlet describing him in 1757.

Three years later he returned to Ireland with his health broken down after an attack of intermittent fever, which he contracted in Holland. He is said to have died shortly afterwards in Dublin, where he had always been popular with the students of Trinity College, one of whom, named Hare, he used to lift by the collar of his coat and hold him out at arm's length, much to the amusement of the others.

They are reported to have stolen his body on the day on which he was to have been waked, which caused a series of combats between the students and the coal-porters of the city, which continued for many years afterwards.

MacGrath's skeleton, which measures 7 feet 8 inches, is preserved at Trinity College, Dublin.

There were two Irish giants who were born about the middle of the eighteenth century, both of whom assumed the name of O'Brien, and hence are sometimes confused. The name of the first was Charles Byrne, who was born about 1761. Before he reached the age of nineteen he is said to have measured 8 feet in height. By the time he was twenty-one, he had gained another 2 inches, and at the date of his death was 8 feet 4 inches. Neither his parents nor any of his relations were people above the ordinary stature.

He came to London in 1782, and his arrival is thus announced in a newspaper of April 24th of that year:

"To be seen this, and every day this week, in his large elegant room, at the cane-shop next door to late Cox's Museum, Spring Gardens, Mr. Byrne, the surprising 'Irish Giant', who is allowed to be the tallest man in the world; his height is eight feet two inches and in full proportion accordingly; only 21 years of age. His stay will not be long in London, as he proposes shortly to visit the Continent."

That he attracted considerable attention and interest is evidenced from a further account which appeared on May 6, 1782:

"However striking a curiosity may be", says the writer, "there is generally some difficulty in engaging the attention of the public; but even this was not the case with the modern living Colossus, or wonderful 'Irish Giant', for no sooner was he arrived at an elegant apartment at the cane-shop in Spring Gardens, next door to Cox's Museum, than the curious of all degrees resorted to see him, being sensible that a prodigy like this never made its appearance among us before, and the most penetrating have frankly declared, that neither the tongue of the most florid orator or pen of the most ingenious writer, can sufficiently describe the elegance, symmetry and proportion of this wonderful phenomenon in Nature, and that all description must fall infinitely short of giving that satisfaction which may be obtained on a judicious inspection."

The "Irish Giant" became the talk of the town and a pantomime produced at the Haymarket Theatre in 1782, in which references were made to Byrne, was called *Harlequin Teague or the Giant's Causeway.*

His rival, whom we shall describe later, appears to have also arrived in London about this time, judging from the following announcement:

"The nobility and gentry are requested to take notice, there was a man shewed himself for some time past at the top of the Haymarket and Piccadilly, who advertised and endeavoured to impose himself on the public for the Irish giant and never was in this metropolis before Thursday, the 11th inst. Hours of admittance every day Sundays excepted from 11 till 3 and from 5 till 8 at half a crown each person."

In an article in a newspaper of August 12, 1782, Byrne is thus described: "This extraordinary young man has been seen by abundance of the nobility and gentry, likewise of the faculty, Royal Society and other admirers of natural curiosities, who allow him to surpass anything of the same kind ever offered to the public.

"His address is singular and pleasing, his person truly shaped and proportioned to his height and affords an agreeable surprize; he excels the famous Maximilian Miller born in 1674 shewn in London in 1733, and the late Swedish giant will scarce admit of comparison. To enumerate every particular would be too tedious, let it suffice to say, that he is beyond what is set forth in ancient or modern history. . . .

" 'Take him for all in all, we shall scarce look on his like again.'
                                        SHAKESPEARE."

In 1782, he removed to "an elegant apartment at the house of Mr. Mittenius, Confectioner, Charing Cross," and subsequently to Piccadilly to the sign of the "Hampshire Hog", where he was to be seen by "Gentlemen and Ladies 2s. 6d. Children and servants in livery 1s."

In 1783, this "truly amazing phenomenon, indisputably the most extraordinary production of the human species ever beheld since the days of Goliath", as he is described, removed to 12, Cockspur Street, where he died on June 30, 1783, at the age of twenty-two.

For a short time he acted as porter at St. James's Palace, but soon tired of the post.

His death is said to have been accelerated by excessive drinking and grief at the loss of his savings, which he had invested in two bank notes, one being for £700 and the other for £70.

According to an account published on April 23, 1783, "The 'Irish Giant', a few evenings since, taking a lunar ramble, was tempted to visit the 'Black Horse', a little public-house facing the King's Mews, and before he returned to his own apartments, found himself a less man than he had been the beginning of the evening, by the loss of upwards of £700 in bank notes which had been taken out of his pocket."

Haunted by the idea that after his death his body would fall into the hands of the surgeons so that his skeleton might be preserved, Byrne left directions that on his decease, fishermen should be paid to take his body and sink it with lead weights in the middle of the Irish Channel.

John Hunter, the famous surgeon and anatomist, who it is said had often asseverated his desire to add the giant's skeleton to his collection, eventually came into possession of the body and according to a story at the time, overbribed the men who had been engaged to carry out Byrne's request, at a cost of five hundred pounds. There is another version published later, which states that Byrne, dreading dissection by Hunter, had, shortly before his death, arranged with several of his countrymen that his body should be conveyed by them to the sea and sunk in deep water, but his under-taker, who had entered into a pecuniary compact with Mr. Hunter, arranged that while the escort was drinking at a certain stage on the march seawards, the coffin should be locked up in a barn. There, some men he had concealed speedily substituted an equivalent weight of paving-stones for the body, which was at night forwarded to Hunter and by him taken in his carriage to Earl's Court. To avoid risk of discovery, immediately after suitable division had been made he boiled it in his great kettle to obtain the bones.

Whether there is any truth in these stories or not, John Hunter obtained the skeleton of Byrne the giant for his collection and it now stands in the Museum of the Royal College of Surgeons of England.

According to accounts in newspapers of the time, Hunter was not alone in wanting to obtain possession of the remains of the unfortunate giant, for "The whole tribe of surgeons", states one journal, "put in a claim for the poor departed Irishman and surrounded his house, just as harpooners would an enormous whale.

"One of them has gone so far as to have a niche made for himself in the giant's coffin, in order to his being ready at hand on the 'witching time of night when churchyards yawn' !"

Another observes that, "Since the death of the 'Irish giant', there have been more physical consultations held, than ever were convened to keep Harry the Eighth in existence. So anxious are the surgeons to have possession of the 'Irish giant', that they have offered a ransom of 800 guineas to the undertakers. This sum being rejected, they are determined to approach the church-yard by regular works and terrier-like unearth him !"

It was given out, that Byrne had been buried in St. Martin's Churchyard, but the true version of the story is, that Hunter was successful in obtaining possession of his remains, together with his slippers, one of his boots and his gloves.

The skeleton measures 7 feet 8¾ inches, and the bones, generally, are well proportioned to the extraordinary height of the individual. The cranium is long and narrow and much depressed, with a low retreating forehead.

His slipper is 15 inches long, his boot 14¾ inches, and his gloves measure 14 inches from the tip of the middle finger to the wrist. A cast of his hand shows it to have been 11½ inches long.

A portrait of Byrne was engraved by Kay in 1783 and published in Edinburgh.

No more striking illustration of the height of a giant as compared with a diminutive dwarf is to be found than in the skeletons of Charles Byrne, the "Irish giant", and Caroline Crachami, the "Sicilian dwarf", which now stand side by side in the Museum of the Royal College of Surgeons.

The other Irish giant who was contemporary with Byrne, was Patrick Cotter, who also adopted the name of O'Brien, in order, as it was said, to give the impression that he was descended from an ancient king of Erin.

He was born at Kinsale about 1760, and when a youth

was apprenticed to a bricklayer. But even at that time he had grown to an abnormal height and attracted the attention of a travelling showman, who persuaded his father to lend him for exhibition for three years for fifty pounds a year. He brought him to Bristol and there hired him out to another showman, but Patrick refused to be exhibited without some payment for himself, whereupon his master had him put in a debtors' prison, from which he was liberated after a time at the instance of a worthy citizen who was interested in him.

On regaining his freedom, he exhibited himself at a fair on his own account, and was able to make thirty pounds in three days, and with this in his pocket he came to England.

We next hear of him at Northampton, where, according to an article in the *Mirror*, a writer states: "He then appeared to be in his seventeenth year. His features were regularly formed, his countenance remarkably healthful, and his standing position erect and commanding. The mildness of his temper was conspicuous, and he possessed intelligence of a superior order to that usually discovered by the individuals of the trade to which he was apprenticed—a bricklayer.

"His stature, eight feet seven inches and three fourths, did not make him appear disproportionate; in every respect he was a well-made man. . . .

"After the exhibition of the day and when the dwarfs of Northampton had retired to their cribs, this proud giant of the earth would take his morning walk, measuring with amazing strides the distance between the 'George Inn' and Queen's-cross.

"Mr. O'Brien expressed himself as being greatly refreshed by these short excursions; they enabled him to enjoy refreshing sleep when he retired to his beds—for the common bed of humanity would have been useless—and therefore he had two joined together.

"Equal courage was combined with his strength and he possessed in the fullest degree the warm temperament of an Irishman.

"An impertinent visitor excited his choler one day by illiberal allusions to the land of his birth. He seized the prig by the collar, held him out at arm's length and gave him three or four mild agitations, something after the manner of Wallace, the lion, with the famous Billy of rat-killing memory.

"Mr. O'Brien enjoyed his early pipe and the lamps of the town afforded him an easy method of lighting it. When at the door of Mr. Dent in Bridge Street, he withdrew the cap of the lamp, whiffed his tobacco into a flame and stalked away as if no uncommon event had taken place."

He appears to have been first exhibited in London in 1782, but there is a doubt if he was the Irish giant alluded to by Byrne and described in a bill as the "Astonishing Irish giant" to be seen at the late bird-shop at the corner of Piccadilly and the Haymarket.

His own announcement was not issued until 1785, when he exhibited himself at 30, St. James's Street. It reads: "Mr. O'Brien has the honour to present his respects to the nobility, gentry and publick, whose patronage and protection he shall be proud to merit, that notwithstanding the innuendo which has been given out by the infant giants. Mr. O'Brien has no art to add to his stupenduous height; he is bold to assure them, that he stands on his own feet without deception and wears his own hair. He acknowledges he is only eight feet three inches and a half high, though Brien Boreau, the puissant ancient king of Ireland, his ancestor, was nine feet high, which he hopes to attain before he is of age, being now between eighteen and nineteen years old.

"To prevent an improper mixture of company, the price of admission from eleven in the forenoon till four is 2s., from four till seven only 1s."

Judging from the accounts in the newspapers of the time, he evidently attracted considerable attention. One states: "It seems as if we should have a war of the giants—the St. James's giant has called the other giants which are in town the infant giants as compared to himself, and positively asserts, they can walk under his arm; if so, they will have but an unequal conflict, yet report says, that a public challenge is expected to be exhibited for the amusement of the town."

The infant giants were probably two brothers called Knipe, who, according to a bill, were to be seen at the Silkdyers, No. 2, Spring-gardens, Charing Cross, in 1785. They were twenty-seven years of age and each measured 7 feet 2 inches.

In July 1785, Cotter appeared on the stage at Sadler's Wells. In the play in which he appeared, a lady was obliged to ascend a flight of steps to salute him, and according to a report of the entertainment, Cotter went round and shook hands with the spectators who occupied the upper boxes, much to the amusement of the audience. In the autumn he again appeared on the stage in company with some dancers, tumblers and performing dogs.

On October 19, 1786, he astonished the town by getting married to a Miss Cave, and the wedding was announced in the Press as follows:

"O'Brien, who last winter exhibited his person in St. James's Street, was lately married at Pancras Church, to a young woman of the name of Cave who lived in Bolton-row, Piccadilly. She may now for more reasons than one, without impropriety, be termed the *Giant's Cave*."

In 1789, he removed to "commodious apartments at the Lyceum in the Strand", and a story is told, that while there, he went out to visit a friend one night in a hackney coach. The coachman did not notice him when he got in, but on seeing him get out stood amazed, and on returning to his rank exclaimed to the other drivers, "Darn me, but I have done more than you all, for I have just carried the Monument."

Dr. Robert Bigsby states, that his father, at a Masonic banquet that was held in Parliament Street, Nottingham, about 1790, saw Cotter draw from his coat pocket a dwarf, whom he believes was the famous Count Boruwlaski.

There was a story published in the *Mirror* in 1830, of a

meeting between Cotter and an equally tall Scottish gentleman, whose name is unknown. The writer states: "We did not know till lately that Scotland had produced a rival to the celebrated O'Brien of Irish birth.

"When that extraordinary man was, some years ago, exhibiting, among other places at Yarmouth, a Scotch gentleman of good family and large fortune, who was passing through the town at the time, sent a note to him stating his height and requesting an interview quite privately with O'Brien, as he did not and could not make of himself a public exhibition.

"They met the same evening at the hotel where O'Brien was staying and upon measuring, the Scotch gentleman's height was found to exceed that of his brother-giant of Erin by half an inch."

O'Brien is said to have returned to London after a tour through the provinces about 1800, and soon after his arrival, for a wager of ten pounds, kissed a young lady who was sitting at a garret window as he passed down the street.

In 1804, according to a bill, he was on exhibition "in a commodious room at No. 11 Haymarket nearly opposite the Opera House. The gentleman alluded to measures near nine feet high. Admittance, one shilling."

Here on May 5, 1804, he was visited by Mr. W. Blair, a surgeon of the Lock Hospital. In the account he gives of the giant he says:[1] "He was of very extraordinary stature but not well-formed. As he would not suffer a minute examination to be made of his person, it is impossible to give any other than a very slight description of him.

"He declined the proposal of walking across the room, and I believe was afraid of discovering his extreme imbecility. He had the general aspect of a weak and unreflecting person with an uncommonly low forehead; for as near as I could ascertain, the space above his eyebrows in a perpendicular line to the top of his head, did not exceed two inches. He told me his age was thirty-eight years and that most of his ancestors by his mother's side were very large persons.

[1] *Gentleman's Magazine*, 1804.

"The disproportionate size of his hands struck me with surprise and in this he seemed to make his principal boast. He refused to allow a cast to be made of his hand and said, 'it had been made many years ago'. . . .

"All his joints were large and perhaps rickety. His legs appeared swollen, misshapen and I thought dropsical. The feet were clumsy and concealed as much as possible by high shoes. His limbs were not very stout, especially his arms, and I judge he had scarcely got the use of them, for in order to lift up his hand he seemed obliged to swing the whole arm, as if he had no power of raising it by the action of the deltoid muscle. He certainly had a greater redundancy of bone than of muscle, and gave me the impression of a huge, overgrown, sickly boy, his voice being rather feeble as well as his bodily energies and his age appearing under that which he affirmed. . . .

"The state of his pulse agreed with the general appearance of his person, viz. feeble, languid and slow in its motions.

"With regard to his actual height, I felt anxious to detect the fallacy he held out of its being almost nine feet.

"Upon extending my arm to the utmost, I reached his eye-brow with my little finger. Allowing his height to have been two inches and a quarter above this, it could not be more in the whole than seven feet ten inches, so that I am persuaded the common opinion founded on the giant's own tale is greatly exaggerated."

Another writer in 1804, gives a very different account of O'Brien. He tells us that he used frequently to walk about the streets to take exercise about two or three o'clock in the morning.

"In one of these nocturnal excursions, it was my chance to overtake him; when he was accompanied by two genteel-looking men of the common size on whose shoulders he supported himself.

"Mr. O'Brien is eight feet seven inches in height and proportionately lusty. His hand, from the commencement of the palm to the end of the middle finger, measures twelve inches and his face, from the chin to the top of his forehead, precisely the same. . . . His thumb is about the size of a moderate man's wrist and his shoe is seventeen inches long."

These measurements given by Caulfield are incorrect. There are two casts of the right hand of Patrick Cotter in the Museum of the Royal College of Surgeons, and from the commencement of the palm to the tip of the middle finger they both measure $10\frac{3}{4}$ inches. The size of the thumb is also exaggerated, as it only measures $1\frac{1}{2}$ inch across the thickest part.

There are also two of Cotter's shoes preserved in the Museum, one of which was made by Batty of Bath and is inscribed "Patrick Cotter O'Brien when thirty-nine years old". Both of these measure $14\frac{1}{2}$ inches long.

Caulfield tells a story that, once when O'Brien was travelling in the special carriage he had built for him, the floor of which was sunk some feet so as to hold his legs conveniently, he was stopped by a highwayman, whereupon the giant, putting his head forward to observe the cause that impeded his progress, the highwayman was struck with such a panic that he clapped spurs to his horse and made a precipitate retreat."

When not staying in London, O'Brien is said to have lived at a house in Essex formerly the residence of a nobleman, but at that time had been converted into an inn. It had particularly high doors and lofty ceilings and he could thus move about the rooms freely.

He was of a thrifty disposition and saved sufficient money from the profits of his exhibitions to enable him to retire when he was about forty-four, and go to live at Hotwells, Clifton, near Bristol. As he grew older he became weak and had some considerable difficulty in walking. It gave him pain to rise from his chair or sit down. Like Byrne, he had a great dread of his body being taken for dissection after his death, and left particular instructions that it was to be protected after burial by iron bars and carefully arched over with brickwork.

He died at Hotwells on September 8, 1806, and according

to his directions was buried in the Roman Catholic Chapel in Trenchard Street, Bristol.

In an account of the funeral given in a contemporary journal, "notwithstanding that the early hour of six o'clock was fixed to prevent as much as possible a crowd, the street was immensely thronged, so that the assistance of the constables was highly necessary. It is supposed that at least 2,000 persons were present. The coffin of lead measured nine feet two inches clear, and the wooden case four inches more. It took fourteen men to bear it to the grave, which was made twelve feet in the solid rock, and every precaution was taken to render abortive either force or stratagem, hence the anatomists are deprived of his body."

According to a Bristol newspaper in 1825, "excavations are being made on the site of the old Roman Catholic Chapel in Trenchard Street, and enclosed in the rock 12 feet below the surface, the workmen came across an enormous lead coffin, which was found to contain a skeleton of heroic dimensions. The plate on the coffin, which was perfectly legible, stated that the remains were those of Patrick Cotter, 'O'Brien', and that his height was 8 feet 3 inches.

"The curious people of Bristol flocked in crowds to the graveyard yesterday to feast their eyes on the giant's remains."

CHAPTER XXII

SOME GIANTS OF THE NINETEENTH CENTURY

THERE are many records of both men and women who reached heights varying between 7 and 8 feet during the last century, and Dana observes, that, although the number of giants publicly exhibited since 1700 was not more than a hundred, only about twenty were advertised as being over 8 feet high.

Among the more noteworthy was Samuel M'Donald, popularly known as "Big Sam", who was born at Lairg in Sutherlandshire, and who is variously stated to have been from 6 feet 10 inches to 8 feet high. During the latter part of the American War, he served as a private in the Sutherland Fencibles, but afterwards entered the Royals, in which regiment he became fugleman.

In 1791, his great stature attracted the attention of the Prince of Wales (afterwards George IV), who made him lodge-porter at Carlton House, where he used to be seen looking over the gates. After holding the office for about two years, he resigned and became recruiting sergeant to the Sutherland Fencibles, to which he had previously belonged.

He is said to have been a man of a mild and gentle disposition, good-natured, and bland in his manners and deportment.

On account of his commanding presence, he was always placed at the head of his regiment when on the march, and was usually accompanied by a great mountain deer. He was exceedingly strong, and one day, it is said, he was challenged by two soldiers on the understanding that he would fight them both at once.

He told them, as he had no quarrel with either, he would first like to shake hands with them. One of them then stretched out his hand, which was at once seized by Sam in a mighty grip, and instead of giving it a friendly shake as the owner anticipated, he swung him off his feet and flung him some distance. The other would-be combatant, not wishing to be served the same way, took to his heels and ran.

"Big Sam" always refused to exhibit himself, but it is said that he once dressed himself up in female costume and was advertised as "The remarkable tall woman", and thereby made so much money, that it attracted the attention of his colonel.

His one public appearance was made at the instance of the Prince of Wales, who wished to see him as Hercules in the play of *Cymon and Iphigenia*. He thus played at the Opera House in the Haymarket, then occupied by the Drury Lane Company until their own theatre was rebuilt in 1809.

It is said that the Countess of Sutherland allowed Sam half-a-crown a day, when he was in the Army, as she did not consider his pay sufficient for his bodily needs.

"Big Sam" died on May 6, 1802, at Guernsey, in the Channel Islands, at the age of forty.

William Bradley, who was born at Market Weighton in Yorkshire in 1798, bid fair to be a man of great stature, as at the age of nineteen he measured 7 feet 8 inches in height, but he died about 1820. A cast of his hand in the Museum of the Royal College of Surgeons measures 11 inches from the wrist to the tip of the middle finger.

About 1822, a French giant named Louis Frenz visited London and took apartments at 22, New Bond Street. At the age of twenty-two he was 7 feet 4 inches in height, and his hand, a cast of which is in the Museum of the Royal College of Surgeons, measures 10½ inches. He is said to have had a brother who was taller than himself and two sisters nearly as tall.

About 1826, there was a London solicitor, popularly known as the "Long Lawyer", who used to cause much amusement about town. He was said to be about 7 feet high, and Cornelius Webb gives the following account of him: "He once affected to ride a cob, but it was soon perceived that he was walking and that the little fellow was only trotting along between his legs—as it were under his auspices. Sitting some time after dinner one day, he remarked on a sudden, that he would get up and stretch himself; if you had seen the consternation or if I could describe it! He would pertinaciously persist in travelling by coach, when he ought to have gone in three, and as he was resolutely bent on riding inside, they made a hole through the roof for his head and shoulders and got informed against for carrying luggage higher than the number of inches allowed by Act of Parliament. His tailor, when he measured him, like a sensible man stood on a flight of steps, but three of his journeymen unused to such a perpendicular position are said to have broken their necks.

"He never laughed till the laughing was over with all the rest of the audience; a joke took some time to travel from his ear to his midriff and tickle it to laughter. When he went to the pit of the theatre, the gods of the shilling gallery cried out 'Sit down, you Sir, in the two!' not perceiving, short-sighted creatures as they are, that he was many feet lower than the midmost heaven."

The romantic story of a giant and giantess which nearly ended in tragedy, is told in the *Observer* of February 6, 1831. It appears from the report, that "On Sunday morning about five o'clock, heavy groans were heard to proceed from the travelling residence (a large caravan) of the celebrated Scotch Giantess (Miss Freeman) near the new Bethlehem.

"On a policeman and others entering, they found a female of gigantic form and a man lying on the floor in a state of insensibility, and it being ascertained that they had taken poison, they were conveyed to Guy's Hospital. The stomach-pump was applied, by which a quantity of arsenic was removed, and they were placed in bed in a very feeble state but their ultimate recovery was expected.

"It appears that the female, who stands six feet six inches, was shown more attention to by a man about her own stature called the 'Spanish Giant', than her husband, who is not more than half the size of his wife, deemed proper, and he wheeled her off in his four-wheeled residence, from St. James's Street, where she was then exhibited, to the open space of ground near New Bethlehem. A few evenings afterwards as the Scottish Giantess and her spouse were comfortably seated in their caravan, the latter to his astonishment perceived his rival, the Spanish giant, looking through the window, which from his surprising height he could do without more trouble. The husband ran out, intending to take vengeance on the disturber of his domestic peace, but the intruder had disappeared. From that moment they lived unhappily and the gigantic wife would frequently seize her husband by the back of the neck and hold him at arm's length till he was nearly choked.

"On Sunday, the husband returned after being out all night, when he found his wife had taken poison, and a portion of it being left in the cup, he drank it off, with the consequences as related."

From time to time giants have served as an attraction in taverns and places of entertainment, and in 1853 a Mr. Smith, the landlord of the "Lion and Ball" in Red Lion Street, Holborn, attracted numerous customers to his establishment by engaging an American giant named Freeman to serve in the bar.

Freeman was said to have been 7 feet 6 inches in height and weighed 21 stone.

His engagement at the "Lion and Ball" is thus announced in a bill:

> "You need not unto Hyde Park go,
>   For without imposition,
> Smith's barman is, and no mistake,
>   The true Great Exhibition.
>
> The proudest noble in the land
>   Despite caprice and whim,
> Though looking *down* on all the world,
>   Must fain *look up* at him.
>
> His rest can never be disturbed,
>   By chanticleer in song,
> For though he early goes to bed,
>   He sleeps so *very long*.

Then come and see the giant Youth,
  Give Edward Smith a call,
Remember in Red Lion-street
  The 'Lion and the Ball'."

Previous to this engagement, Freeman appeared on the stage of the Olympic Theatre in company with a dwarf named Hervio Nono, in a play called *The Son of the Desert and the Demon Changeling*, which was written expressly for them. At the conclusion of the performance, in which the giant is said to have acquitted himself well, much amusement used to be caused by the dwarf leading the gigantic actor before the curtain to receive the plaudits of the audience.

Freeman's skeleton, which measures 6 feet 9 inches, is also preserved in the Museum of the Royal College of Surgeons, where it can be compared with that of Byrne, the Irish giant.

Frank Buckland mentions a gigantic Irishman called Murphy, who was born at Killowen, near Rostrevor, and who died in Marseilles. In early life he had worked as a dock-labourer in Liverpool, but after obtaining a situation at an hotel where he attracted many customers, he exhibited himself in various parts of the country and finally on the Continent. Here he made a considerable sum of money, and was introduced to the Emperor and Empress of Austria, who became interested in him. At the age of twenty-six he is said to have been only a few inches short of 9 feet in height.

Another giant mentioned by Buckland was James Brice, a Frenchman, who came to London about the time of the Great Exhibition in 1862. Buckland, who had him carefully measured, states, that his height was actually 90 inches; and his shoes measured 16 inches in length.

He was born at Ramonchamp in the Vosges, and coming from that district called himself "The Giant of the Mountains". His parents were farmers and both of normal stature. It was not until after a short illness in childhood, that he began to grow to gigantic proportions, and by the age of thirteen was as tall as his father.

When he was sixteen, he visited some of the principal towns in France and eventually came to Paris, where he was received by the Emperor.

After his stay in England, he went to Ireland and there fell in love with an Irish girl, whom he married. In October 1865 they both came to London, and he was engaged by Anderson, the conjurer, to appear at St. James's Hall, Piccadilly, where he was announced as "Anak, King of the Anakims or the Giant of Giants".

Buckland states, that he invited Brice to go and see Regent's Park Barracks, and when he went into the stables to see the troop-horses, they shied and snorted at him because he was so tall.

During his travels he says that he met with only three persons who in stature approached his own height. One was a lawyer, who came to see him at Haverford West, who was 6 feet 8½ inches, another was a policeman at Newcastle, who measured 6 feet 9½ inches, and the third was John Greeve of Pontefract, who was 6 feet 10½ inches in height.

A giantess who claimed to belong to the Polish nobility was exhibited at Saville House, Leicester Square, in 1863. She called herself the Countess Lodoiska, and came from Warsaw, where her parents, who were not above the ordinary stature, lived. She was 7 feet in height and could lift without any difficulty 160 pounds weight with one hand. She is said to have been charming in appearance and to have had most pleasing manners, besides being remarkably well-formed. At the time of her visit to London she was about twenty years of age.

The Chinese have long had traditions of a gigantic race of people who once lived in some remote part of their country, and there is a legend which dates from the fifteenth century, that a certain Emperor had a bodyguard of archers composed of men of immense stature. But no Chinese giants appear to have achieved notoriety in Europe until Chang Woo Gow came to England in 1866.

He was born in the city of Fy-chow of respectable

parentage, his father being a man of considerable height, although his mother was of normal stature.

Chang came to England at the age of nineteen, accompanied by his wife, who was called King-Foo, "The fair lily", and a dwarf named Chung. He was at that time 7 feet 9 inches in height and weighed 20 stone, but later he reached the height of 8 feet.

Some will doubtless remember this genial giant when he was exhibited at the old Egyptian Hall in Piccadilly. He had a mild, agreeable face, with the prominent cheekbones and narrow eyelids typical of the Mongol race, while his long, straight, figured robe seemed to add to his height.

He was both intelligent and well-educated and used to smile blandly when he extended his arm for visitors to walk beneath. When he visited the Prince and Princess of Wales, at their request, he wrote his name on the wall of the room in which he was received and this measured nearly 10 feet from the ground. He stated that he had a sister called Chen-Yow-Tzu, who was 10 inches taller than himself, but she had died on reaching the age of womanhood.

Chung, the dwarf, who used to stand alongside of him on the platform, was 36 inches high and presented a great contrast to his gigantic countryman.

The marriage of two giants is not a matter of everyday occurrence, so it is little wonder that the nuptials of Captain Martin van Buren and Miss Anna Swan attracted considerable interest on June 17, 1871. The ceremony took place at St. Martin-in-the-Fields in London. Both the bride and bridegroom were over 7 feet high, their combined height being 14 feet 8 inches.

Van Buren, or Bates, was born in Kentucky in 1845, and was admitted to the Southern Army in America at the age of sixteen on account of his stature. At the close of the war, his height was 7 feet 2½ inches, and on leaving the army he toured on exhibition through the United States and afterwards through the chief countries of Europe.

He came to London in 1871, and there met Miss Anna

Swan, who was then being exhibited as the "Nova Scotia Giantess". She was three inches taller than Van Buren and measured 7 feet 5½ inches. They became engaged to be married and directly after the ceremony at St. Martin-in-the-Fields, left on an exhibition tour through the provinces.

They eventually returned to America, and settled down to a quiet life on a farm at Guilford, Medina County.

In 1882, a girl who measured 8 feet 6 inches was exhibited in London. She was known as "Miss Marian, the Queen of the Amazons", and was barely eighteen years of age. She appeared at the Alhambra in Leicester Square and attracted a great deal of interest at the time.

Within recent times a giant of unusual size was to be seen in London in the person of Jim Tarber, who was said to measure 8 feet 4 inches in height.

According to his own account he was born on a ranch in Texas, his parents being of ordinary stature, and he did not reach his great height until he was twenty-eight years of age.

He is said to be a man of mild and friendly disposition, who shuns publicity and whose great desire is to be back again on the farm.

Although in many cases the parents of giants are said to have been people of ordinary stature, there are several cases recorded in which abnormal height has been common in parents and their families.

Among these were the children of Hales, a gigantic man, the father of Robert Hales, known as the "Norfolk giant", who was born at Somerton, near Great Yarmouth, in 1820.

Hales, who measured 6 feet 6 inches, married Elizabeth Dimond, who was 6 feet in height. They had four sons and five daughters, all of whom grew beyond ordinary stature. The sons averaged 6 feet 5 inches in height and the daughters 6 feet 3½ inches. Robert, who was called the giant, was the tallest of the family and reached the height of 7 feet 6 inches. He went to America, and after remaining there two years returned to London in 1851, where he became the landlord of the Craven Head Tavern in Drury Lane.

By his geniality and affability he attracted a number of customers.

In 1851, he was commanded to attend Buckingham Palace, where he was introduced to Queen Victoria, Prince Albert and six members of the Royal Family.

Another case of a family of gigantic stature was recently reported from America.

The account states that "Mr. Hiram C. Bogue, a farmer of Underhill, Vermont, who is seven feet in height, has a family of twelve children whose heights are as follows: Max, 7 feet 2 inches, Leland, 6 feet 8 inches, Ray and Alvin, 6 feet 7 inches, Arthur and Howard, 6 feet 6½ inches, Homer, 6 feet 6 inches, and Ida, Anna and Glenna, the daughters, 6 feet. Mrs. Bogue, their mother, is 5 feet 10 inches in height. Their combined measurements total seventy-seven feet five inches, a gigantic family indeed, which shows we are not yet past the age of giants."

CHAPTER XXIII

EARLY TRADITIONS CONCERNING DWARFS AND PIGMIES

TRADITIONS concerning a race of people of abnormally small stature have been common in all countries from an early period of the world's history. Homer refers to the pigmies who were believed to be found in Thrace, and Herodotus tells us of a people of extremely small stature who dwelt in the deserts of Libya.

Dwarfs also figure in the mythological lore of several nations in East and West. There is an ancient Hindu legend, that Vishnu presented himself to King Mahabali under the guise of a Brahmin dwarf, who was so small that he imagined a hole made by a cow's foot full of water to be a lake.

There was an old Saxon tradition that four dwarfs supported the celestial dome which was created by the god Odin, and there is another quaint legend which affirms the belief that dwarfs were made by the devil. Concerning this, Delrio says: "There is no doubt but that the Devill may make Pigmies and prohibit men from ever coming to the just stature of humane body, as we see by man's artifice, to wit, by giving them burnt wine and enclosing them in little pots as those little dogs wherewith women are so delighted are procured, and parents greedy of gaine, very wickedly, with certaine medicaments cause their children's growth to be stunted that they prove dwarfs.

"But he cannot make a giant of a pigmie for the thanks that the Devill cannot so extend the bones of a little man to make them of a giant-like magnitude, and therefore Petrus Chieza accounts that a fable which the Indian Cichorani brag they can do with certaine herbs."

Schweinfurth confirmed the stories of Homer, Herodotus and Aristotle that there was a race of pigmies in Africa who inhabited a district near the source of the Nile. These people, called Akkas, live south of the Niam-Niam and average in height from 4 feet to 4 feet 10½ inches.

Stanley met with a similar race in his journey through

Central Africa and remarks on their activity and cunning, while tribes with similar characteristics have been found in other parts of the Dark Continent.

The legendary story of Tom Thumb, common to several European countries, is probably of Scandinavian origin and is thus referred to in a rhyme called *Tom Thumbe: His Life and Death*, written in 1630:

> "In Arthur's court Tom Thumbe did live,
>   A man of mickle might,
> The best of all the table round,
>   And eke a doughty knight;
> His stature but an inch in height
>   Or quarter of a span;
> Then thinke you not this little knight
>   Was prov'd a valiant man?"

Tradition states, that the original Tom died at Lincoln, and a memorial stone was at one time placed to his memory in the Cathedral.

The Romans were credited with the knowledge of making children dwarfs by giving them insufficient food when young, but they naturally soon became rachitic and many perished.

There are little people, whose diminutive height is caused by arrested development, who are rachitic and usually die young, and others, who are really dwarfs from birth, who develop naturally, are robust and intelligent, and often live to a mature age.

Many of the latter have proved to be quick in learning and have become celebrated for their cleverness and wit.

The custom of keeping a dwarf in the retinue of Royal and other personages of position and wealth, is one of considerable antiquity. Wilkinson states, that the ancient Egyptians probably kept them in their houses, on account of some superstitious regard for men who bore the external character of one of their principal gods, Ptah, who is sometimes represented as a dwarf.

Later on, the custom spread to different parts of Europe,

and the Romans, especially under the first Emperors, placed dwarfs among the objects of their luxury and ostentation.

Suetonius mentions a dwarf in the service of Augustus who was less than two feet high, and who had a very strong voice. He had a particular liking for having dwarfs about him, and caused them to be collected and sent to him from all parts of the world. He stipulated that they should be perfectly formed, handsome and lively, and he used to amuse himself with their prattle and played with them for nuts.

Tiberius also kept a dwarf whom he often consulted on State affairs, and Mark Antony had one, whom he called Sisyphus, who was less than 2 feet in height. Domitian is said to have gathered so many dwarfs round him, that he formed them into a little troop of gladiators. Julia, the niece of Augustus, kept two dwarfs in her suite, each of which was not more than 2 feet 4 inches in height. One called Conopas, "whom she set great store by, was a man and the other, named Andromeda, was a freed maid."

These dwarfs in Roman times, who became the pets of emperors and great ladies, commonly went naked, and were richly decked with jewels and festooned with bands studded with precious stones.

There were several men of dwarfish stature about this period who attained some eminence. Among them were Marius Maximus and Marcus Tullius, both of whom were but two cubits or 2 feet 11 inches in height, and yet both were Knights of Rome.

Philus of Cos, the tutor of Ptolemy Philadelphus, was also a dwarf, while Alypius of Alexandria was under 2 feet high and Lucinus Calvus but a foot taller.

We are told of Alypius of Alexandria, that he was "a most excellent logician and philosopher and was of so small a body that he hardly exceeded a cubit (1 foot 5½ inches) in height.

"Such as beheld him would think he was scarce anything but spirit and soul; so little grew that part of him which was liable to corruption that it seemed to be consumed with a kind of divine nature."

The custom of keeping dwarfs as dependents in noble families survived, and later, in the Middle Ages, they were to be found attached to nearly every Court and the lively dwarf, with his quips and cranks, frequently played the part of jester.

They were given unlimited licence of speech, and often became the pets and favourites of their Royal masters or the Court ladies of the time.

They were introduced into pictures and their portraits were painted by many of the great masters. Velasquez depicted some who were attached to the Spanish Court, while Domenichino represented others who were in the suite of the Emperor Otho. Raphael introduced them into his pictures illustrating the history of Constantine, and others are immortalized in the works of Paul Veronese and Mantegna.

Mention should also be made of the famous painting representing the Infanta Margarita with her two dwarfs, Maria Borbola and Nicolasico Pertusano, by Velasquez, now in the Prado.

The same master also painted the portrait of Don Antonio el Ingles, a dwarf, with a large dog, and in the "Triumph of Caesar" by Mantegna several dwarfs are introduced by the artist into the picture.

Lady Montagu describes the dwarfs at the Viennese Court as "devils bedaubed with diamonds", to such an absurd extent were luxuries of all kinds showered on these little Court favourites.

Charles IX and his mother had a great partiality for them and sent emissaries to fetch them from various countries. In 1572, Charles received three dwarfs as a present from the Emperor of Germany, and in the same year added others to his suite who were brought from Poland.

One of these, Majowski, was given to the Queen-mother, and among her papers, mention is made of payments to "Cochon, governor of the dwarfs, to Rondeau their tailor and Bourdin their valet".

Another historian states, that Charles IX had nine

dwarfs, Catherine de' Medici, three couples at one time, and in 1579 had still five pigmies named Merlin, Mandricart, Pelavine, Rodomont and Majowski.

In Italy also the craze persisted, and in 1566 it is stated, that Cardinal Vitelli gave a sumptuous banquet in Rome at which the waiters were thirty-four dwarfs.

As late as 1710, dwarfs were greatly in favour at the Russian Court, and Peter the Great, at the celebration he gave in honour of the marriage of his favourite Valakoff with the dwarf of the Princess Prescovie Theodorovna, had seventy-two dwarfs of both sexes assembled to form the bridal party.

With respect to the great intelligence often developed by dwarfs, Evelyn, writing in 1687, mentions a dwarf named "Mr. Ramus (Pumilo to Thomas Earl Marshal of England) who being learned and in the magnificent train of that noble lord when he went ambassador to Vienna, made a speech in Latin before his Imperial Majesty with such a grace and so much eloquence, as merited a golden chain and medal of the Emperor." About the middle of the seventeenth century, Godeau, who was a French dwarf, showed such talent in literature that Richelieu named him Archbishop of Grasse.

The custom of keeping dwarfs in the houses of noble families lingered in Russia and Sweden well into the nineteenth century, and Porter states in his *Travels in Russia and Sweden*, 1805–8: "They are here the pages and playmates of the great and at almost all entertainments stand for hours behind their lord's chair, holding his snuff box or awaiting his commands. There is scarcely a nobleman in this country who is not possessed of one or more of these frisks of nature.

"These little beings are generally the gayest dreast persons in the service of their lord and are attired in a uniform or livery of very costly materials.

"The race of these unfortunates is very diminutive in Russia and very numerous. They are generally well-shaped and their hands and feet particularly graceful. Indeed, in the proportion of their figures, we should nowhere discover them to be flaws in the economy of nature, were it not for a peculiarity of feature and the size of head, which is commonly exceedingly enlarged. It is very curious to observe how nearly they resemble each other; their features are all so alike, that you might easily imagine that one pair had spread their progeny over the whole country."

The size of the head in proportion to other parts of the body is a notable feature in all dwarfs.

The custom of keeping dwarfs in palaces was also a common one with the Turks, where they served as pages in the households, or for the amusement of their masters.

In *Don Juan*, Byron alludes to the

> "Dwarfs and blacks, and suchlike things, that gain
> Their bread as ministers and favourites,"

and in describing the Sultan's palace in Turkey he makes mention of

> "Two little dwarfs, the least you could suppose,
> Were sate, like ugly imps, as if allied
> In mockery to the enormous gate which rose
> O'er them in almost pyramidic pride."
>
> .   .   .   .   .
>
> They were misshapen pigmies, deaf and dumb—
> Monsters, who cost a no less monstrous sum."

Dwarfs were sometimes credited with occult powers, as instanced in the case of Zep, a dwarf who was adopted by Tycho Brahe, the famous Danish astronomer in 1580. He was brought up and lived with the family in the Castle of Uraniborg on the Island of Hveen.

Zep used to follow his master about and sat at his feet during meals and was fed with morsels from his hand. He chattered incessantly and was believed to be clairvoyant, so his words were listened to with great attention.

When any person on the island fell sick, the dwarf was usually called in to give an opinion on the chance of recovery or to say if the illness was likely to prove fatal or not.

CHAPTER XXIV

DWARFS AT THE ENGLISH COURTS

QUEEN MARY was one of the first English monarchs to have a dwarf as a page of honour: Little is known about him beyond his name, which was John Jervis, and his height, which was 3 feet 8 inches. He lived to reach the age of fifty-seven and died in 1558.

Richard Gibson, however, who became page of the back-stairs to Charles I, was quite a notable personage in his time. He was born in the time of James I and lived through four reigns and died at the age of seventy-five years on July 23, 1690, after William and Mary had come to the throne. He was 3 feet 10 inches in height and was gifted as an artist, especially in the painting of miniatures.

He was first instructed by De Clein, master of the tapestry works at Mortlake, and afterwards studied under Sir Peter Lely and was appointed drawing-master to the Princesses Mary and Anne. He painted miniatures of Oliver Cromwell and other famous personages, and also a picture representing the parable of the Lost Sheep, which was greatly valued by Charles I.

He married Anne Shepherd, a dwarf who was in the suite of Queen Henrietta Maria, and both the King and Queen took a great interest in the union.

King Charles was present at their wedding and gave the bride away and the Queen gave her a diamond ring as a wedding present. Both dwarfs were equal in height, and although they had nine children, five of whom lived to grow up, they were all of ordinary stature. Mrs. Gibson survived her husband and died in 1709, at the advanced age of eighty-nine.

Another famous dwarf of this period was Jeffrey Hudson, who was born at Oakham in Rutlandshire in 1619. He was the only member of his family who was of diminutive stature, and at the age of eight is said to have been "scarce a foot and a half high". He remained that height until he reached the age of thirty, after which he grew to 3 feet 9 inches and afterwards remained at that stature.

At Burleigh-on-the-Hill, where his father kept and ordered the baiting bulls for George Duke of Buckingham, he came under the notice of the Duchess, who took him into her service, where he was well looked after and clad in a suitable livery.

When King Charles I and the Queen were entertained at Burleigh after their marriage, there is a story that one day, Jeffrey was brought to the table inside a great cold pie, which so amused the Queen that she retained him in her service and took him to Court. He is said to have become great friends with William Evans, the King's giant porter, and they had many escapades together. On one occasion, Evans is stated to have put the dwarf in his pocket and produced him during a masque at Court together with a long loaf.

They are represented together in the stone relief already referred to, which is still to be seen in Bullhead Court, Newgate Street.

Jeffrey is thus alluded to by Heath in his *Clarastella* in 1658:

"Small Sir! methinkes in your lesser selfe I see
Exprest the lesser world's epitome.
You may write man, in th' abstract so you are
Though printed in a smaller character.
The pocket volume hath as much within't
And is more useful too. Though low you seem,
Yet you're both great and high in men's esteem;
Your soul's as large as others, so's your mind;
To greatness virtue's not like strength confin'd."

Sir Walter Scott introduces Jeffrey into *Peveril of the Peak* and describes him as, "although a dwarf of the least possible size, had nothing positively ugly in his countenance or actually distorted in his limbs".

Owing no doubt to his quick intelligence, he was employed by the King on several important missions, in some of which he had exciting adventures. In 1630, he was dispatched to France to bring a midwife for the Queen, who was then expecting her accouchement. On the return journey with the nurse and the royal dancing-master, bringing many valuable presents to the Queen from her mother, Marie de' Medici, he was captured in the Channel by a Flemish privateer and lost not only the rich gifts entrusted to him, but also effects said to have been worth £2,500 which had been given to him at the French Court.

Later on, when at sea, he was taken prisoner by a Turkish pirate and conveyed to Barbary, where he was sold as a slave and passed through many hardships until he was redeemed and made his way back to England.

On the outbreak of the Civil War, he was appointed a Captain of Horse in the Royal Army and accompanied the Queen to France.

In 1653, during a dispute with Mr. Crofts, a brother of Lord Crofts, he became so enraged, that he challenged him to fight a duel. It was arranged that the fight should take place on horseback. Mr. Crofts, who was more amused than offended at the dwarf's effrontery, arrived at the rendezvous armed only with a squirt. This aroused Jeffrey to still greater anger and, drawing his pistol, with the first shot he wounded his antagonist fatally.

Jeffrey was arrested and at first imprisoned, but was afterwards released and expelled from Court. He retired for a time to the country and lived on an allowance made to him by the Duke of Buckingham and some others. On returning to London later, to try and regain his old position at Court, being a Roman Catholic, he was suspected of complicity in the Popish plot of 1679, and was committed to the Gate-house at Westminster.

He died shortly after his release in 1682, at the age of sixty-three years.

There is a portrait of Jeffrey Hudson by Mytens at Hampton Court Palace, and his waistcoat of blue satin, slashed and ornamented with pinked white silk, with stockings and breeches of blue satin all in one piece, are preserved in the Ashmolean Museum at Oxford.

Another eccentric dwarf of remarkable ability, who

actually became Prime Minister to the King of Lombardy, was Bertholde, who was born at Bertagnona near Verona.

His parents were very poor and, being one of a family of nine, he was often half-starved, but his liveliness and wit made him a favourite with all the villagers and people in the district, in so much they offered to contribute to his support. On Sundays he would amuse the children of the village and on week-days gave them instruction.

He is described as having "a very large, round head with straight red hair, as coarse as a hog's bristles, two little bleary eyes, edged round with a border of bright carnation and over-shadowed by a large pair of eyebrows. He had a flat, red nose and a wide mouth, from which proceeded two long crooked teeth, not unlike the tusks of a boar and pointing to a pair of ears like those which formerly belonged to Midas. A lip of monstrous thickness which hung down on a chin that seemed to sink under the load of a beard, thick, straight and bristly. He had a very short neck, which nature adorned with a kind of necklace formed of ten or twelve small wens.

"The rest of his body was perfectly agreeable to the grotesque appearance of his face, so that from head to foot he was a kind of monster, who by his deformity and the hair with which he was covered, had a greater resemblance to a bear half-licked into form than to a human creature." Such is the far from prepossessing description given by a contemporary writer of Bertholde.

At length, unwilling to be a burden to his friends, he decided to journey to Verona, where Alboin, the first King of the Lombards, had his Court, and he set out thither.

On his arrival at the palace, seeing the door open, he boldly marched in, and ascending the grand staircase to the Royal apartments, entered the one in which the King was seated surrounded by his courtiers.

Before speaking a word, Bertholde approached him, and, without removing his hat, seated himself in a chair that happened to be vacant by the side of the King.

Amazed and surprised at the grotesque appearance of the

rustic, the King exclaimed: "Who are you? How did you come into the world? What is your country?"

"I am a man," replied the dwarf, unabashed. "I came into the world in the manner Providence sent me and the world itself is my country."

The King, astonished at his answers and seeing he had to do with no ordinary person, then began to question him thus:

"What thing is that which flies the swiftest?"

"Thought", replied Bertholde, promptly.

"What is the gulf that is never filled?"

"The avarice of the miser", answered the dwarf.

"What is most hateful in young people?"

"Self-conceit, because it makes them incorrigible", was the reply.

"What is most ridiculous in the old?"

"Love", responded Bertholde.

"What are the things most dangerous in a house?"

"A wicked wife and the tongue of a servant."

"What way will you take to bring water into a sieve?"

"I'll stay till it's frozen."

"How will you catch a hare without running?"

"I will wait till I find her on the spit", the dwarf answered.

The King was astounded at the readiness with which he replied to his questions and was so pleased at his intelligence, that he promised to give him anything that he desired.

"I defy you to do that", said Bertholde, bluntly.

"How so?" asked the King. "Do you doubt my good will?"

"No," answered the dwarf, quietly, "but I aspire after what you do not possess and consequently cannot give me."

"And what is this precious thing?" asked the King.

"Felicity, which was never in the power of kings; who enjoy less of it than the rest of mankind", replied Bertholde.

"What then are you seeking at my Court?" queried the King.

"What I have not been able to find, for I had imagined a king to be as much above other men as a steeple is above common houses, but I have found that I have honoured them more than they deserve."

The King, annoyed at the strange dwarf's rudeness, thereupon told him to leave the palace immediately.

He obeyed with the remark, that he was of the nature of flies, which the more you attempted to drive them away, the more obstinately are they bent to return.

"I will permit you to return like them", rejoined the King, "provided that you bring them along with you, but if you appear without them, you shall forfeit your head."

"Agreed", the dwarf called out, as he departed down the stairs.

According to the story, he made with all haste to his native village and running to a stable belonging to one of his brothers, he took out an old ass, whose back and hind-quarters had lost the friendly covering of a sound skin, and, mounting on his back, returned to Verona, accompanied by an infinite number of flies behind him.

He thus arrived at the palace and announced himself to the King, claiming he had kept his promise.

The King was so amused with his strategy and wisdom, that he gave him leave to remain at Court, where he soon attained a prominent position.

Some time afterwards, he fell under the Queen's displeasure and she determined to put an end to his career. She sent for him and placed four large and fierce dogs in the courtyard through which he had to pass, in order that they might attack him and tear him to pieces.

The dwarf, however, who had been previously informed of her intentions, got a brace of live hares. He boldly crossed the courtyard and, on the approach of the dogs, let the hares loose, and so was at once delivered from their attention.

The Queen, much enraged on hearing how she had been outwitted, had Bertholde seized and put into a sack and thrown into a room, where he was to be kept until he could be dropped into the river next day. But the dwarf persuaded the guard to let him out and lend him clothes, and thus disguised he escaped.

The following day he was captured, and the King, in order to satisfy the Queen's resentment, ordered him to be hanged on a tree.

Bertholde besought the King to take care of his family, and, as a last request, to allow him to choose the tree on which he was to die. To this the King consented, and instructed the guard to see that the executioner gave him his choice.

The trees of every wood for many miles round were examined, but Bertholde very wisely objected to all that were proposed, until at last the executioner and his guard, wearied out by the search, let him go free.

"On their return to the palace, they found the King lamenting at the loss of so faithful and able a servant, and he rejoiced to learn from them that he was still alive. He sent them back again to find his hiding-place and to persuade the dwarf to return to the palace. This they did, and on his return after a while he became reconciled to the Queen.

"Bertholde grew in favour and the King eventually made him his Prime Minister, and so under his influence the reign of this prince was happy and prosperous."

Bertholde left a characteristic will, which he addressed to:

"All those who shall see or read of this present writing, health and a good appetite."

The following are extracts from this extraordinary document:

"I Bertholde, great grandson of Bertolazzo, grandson of Bertazzo di Bertin and son of Bartolin of the village of Bertagnona;

"Knowing that we are all mortal and neither more nor less than bladders filled with wind which the least accident reduces to nothing, and that when we have arrived at the age of seventy, as I have this day, it is time to think of beating a retreat.

"For these causes finding some grains of good sense in my bald head I am willing to set my affairs in order by making this my last will and testament.

"To my brother, the venerable cobbler of our village, I leave my shoes and 8d. in good money.

"To Sambuco, my uncle, gardener, my straw hat.

"To Master Allegratto, the King's butler, my large leather belt and my purse for having many times filled my roundlet with wine.

"To Master Martin, cook to the servants, my knife and fork.

"To my aunt Pandora, washerwoman, my straw bed, two chairs with holes in them and a little crazy, and two ells of linen to make her three aprons, for having washed my shirts and my large woollen stockings.

"To Fechetti, page of the Court, 25 lashes with a whip for having tied crackers to my tail, and many other tricks and impertinent fooleries.

"I have nothing to leave my King, but as I believe he has received some benefit from my advice, I will now give him such counsel as shall not be less salutary both to him and his people.

"I advise him then, for the good of his subjects and himself, constantly to hold the balance between the rich and poor with an even hand.

"To examine carefully before he determines. Never to pronounce a sentence whilst moved by anger. To recompense good and wise men, to chastise the wicked, to drive away flatterers, liars and calumniators, and in general all those pests of the Court who carry fire in their tongues and to protect widows and orphans.

"To cause speedy judgments in all courts of law and put a stop to all tricks and quibbles of courts.

"If he follows these few rules, he will live happily, his reign will be immortal, and he will be proposed as a pattern of wisdom and perfection to all the kings of the earth till the end of time.

"Amen.

(*Signed*) "BERTHOLDE."

CHAPTER XXV

SOME DWARFS AND PRODIGIES OF THE SEVENTEENTH CENTURY

FROM the evidence afforded by their bills, many interesting dwarfs and prodigies were exhibited in London in the seventeenth century.

Among them was John Worrenburg, who was born at Hartshousen in Switzerland in 1659. When he came to London at the age of thirty-nine he was 2 feet 7 inches in height, but had the strength of a full-grown man in his arms and legs.

He was exhibited at the "Plume of Feathers", over against the "King on Horseback", in Stocks Market, and he is described as "A man of the least stature that has been seen in the memory of any, being but two foot and seven inches in height, of seven and thirty years of age. He has a very long beard and sings well. He has been seen by the King and Nobility at White-hall. He speaks good High Dutch and is so very well proportioned to his bigness that all that sees him, admires him."

He came to a curious end when travelling to Holland in 1695, for when being carried in a box over a plank from the ship to the quay at Rotterdam, the plank broke and he fell into the river and, being encumbered in the box, he was drowned.

Another dwarf, together with his wife and a diminutive horse, were exhibited at the "Duke of Marlborough's Head, over against Salisbury-court in Fleet-street".

According to his bill, "this little Blackman was but three feet high or a yard, aged thirty-two years". James Paris, who saw him, states: "He was straight, well-shaped and proportionable. He was called the 'Black Prince'. He had a wife which was not 3 feet high at thirty years of age. They called her the 'Fairy Queen', and she could dance extraordinarily well. And also their 'little Turkey horse', that was but two foot odd inches high and above

By Her Majesty's Permiſſion.

At the Duke of Marlborough's-Head, over-againſt Salisbury-court in Fleet-ſtreet, They is now come to that Place, a large Collection of Strange and Wonderful Creatures, from moſt Parts of the World, all alive.

First, Two strange Monstrous Creatures, that was taken in the Woods in the Deſarts of ÆTHIOPIA, in Preſtor Johns Country in the remoteſt parts of AFFRICA; from their Heads downwards they reſemble Humane Nature, having Breaſts, Bellies, Navels, Niples, Legs and Arms like a Man or Woman, with long Monſtrous Heads, no ſuch Creatures was ever ſeen in this part of the World before, the Female ſhowing many ſtrange and wonderful Actions which gives great Satisfaction to all that ever did ſee her. The next is the Noble Picary, which is very much admir'd by the Learned. The next is a Creature call'd a Poſom, from the Weſt-Indies, which is the moſt Wonderful Creature in Nature, having a falſe Belly for her Young ones to run into to ſave them from Danger, having a Tail much like a Rattle-Snake, by which ſhe gets up into a Tree, and hangs by the Tail upon a Branch till her Enemies are gone. Likewiſe a ſmall Egyptian Pamper, Spotted like a Leopard. Alſo a Small Monſtrous Creature brought from the Coaſt of BRAZIL, he having a Head like a Child, and his Body, Leggs and Arms, being of ſuch Strange and Wonderful Shapes that the like of him never before was ſeen in this Kingdom.

Alſo a little Black Man, being but 3 Foot High and 31 Years of Age, ſtraight and proportionable every Way; Who is diſtinguiſhed by the Name of the Black Prince: And has been ſhown before moſt Kings and Princes in Chriſtendom. Likewiſe his little Turkey-Horſe, being but a Foot odd Inches High, and above 12 Years Old, the leaſt Man and Horſe that ever was ſeen in the World Alive. The Horſe being kept in a Box. And as no ſuch Collection was ever ſhown in this Place before, we hope they will give you Content and Satisfaction, aſſuring you that they are the greateſt Rarities that ever was ſhown Alive in this Kingdom, and are to be ſeen from 9 a Clock in the Morning till 9 at Night, where t us attendance ſhall be given at the afoteſaid Place.

"THE BLACK PRINCE AND HIS LITTLE TURKEY HORSE."

From his bill, XVII century

twelve years old, that shewed many diverting and surprising tricks at the word of command. The horse being kept in a box."

Paris also mentions John Grimes, who was born at New-castle-on-Tyne and who, at the age of fifty-seven, stood only 3 feet 8 inches high.

"He was so strong that he could lift two men from the ground at once.

"He married one wife by whom he had four children, and he was as broad as he was long. He sold himself to a surgeon near the Fountain Tavern in the Strand, some years before his death, for sixpence a week, to be dissected after his death. He died in 1736."

"The Dwarf of the World", however, was a little German woman, who was forty-nine years of age and was to be seen in 1700 at the "Brandy Shop" over against the "Eagel and Child" in Stocks Market, any hour of the day from 8 in the morning till 8 at night. She was but 2 feet 8 inches in height and the mother of two children. "She was as straight as any woman in England. She sings and dances incomparable well, she has had the honour to be shown before Kings and Princes and most of the Nobility of the land. She is carried in a little box to any Gentleman's house if desired."

A dwarf known as the "Little Scotchman" was exhibited in London in 1682. He is said to have measured 2 feet 6 inches and had reached the age of nearly sixty years.

"He has been married several years", states the bill, "and has two sons (one of which is with him). He sings and dances with his son. He formerly kept a writing-school and discourses of the scriptures and of many eminent histories very wisely. If need requires, there are several persons in this town that will justifie that they were his schoollars and see him marry'd.

"He is to be seen at the lower end of Brookfield Market, near Market House."

A remarkable dwarf, according to his bill, was to be seen at the "Young mans Coffee-House" at Charing Cross. He was "a little man, fifty years of age but two feet nine inches high and the father of eight children. He was born without any joints in his wrists, and notwithstanding has the use of both hands to great perfection. His feet are double-jointed and he has two pan-bones to each knee. He is straight, well-proportioned and well-made in every way. He performs the beat of a drum in a surprising degree and sings with a loud voice at the same time.

"When he sleeps he puts his head between his two feet to rest on by way of a pillow and his great toes in each ear, which posture he shews and performs several other things too tedious to mention, to the general satisfaction of all the spectators.

"If any gentlemen or ladies desire to see the above surprising little man at their houses, he will wait on them at any hour between 9 in the morning and 3 in the afternoon, on notice given him at his lodging and the price left to their own generosity."

Besides the dwarfs there were numerous prodigies who attracted the town at this period, and among those who appear to have been highly popular, were the bearded-women.

One of these ladies who achieved notoriety was Barabara Urselin or Van Beck, who is said to have been born at Augsburg. She is described as having a very large, spreading beard, the hair of which hung long and flowing.

John Evelyn thus records a visit he paid to her in his *Diary* on September 15, 1651: "I saw the hairy woman, twenty years old, whom I had before seen when a child. She was born at Augsburg in Germany. Her very eyebrows were combed upwards and all her forehead as thick and even as growes on any woman's head, neatly dressed.

"A very long lock of hair out of each eare. She also had a most prolix beard and mustachios, with long locks growing on ye middle of the nose, like an Iceland dog exactly, the colour of a bright browne, fine as well-dressed flax.

"She was now married and told me she had one child and it was not hairy nor were any of her relations. She was very well-shaped and plaied well on ye harpsichord."

Some years later, on December 21, 1668, Pepys thus records a visit he paid to a hairy or bearded woman: "I went into Holborne and there saw the woman that is to be seen with a beard. She is a plain little woman, her name Ursula

THE HAIRY WOMAN
Aldrovandus, 1642

Dyan, about forty years of age, her voice like a little girl's, with a beard as much as ever I saw a man with, almost black and grizly. It began to grow at about seven years old and was shaved not above seven months ago, and is now as big as any man's, almost as ever I saw. I say bushy and thick. It was a strange sight to me, I confess, and what pleased me mightily."

"The Bold Grimace Spaniard", who was exhibited by Mr. David Cornwell, "a professed operator of Teeth", at the "Ram's Head Inn" in Fenchurch Street, was also a popular attraction.

His bill states: "This creature was brought from Bilboa and lived fifteen years among wild creatures in the mountains and is said to have been reared by them.

"He performs the following grimaces. He lolls out his tongue a foot long, turns his eyes in and out at the same time. Can contract his face as small as an apple, extends his mouth six inches and turns it into the shape of a bird's beak and his eyes like to an owl's, turns his mouth into the form of a hat cock'd up three ways, licks his nose with his tongue like a cow, and changes his face to such a degree, as to appear like a corpse long bury'd.

"Altho' bred wild so long yet by travelling with some comedians eighteen years, he can sing wonderfully fine and accompanies his voice with a thorow bass on the lute."

Another "strange monstrous female creature", who was to be seen about the same time, is declared to have been "taken in the woods in the deserts of Aethopia in Prestor John's country, in the remotest parts of Africa, being brought over from Cape de Bon Espérance alias Cape of Good Hope. From her head downwards she resembles Humane Nature having breasts, legs and arms like a woman with a long monstrous head.

"No such creature was ever seen in this part of the world before, she showing many strange and wonderful actions which gives great satisfaction to all that ever did see her."

Then early in the eighteenth century there was the "Suffolk boy with bristles like a hedgehog who was exhibited at the sign of the 'Prince and Princess of Orange', over against the Opera-house in the Haymarket".

He is described as "a fresh lively country lad just come

from Suffolk who is all cover'd all over his Body with Bristles like a Hedge Hog as hard as horn which shoot off yearly.

THE CAT WOMAN
Schnach, 1679

"He was described before the Royal Society and his skin is said to be compared to the bark of a tree. Others thought it looked like seal-skin or the hide of an elephant or the skin of a rhinosceros.

"He was shown in so decent a manner, that Ladies may have the opportunity of seeing so great a curiosity as well as gentlemen."

Prodigies called "Changlings or Fairy children", also seem to have had a vogue about this time.

A bill of 1680 announces the arrival in London of a "Changling Child" who was to be seen next door to the "Black Raven", in West Smithfield.

"This Fairy child suppos'd to be born of Hungarian parents but chang'd in the nursing, aged nine years, does not exceed a foot and a half high. The legs, thighs and arms are so very small, that they scarce exceed the bigness of a man's thumb, and the face no bigger than the palm of one's hand, and seems so grave and solid as if it were three score years old.

"You may see the whole anatomy of its body by setting it against the sun. It never speaks and when passion moves it, then cries like a cat. It has no teeth but is the most voracious and hungry creature in the world, devouring more victuals than the stoutest man in England."

Another of a similar kind, who is called the "Little Farey Woman", came from Italy, being but "two feet two inches high and no ways deformed". She was to be seen at the "Harts-Horn Inn" in Pye Corner early in the reign of Queen Anne.

The "fairy changling" arose from the old tradition, that fairies or goblins stole into a house and sometimes changed a human infant for one of their own.

A girl without any perfect bones in her body was the attraction at the "Shooe and Slap" in West Smithfield, according to a bill of 1677:

"This Wonder of Nature viz. a girl above fifteen years of age, born in Cheshire and not much above eighteen inches long, having never a perfect bone in any part of her, onely the head, yet she hath all her senses to admiration and discourses, reads very well, sings, whistles and all very pleasant to hear."

Short Janetie, a female dwarf who married a giant, is depicted in a Dutch engraving published about 1685. The lady has short curled hair and wears an elaborately figured gown with short sleeves. She wears earrings, a necklace and carries a fan.

From an inscription on the picture, "Short Janetie", as she was called, came from Waddigsveen in Holland and was a little over 3 feet in height when she was forty-six years of age. Her husband was "Tall Jacob of Sneek", who is said to have been 8 feet high and forty years of age.

A verse below the print reads:

> "This is short Jannetjen, married to a tall fellow,
> A wise fellow who remembers this golden proverb;
> A woman is an evil, a pest in the house;
> And if you want to play the fool
> (Or rather if you must), choose the smallest of all evils."

The "Rummer Tavern" at Charing Cross appears to have been a favourite resort of dwarfs and prodigies, and it was here the "Wonderful Strong and Surprizing Persian Dwarf" was on view. "He was three feet eight inches high, born in Persia, was fifty-six years old, spoke eighteen languages and in Italian, danced to admiration and with ropes tied to his hair when put over his shoulders, lifts a great stone."

His bill tells us, that "he has had the honour to divert the greatest part of the nobility, gentry and others in most parts of Europe with his wonderful performances. 1st. He carries upon each hand the largest men, dancing about the room. 2nd. He holds a chair on his hands with his whiskers or moustaches, which are six inches long and takes up from the floor a piece of money.

"3rd. He takes up from the floor with his whiskers the said piece, three of his fingers being on the floor, lifting at the same time one of his legs up in the air and with his arm thro' a chair, represents a Scaramouch. 4th. He takes up the said piece of money with his whiskers and holds up two chairs in his arms in the form of a Scaramouch's wings. 5th. He bears a stone of four hundred weight hanging on his hair above six inches from the floor, dancing about the room. 6th. He lays his head upon a chair and his feet on another, with his body extended, and bears the said stone and two men on the top of his stomach with ease.

"With many more wonderful performances by strength and dexterity too tedious to mention that surpasses imagination, and he is justly called the Second Sampson.

"He has had the honour to be seen by the Prince and

TO BE SEEN,

By one, or more (in so decent a Manner that Ladies may have the Opportunity of seeing so great a Curiosity as well as Gentlemen) without Loss of Time, at the Sign of the Prince and Princess of Orange, over-against the Opera-House in the Hay-Market,

"THE SUFFOLK BOY WITH BRISTLES"
From his bill, XVIII century

Princess of Wales at Cliefden House and by the princesses at St. James's."

The arrival at the "Rummer" of a "Little Wild man" is announced in another bill. "He was born in St. David's Straits and at the age of twenty-seven years was thirty-four inches in height, straight and well-proportioned. He was clothed in the proper dress of his country and has had the honour to be shew'd to their Royal Highnesses the Prince and Princess of Orange."

CHAPTER XXVI

REMARKABLE DWARFS AND PRODIGIES OF THE EIGHTEENTH CENTURY

AMONG the prodigies who became famous for their intelligence and skill in the eighteenth century was Matthew Buchinger, who besides being a dwarf, was without hands, feet, legs or thighs.

He was born at Anspach in Germany in 1674, and when he came to England early in the eighteenth century, he was 29 inches in height. In spite of his natural disabilities, by the aid of two excrescences which grew from his shoulder-blades, like fingers without nails, he was able to draw and write with remarkable dexterity and skill.

He excited the interest of King George I and was patronized by Robert Harley, Earl of Oxford, for whom he executed several specimens of his skill in penmanship, which are still preserved among the Harleian Collection of manuscripts in the British Museum.

According to one account of his accomplishments, "he makes a pen and writes several hands as well as any writing-master; he draws faces to the life, and coats-of-arms, pictures, flowers, etc. with a pen very curiously. He threads a fine needle very quick; shuffles a pack of cards and deals them very swift. He plays upon the dulcimer as well as any musician; he does many surprizing things with cups and balls; he plays skittles several ways, very well; shaves himself very dexterously and many other things."

Another account of this prodigy states: "Though wanting the useful benefits of nature, having neither hands, feet or thighs, yet he excels all persons who enjoy those happy advantages in their several faculties. He plays on various sorts of musick as the hautboy and strange flute in consort with the bagpipe, dulcimer and trumpet which is esteemed the greatest curiosity by the most ingenious musicians of the age.

"At the 'Two Blackamoors' Heads' in Holbourn near

Southampton Street, he is daily at work in his room, where those who come to see his performances may see him making a curious piece of machinery to play upon the violin and german flute."

Matthew was the youngest of a family of nine. He married four times, and during that period became the father of eleven children. His second adventure into matrimony does not appear to have been a particularly happy one, for it is said, that his wife "was a very perverse woman, who would spend all his money very prodigally and luxuriously, in nice eating, drinking and clothes.

"She would not permit him to eat nor drink as she did, and did beat him cruelly which he bore very patiently; but one day, she having beat him before company, that so provoked him, that he flew at her with such force, that he threw her down and getting upon her so beat her with his stumps, that he almost killed her. Threatening her to treat her in the same manner if she ever did so any more, and she became ever after a very dutiful and loving wife."

James Paris states, that he saw him in London on March 10, 1731, and "he did with his stumps what many could not do with their hands and feet so well as he in playing at cards, dice, ninepins, shuffel-board and rolly-poly. He did cutt paper in several curious shapes, forms and figures. He writ, cast accounts, and designed very prettily; comb'd, oyl'd and powdered his perruque very well; load and discharge a pistol and did never fail of hitting the mark. He darted a sword at a mark exactly at a great distance and performed a great many other strange things.

"He was very well-shaped and had a handsome face."

His greatest skill was shown in his remarkable penmanship, which was wonderfully minute. He drew his own portrait exquisitely on vellum, inserting in the flowing curls of the wig, six of the Psalms together with the Lord's Prayer. Another specimen of his work is "Publius Lentulus' Letter to the Senate of Rome concerning our Blessed Lord and Saviour", with an ornamental border surmounted with a picture of Christ drawn with a pen and ink in lines and dots. He designed and drew a fan-mount for the Countess of Oxford on which he spent fifteen months' work.

In a letter accompanying it addressed to the Earl he writes:

"I have finish'd a curious fan of my own drawing which I had not an opportunity till lately, I have to send to your Lord^P with my wife and there not being such another piece of work and I dispair of ever performing the like again, I was feiffteen months a drawing of it, and if your Lord^P have a fance for it, as for the price I leave to your Lord^P."

Leaving London, Buchinger travelled throughout Scotland, and when in Edinburgh executed a specimen of his penmanship for the corporation and magistrates of that city.

He appears to have taken a fancy to Highland costume, for on his return, when he took up his residence at the "Corner House of Great Suffolk Street near Charing Cross", he announces that besides his other accomplishments, "he dances a horn-pipe in a Highland dress, as well as any man without legs, with a dance performed by a Highland-man. The fore-seat one shilling, the back seat sixpence.

"He had the honour of shewing three successive Emperors of Germany, the most of the Kings and Princes of Europe and in particular, several times before his late Majesty King George."

He is said to have died at Cork in Ireland in 1732, and an elegy which appeared in Dublin afterwards contains the following lines:

> "Poor BUCHINGER at last is dead and gone,
> A LIFELESS TRUNK who was a LIVING one;
> TRUNK, did I say, wherein all Virtues met?
> I shou'd ha' call'd him a rich CABINET.
>
> He never made one FALSE STEP all his life,
> Except in marrying his second Wife;
> And tho' they went together in pure Love,
> They did not hit it, nor were HAND IN GLOVE.
>
> He of his pen had very great Command,
> If he wrote any, 'twas NO RUNNING HAND.
> He play'd all games with Skill, but was most nice,
> Tho' WITHOUT SLIGHT OF HAND, at Cards and Dice."

A dwarf of astonishing strength was Owen Farrell, who was born in the County Cavan in Ireland. His parents, who were peasants, were very poor, and in 1716 he took a situation as footman with a colonel who lived in Dublin.

He was strongly and heavily made, and though only 3 feet 9 inches in height, he developed extraordinary strength. It is said that he could carry four men at one time, two sitting astride on each arm. Assured that he could make more money by exhibiting himself, he gave up his situation and travelled from place to place, where for a time he attracted some attention.

Eventually he found his way to London, but his performance was not successful and he chiefly subsisted by begging about the streets. Clumsy and uncouth, in ragged clothes, his toes protruding through his shoes, and holding a big staff as tall as himself, he used to stand in Covent Garden with a battered old hat in his hand and besought the attention of passers-by.

He thus became well known in town, and his portrait was painted by more than one artist and engraved.

A contemporary writer says: "He was so gross and massive in proportion to his height, that he presented us with a very disagreeable image". Granger remarks: "Nature deviated widely from its usual walk in giving this dwarf little more than half the stature of a man, with the strength of two."

Some time before he died he sold his body to a Mr. Omrod, a surgeon, for a weekly pittance, a not unusual proceeding at the time, and after his death, about 1742, this gentleman took possession of it. His skeleton eventually went to form part of the collection of William Hunter, which is now preserved in the Museum of the University of Glasgow.

A more diminutive dwarf who excited attention in London about 1751, was John Coan, who was born at Twitshall in Norfolk.

At the age of sixteen, he measured just 36 inches and weighed 27½ pounds. He was first exhibited in Norwich, and from an account given by Arderon, who saw him on April 3, 1750, when he was twenty-two, his height with his hat, wig and shoes on, was 38 inches. "His limbs were no larger than those of a child of three or four years old; his body was perfectly straight. He had a good complexion; was of a spritely temper; discoursed readily and pertinently considering his education, and read and wrote English well. His voice was a little hollow but not disagreeable; he could sing with tolerable proficiency; and he amused the company who went to see him by mimicking very exactly the crowing of a cock."

On December 5, 1751, Coan was shown to the Royal Society at their house, which was then in Crane Court, and in the following year was presented to King George II at St. James's Palace.

According to the *London Gazette* for January 10, 1752: "On Wednesday evening, Mr. John Coan, the Norfolk dwarf, was sent for to Leicester House by her Royal Highness the Princess Dowager of Wales and was immediately introduced before her, his Royal Highness the Prince of Wales, Prince Edward, Princess Augusta, and all the other princes and princesses being present, where he staid upwards of two hours; and we are assured by the pertinency of his answers, actions and behaviour, their Royal Highnesses were most agreeably entertained the whole time and made him a very handsome present."

An advertisement in the *Gazette* about this time states: "Mr. John Coan, the Norfolk dwarf, is now to be seen at the watchmakers, facing the Cannon Tavern, Charing Cross."

Owing to the Royal patronage, Coan achieved considerable notoriety and, according to a newspaper, he "had the favour of being sent for to the Guildhall at Bristol, when at St. James's Fair, with the dog that reads, writes and casts accounts and the African Prince. The Mayor and Aldermen ingeniously declared, that there was not a subject besides him publicly exhibited at the fair worth seeing, and peculiarly to express their satisfaction, made Mr. Coan a very handsome present."

He delighted in giving recitations from plays, and at Tunbridge Wells, played in the *Fine Gentleman in Lethe*. He is said to have developed a good voice and by his humorous delivery and quaint antics, would send his audience into roars of laughter, especially when he mounted a table and sang his favourite song *The Cock*.

He took a great pride in his appearance, and was fond of gorgeous costumes, sometimes wearing a coat and breeches of blue and gold and at others of light blue and silver, with a bag-wig.

Like other prodigies, when public interest began to wane, he exhibited at Bartholomew Fair, together with Edward Bamford, the giant hatter of Shire Lane, Temple Bar, who was 7 feet 4 inches in height.

In 1762, he was engaged by Pinchbeck, the proprietor of the "Dwarf Tavern in the Five Fields at Chelsea", to which a tea-garden was attached, and used to amuse the visitors, but his health began to fail and here at the age of thirty-nine he died.

His body was exhibited and lay-in-state at the tavern for a time, and even after he was buried the proprietor endeavoured to attract the curious by showing an effigy of the dwarf dressed in his clothes.

A German dwarf named Coppernin is said to have been the last to have been attached to an English Court. He was retained in the service of Wilhelmina Carolina of Brandenburg, the wife of George II.

CHAPTER XXVII

THE COUNT BORUWLASKI AND OTHER COURT DWARFS

FEW dwarfs who achieved fame had a more interesting career than Joseph Boruwlaski, the Polish dwarf, who later became known as "Count Boruwlaski". He was born near Chaliez in Polish Russia in November 1739, and although of humble parentage, he had the good fortune to obtain the patronage of several ladies of influence and wealth, who brought him into prominence.

He was one of a family of six, all of whom were normal but three, his brother, a sister and himself. The sister, who was seven years younger than Joseph, was so short that she could stand under his arm and is said to have been a "model of symmetry and beauty". At the age of twenty, she was 2 feet 4 inches in height and perfectly formed, but was attacked with smallpox and died after two days' illness.

The Starostin de Caorlix, who afterwards became the Countess de Tarnow, became interested in Joseph and wished to look after him, but it was some time before his mother would consent to the proposal.

On the marriage of the Starostin, her friend, the Countess Humiecka, wished to take charge of Joseph, and she took him with her to her estate at Rychty in Podolia, where he remained for some years.

At the age of fifteen, he had grown to the height of 25 inches, and the Countess took him with her to Vienna, where he was presented to the Empress Maria Theresa.

The Empress became very attached to the little dwarf, and a story is told, that on one occasion, taking him on her knee, she asked him what he thought was most curious and interesting at Vienna.

Joseph replied, that of the most wonderful things he had seen, nothing seemed so extraordinary as that which he then beheld.

"And what is that?" asked the Empress.

"To see so little a man on the lap of so great a woman," replied the astute dwarf.

The Empress happened to be wearing a very beautiful ring on her finger which bore her cypher in brilliants, and noticing that Boruwlaski was gazing at it intently, she asked him if he admired it.

"I beg your majesty's pardon," he replied, "but it is not the ring that I am looking at but the hand, which I beg your permission to kiss", at the same time raising it to his lips.

The Empress was so pleased at his answer, she took a diamond-ring from the finger of Marie Antoinette, then a child, who was present, and gave it to Boruwlaski, much to his delight.

On leaving Vienna, the Countess took the dwarf with her to Lunéville to visit Stanislaus Lesczinski, the ex-King of Poland. He also kept a little French dwarf known as Bébé at his palace, who was slightly taller than Boruwlaski. Seeing that his master was so much interested in the new arrival, Bébé became intensely jealous of him and deeply resented any attention the King paid to Joseph.

One day, after Stanislaus had been amusing himself with the two dwarfs, he left the apartment for a time, and Bébé seized the opportunity to take revenge on his rival. Taking Boruwlaski unawares, he seized him round the waist and tried to throw him on the fire. The noise of the struggle was heard by the King, who re-entered the room only just in time to separate them, and handing Bébé over to a footman, ordered him to be beaten and not allowed to enter his presence again.

Boruwlaski begged the King to forgive him, to which the King consented after Bébé had been thrashed and had asked his rival's pardon.

The Countess, on leaving Lunéville, took the dwarf with her to Paris, where he soon became a great favourite at the French Court and was patronized by the Royal Family. He was much in demand on the occasions of masks and pageants, and on one evening, at a banquet given by the

Count Oginski, Boruwlaski was served up at the table in a tureen. Bouret, the farmer-general, is said to have given an entertainment in his honour, at which the plates, dishes, forks and spoons, and even the food, consisted of things in miniature and proportionate to his size.

An interesting account of Boruwlaski was given to the Royal Academy of Sciences of Paris by Count Tressan in 1760. He states, he is now "twenty-two years of age and about twenty-eight inches high.

"He is well-proportioned; his eyes are fine and full of fire; his features agreeable and indicate gaiety and sprightliness of mind.

"He enjoys a perfect state of health, drinks nothing but water, eats little, sleeps well and can bear a great deal of fatigue. He dances well and is very nimble. His manner is extremely graceful and his repartees, smart and spirited. He speaks sensibly of what he has seen and has a very good memory; his judgment is sound and his heart susceptible of the most tender impressions. He loves to be treated with the decorum due to his rank, yet is not offended with those who make free with him on account of his stature."

From Paris, the Countess took her dwarf to Holland, where he also became very popular with the ladies of the Court at The Hague.

On leaving Holland they travelled back through Germany to Warsaw, and while there, Boruwlaski fell in love with an actress belonging to a company of French comedians then playing in the city. He obtained an introduction to the object of his passion, but unfortunately she was more amused than impressed by his sentiments and his benefactress was greatly displeased at his intrigue.

Later on, when Stanislaus II came to the throne of Poland, he took Boruwlaski under his protection, though he still remained a favourite with the Countess. She had meanwhile taken a young girl named Isalina Barbutan into her household as a companion, and the dwarf again fell in love. She, however, ridiculed his attentions, but her indifference only made him more ardent. She was at length compelled to appeal to the Countess, who eventually ordered the dwarf to leave her house, and so Boruwlaski was for the first time turned adrift in the world without resources.

Through the interest of Prince Casimir, the King promised to provide for him, and this caused him to renew his addresses to Isalina Barbutan. This time, however, he was received with more favour and with the King's approval, who promised to settle an annuity of one hundred ducats upon him, he at last married the lady of his choice.

Soon after the marriage, he found that his allowance was not sufficient to provide the luxuries to which he had been accustomed, and his friends suggested that he should take a tour round the countries of Europe, where he had already made many influential friends.

The King approved of the plan, and provided him with a suitable travelling-carriage and letters of introduction to several of the Royal Courts. Thus equipped he set out from Warsaw with his wife in November 1780.

They had to remain in Cracow for some time, where his wife gave birth to a daughter, so they did not reach Vienna until February 1781. Here he sought the assistance of Count Kaunitz, one of his former friends, and through him, he was introduced to Sir R. M. Keith, the British Ambassador, who suggested that he should visit England.

Both Boruwlaski and his wife were musical, and he was an excellent performer on the guitar, on which he played pieces of his own composition.

After giving a concert in Vienna, which was attended by most of the notabilities of the city, they continued their tour through Germany, and afterwards visited Turkey, Lapland and Finland. He then decided to visit England, and, embarking on a vessel at Ostend, they reached Margate after a tempestuous voyage that lasted six days, during which the ship lost her masts in a terrible storm.

On arrival in London, he obtained the patronage of the Duke and Duchess of Devonshire, and was afterwards presented to the Prince of Wales, who later became George IV. Through the influence of the Countess of Egremont, he was also received by the King and Queen and several members of the Royal Family.

In order to add to his income, he organized a series of subscription concerts, at which he appeared and performed, but they did not prove very successful. An advertisement of the postponement of one of his concerts was as follows:

"Carlisle House. (By very particular desire.)

"Comte Boruwlaski, the most celebrated dwarf now in England, is compelled to put off his concert from Monday the 17th to Wednesday the 19th instant, when it will be performed at this place under the direction of Mr. Cramer, who was unavoidably prevented from attending on the first night.

"Tickets for the 17th inst. will be admitted and may be had of Comte Boruwlaski, No. 55 Jermyn-street, near St. James's Church."

Through Mathews, the comedian, who was a friend and admirer of the dwarf, Boruwlaski was again received by King George IV. Mrs. Mathews in the *Memoirs* of the actor says: "When my husband and his little charge were ushered into the presence of the sovereign, the King rose from his chair and raising up Boruwlaski in his arms said: 'My dear old friend, how delighted I am to see you,' and then placed the little man on a sofa."

The King gave Boruwlaski a miniature watch, chain and seals and remarked to Mathews: "If I had a dozen sons, I could not point out to them a more perfect model of good breeding and elegance than the Count. He is really a most accomplished and charming person."

While Boruwlaski was in London he was introduced one day to O'Brien, the Irish giant. "Our surprise", says the dwarf, "was mutual. The giant remained for a moment speechless with astonishment, then stooping half-way he presented his hand, which could easily have enveloped a dozen of mine, and made me a pretty compliment. I nearly reached the giant's knee."

In 1783, he made a tour of the principal provincial towns, including those of Scotland and Ireland, which proved more successful, and he returned to London in 1786 with the money he had made. The news of this reaching Poland, the King withdrew his annuity, which caused Boruwlaski to return for a time to his own country, but after settling matters there, he came back to England, and in July 1791 we hear of him next at Southampton, where he gave a ball in the Long Rooms and performed on the guitar for the amusement of those present.

He was now getting on in years, and through some ladies named Metcalf, of Durham, he was offered a cottage near that city, together with an annual allowance if he would take up his permanent residence there. This he accepted, and remained at Bank's Cottage until his death, on September 5, 1837, at the advanced age of ninety-eight years.

His remains were interred near those of Stephen Kemble in Durham Cathedral. One of his shoes, the sole of which measures $5\frac{7}{8}$ inches, is preserved in the Philosophical Institution at Bristol.

Bébé, the dwarf of King Stanislaus of Poland, who in a fit of jealousy attempted to burn Boruwlaski, was born at Plaisnes in the Vosges. His real name was Nicholas Fény, and at the time of his birth he measured 8 inches. He was carried to church to be baptized, "on a plate overspread with the tow of flax, and a wooden shoe served him as a cradle". In an account of his life given to the Academy of Sciences in 1726, it is stated that, he was only reared with great difficulty, being suckled by a goat. He was able to walk at the age of two years, and a pair of shoes then made for him measured $1\frac{1}{2}$ inches long. When he was six, his height was 15 inches, and he was then well-proportioned and healthy.

The King having heard of him, had him brought to Lunéville, where he was lodged in the palace and well looked after. He made a great pet of the little dwarf and gave him the name of Bébé.

He was incapable of reasoning, but later on developed a great liking for music, and loved to beat time, which he did with accuracy.

Bébé was of a very jealous disposition and formed strong attachments. The Princess of Talmond endeavoured to give him instruction, but he was so jealous of her attentions to anything else, that one day, seeing her caress a dog, he snatched it from her arms and threw it out of the window, exclaiming: "Why do you love him more than me?"

About 1761, he fell in love with a female dwarf named Anne Thérèse Souvray, but he died before they could be married. In his twenty-third year he fell into a lethargic condition, and was unable to walk and could only speak with difficulty. From this he never recovered and died on June 9, 1764. At the time of his death he measured 33 inches.

Anne Thérèse Souvray afterwards adopted his name, and was exhibited in Paris in 1819, when she was seventy-three years of age and at that time 33 inches in height. In spite of her advanced age, she danced and sang with great vivacity, and is said to have been full of gaiety and life.

A pair of remarkable dwarfs were married at the church of St. Martin-in-the-Fields in 1719. The husband, Robert Skinner, was forty-four years of age and was 2 feet 1 inch in height, while his bride was but one inch taller. He was a native of Ripon in Yorkshire and his wife was born in Wales. They were both of good appearance, perfectly straight, well-proportioned and intelligent.

It was not until after they had been married twenty-three years and had a family of fourteen children, they were exhibited at Westminster, where they attracted a good deal of attention.

Crowds of people flocked to see the little couple, and in the space of two years they had made sufficient money to retire.

They used to travel about in a small carriage drawn by two dogs, driven by a small boy in a yellow and purple livery, and were thus frequently to be seen in St. James's Park.

Mrs. Skinner died in 1763, and her husband was so stricken with grief, that he shut himself up in one room for twelve months, refusing to be seen except by a faithful old servant who looked after him. Eventually he left London and returned to his native place in Yorkshire, where he died two years afterwards. He is said to have left twenty-two thousand pounds, which was to be equally divided among his children.

An amusing bill printed in the early part of the last century announces the arrival at Bartholomew Fair of "Mr. Thomas Allen, the most surprising small man ever before the public, also Miss Morgan, the celebrated Windsor Fairy, known in London and Windsor by the addition of 'Lady Morgan', a title which his Majesty was pleased to confer upon her.

"This unparalleled woman is in the 35th year of her age and only 18 pounds weight.

"Her form affords a pleasing surprise and her admirable symmetry engages attention. She was introduced to their Majesties at the Queen's Lodge Windsor on Saturday the 4th of August 1781 by the recommendation of the late Dr. Hunter; when they were pleased to pronounce her the finest display of human nature in miniature they ever saw. But we shall say no more of these wonders of nature; let those who honour them with their visits judge for themselves.

'Let others boast of stature or of birth,
This glorious truth shall fill our souls with mirth,
That we now are, and hope for years to sing,
The smallest subjects of the greatest king.'

"Admittance to ladies and gentlemen, 1s.; children, half price. In this and many other parts of the kingdom, it is too common to show deformed persons with various arts and deceptions under denominations of persons of miniature, to impose on the public. This little couple are beyond contradiction the most wonderful display of nature ever held out to the admiration of mankind!

"N.B. The above lady's mother is with her and will attend any lady or gentleman's house, if required."

On a report being circulated which "Lady Morgan" considered derogatory to her reputation, she very indignantly wrote a letter to the editor of the *European Magazine*, of which the following is an extract:

"Sir,

"I must confess, that I was a good deal surprised to find that you have chosen to make free with the short woman, and still more hurt to learn that my friends will have it I am designated by that appellation, and that you have dared to take those liberties with me, whom they say the judicious manager chose from the pigmy race to lengthen out a piece. Now this, give me leave, sir, to say, I flatly deny. . . .

"I can assure you, that, although diminutive, I am a person of no small importance. My grandfather was Timothy Tuck Esq. the little hero mentioned in the *Guardian*; my great-uncle, Thomas Tiptoe Esq., the little lover, who was maliciously accused by a lady of purloining her sizzars-sheath to make him a scabbard for his sword. My father, Ragotin Tuck Esq., was the little beau of the last age so well known in the green rooms for pestering the actresses, and although there is no truth in the story that one of them shut him up in a clothes trunk, yet the thing might have been a dramatic effect.

"Thus you see, sir, I have a line of ancestry to boast, though not great, certainly splendid.

"Of myself, I shall say little, the influence of correction rather than vanity guides my pen, therefore I have only to request that you will set the public right with regard to me or I declare, I will never hereafter consider you or your works with the least degree of favour, nor shall you or your publisher in future even so much as squeeze the little finger of

'Lady Morgan.' "

The "Timothy Tuck and Thomas Tiptoe" alluded to in the letter, refer to a humorous notice of a club of little men published in the *Guardian* on June 25, 1713, and in the following number of that journal, of which no man above five feet in height was allowed to become a member. Among those who belonged to it were "Tom Tiptoe, a dapper black fellow, the most gallant lover of the age, who was particularly nice in his habiliments, and Tim Tuck, who was full as large when he was fourteen years old as he was then".

An engraving by Mills, published in 1803, represents Thomas Allen and Lady Morgan hand-in-hand. The former was then thirty-five years old and 3 feet 3 inches high, and the latter was forty-five years of age and 3 feet in height. Allen is clad in a loose tail-coat and wears a wig and Hessian boots, and Lady Morgan is attired in a long-skirted dress, earing high-heeled shoes, and carries a fan in her left hand.

A remarkable female dwarf known as the "Corsican Fairy" was exhibited in London in 1773, and excited much interest. She was 34 inches in height and weighed 26 pounds. Her name was Madame Teresa, and she was a native of Corsica. She was symmetrical in form, had a pleasing and vivacious manner and could speak Italian and French. She was very spritely and danced with much grace. A portrait of her, painted by Hincks when she was in London, is among the collection of pictures at the Royal College of Surgeons.

CHAPTER XXVIII

SOME ECCENTRIC AND MUSICAL DWARFS

Two dwarfs of Dutch birth achieved notoriety in the early part of the nineteenth century, both of whom excited considerable interest when they appeared in London.

One of these was Simon Paap, who was born on May 25, 1789, at Zand Voort in Holland. He was the son of a fisherman and was of normal proportions until he reached the age of three years, when he ceased to grow, and never afterwards increased in height.

At the age of twenty-six, he was 28 inches and weighed 27 pounds. He is said to have been "handsome and well-proportioned in his limbs and body, but his head was rather large for his size. His appetite seldom exceeded that of a child of three or four years of age. He was fond of wine, smoked a pipe and took snuff, all in moderation. He had pleasant manners and spoke Dutch, French and English.

After being exhibited in most of the principal towns of his native country, he came to England about 1815. He was presented to the Queen, the Prince Regent and other members of the Royal Family, at Carlton House, on May 5, 1815, and was also introduced to the Lord Mayor on September 1st of the same year.

He dressed in a fantastic costume, consisting of a jacket of blue silk, large, loose breeches of blue-figured satin of the Dutch style, white silk waistcoat and white silk stockings, with buckles on his shoes. He wore a miniature portrait of the Prince of Orange set in gold on his left side, a gift from the Princess, and two large gold buttons on the front of his jacket, while his fingers were decked with several fine rings.

When he walked the streets in the West End, he dressed as a small child of about four in order to escape attention. He usually carried a small whip in his hand and was attended by a woman, like a nursemaid.

As well as exhibiting at the fairs he appeared twice at Covent Garden Theatre, his performance consisting of manual and military exercises, during which he discharged a small gun.

According to an advertisement which appeared in a newspaper on September 8, 1816, he was then on exhibition at the "Ram Inn, in West Smithfield," under the management of a Mr. Gyngell, who states:

"Owing to the very flattering encouragement he experienced at his new Jubilee Pavillion during the Fair by the most respectable company, is induced to exhibit the whole of his mechanical and scientific entertainments at the Ram Inn, West Smithfield, to-morrow Monday and two following evenings. . . .

"After which, Mr. Paap, the smallest man in the world, will be exhibited, being only 28 inches in height, weight 27 lbs., and twenty-seven years old."

Dr. Bigsby says he saw Paap in a caravan in the market-place at Nottingham about 1815, and he was seen in Oxford in 1818.

He used to present his visitors with his autograph with a few words, written in a small but distinct handwriting.

He died at Dendermonde in Holland on December 2, 1828, at the age of thirty-nine, and his height is recorded on a pillar in the porch of the Brouwer's chapel in the great church at Haarlem, close to that indicating the height of Cajanus, the giant.

Rather less in height, but more bulky and clumsy in appearance, was Wybrand Lolkes, who was born at Jelft, in West Friesland, in 1790.

He also was the son of a fisherman and one of a family of eight, all of which but Wybrand were of normal height. At an early age he showed a taste for mechanics, and when he was old enough, through some people who took an interest in him, he was apprenticed to a watchmaker in Amsterdam. After serving four years with his master, he commenced business for himself in Rotterdam, but when trade began to fall off, he began to attend the local fairs, where he attracted attention and made quite a considerable sum of money.

After a time, he resolved to visit England, and on landing at Harwich, was received by a crowd of curious people who had heard of his arrival.

Philip Astley, hearing of him, engaged him to come to London at a weekly salary of five guineas, and he made his first appearance at the Amphitheatre near Westminster Bridge on Easter Monday 1790.

His wife, whom he had married in Rotterdam, was a tall young woman of pleasing appearance, and she accompanied him on his travels. They usually came on the stage hand-in-hand, she being compelled to stoop in order to reach his fingers. He had a large head with a full face, long arms, short thighs and scarcely any legs.

But in spite of his clumsy appearance, he was very active and nimble, particularly in jumping and standing on his head, which he would perform with all the agility of a young man. He was remarkably strong, and could easily spring from the floor on to a chair of ordinary height. Dignified in manner, he was very vain and of somewhat a morose disposition. He had three children, all of whom were normal in stature. At the age of sixty, he was 27 inches in height and weighed 56 pounds. He did not remain long in England, and is said to have returned to his native country with a considerable sum of money.

The original "Black Dwarf", immortalized by Sir Walter Scott in his well-known novel, is said to have been a little man named David Ritchie, a native of Tweeddale, who was the son of a quarryman of Stobo.

Ritchie is said not only to have been hideously misshapen in form, but also to have had a most repulsive appearance.

He is described in 1817 by Robert Chambers as having "a skull of an oblong and rather unusual shape, which was said to be so strong that he could strike it with ease through the panel of a door or the end of a barrel. His laugh is said to have been quite horrible and his screech-owl voice, shrill, uncouth and dissonant, corresponded with his other peculiarities. He usually wore an old slouched hat when he went abroad and when at home, a sort of cowl or nightcap.

"He never wore shoes, being unable to keep them on his misshapen fin-like feet, but always had both feet and legs quite concealed, wrapped up with pieces of cloth. He always walked with a sort of pole or pike-staff considerably taller than himself. His habits were in many respsect singular and indicated a mind congenial to its uncouth tabernacle. A jealous, misanthropical and irritable temper was his prominent characteristic."

He was brought up as a brushmaker in Edinburgh and then plied his trade as he wandered about the country, but his misshapen figure and disagreeable visage caused him to be loathed and derided wherever he went.

At length, driven to distraction by the treatment he generally received, he sought some spot far from the haunts of men where he might be at peace.

Knowing the country well, he settled himself on a patch of remote wild moor-land at the bottom of a bank on the farm of Woodhouse, in the valley of the small river Manor, in Peebleshire. Here, with some toil, he built himself a miniature dwelling, the walls of which he constructed of stone of some thickness.

The door of the cottage was about 3 feet 6 inches high, and he could just stand within it.

He was regarded as a formidable personage possessed with occult powers by the dalesmen of the Border, and was generally blamed if any misfortune befell the sheep or cattle, but otherwise he appears to have been left unmolested. The few people who passed his dwelling avoided "Bow'd Davie", as he was called, on account of his reputation of being able to cast the evil eye, and so the unfortunate dwarf became almost an outcast.

Scott, who visited him in 1797, says, he was "fond of reading Shenstone's *Pastorals* and Milton's *Paradise Lost*", and seems to have regarded him as a man of thought and some intelligence. He died early in the nineteenth century.

Quite a number of dwarfs appear to have been endowed with a taste for music, and among those who developed considerable proficiency in the art, were Nannette Stocker and John Hauptman, who appeared together in London in March 1815.

Nannette was a pianist of some ability and Hauptman was an accomplished violinist. They attracted crowds of people to their concerts. Nannette, who was born at Kammer in Upper Austria, was 33 inches in height and weighed 33 pounds, while Hauptman was a little over 36 inches high.

Nannette started her career after the death of her mother, and began travelling with a show in October 1797.

According to an account in a newspaper, she visited Berlin in 1799, and her arrival was thus announced:

"There is now exhibiting at Berlin, a female dwarf of a more diminutive and well-proportioned stature than any 'Jeu de Nature' hitherto seen. . . . Her name is Nannette Stocker; she is now seventeen years of age and of the ordinary size and growth of a child of seven years old, exceedingly well-proportioned, full of vivacity and quick of apprehension. Her parents were peasants in Saxony and both of them above the ordinary middle stature."

Nannette was introduced to John Hauptman when she was visiting Strasbourg in 1798. He was born at Ringendorff, near Bousvillers, on the Lower Rhine, and was still under the care of the authorities of the town when they met, but Nannette's guardian, who travelled with her, seeing what a great attraction the two dwarfs would prove if they were able to appear together, eventually arranged the partnership, and they made their first appearance at the Grand Theatre at Clermont.

Hauptman's violin solos were accompanied by Nannette on the piano, and she made a further contribution to the entertainment by dancing.

They first performed in London at 22, New Bond Street, and drew large audiences to their recitals. Nannette is described by a writer of the time as being "the most lively little person imaginable, full of talk and always appearing with a smile. When not playing on the pianoforte, she was either knitting or working at her needle. She spoke English very well. Hauptman was more reserved, and when not accompanying the lady with his violin, generally walked about the room. He was not a master of the English language, and he appeared rather heavy. It was said that he had offered Nannette his hand and heart, which favours she had declined."

In the summer of 1823, Caroline Crachami, a little Sicilian dwarf, about nine or ten years of age, was exhibited in London, who was but 19¾ inches in height.

She was the daughter of a musician, and was born in Palermo in 1815. The Duchess of Parma took an interest in her, but she was not exhibited in public until she was brought to England in 1823, when she attracted considerable interest.

After being twelve months in this country, one evening, after receiving upwards of 200 visitors, she collapsed, and died shortly afterwards.

A rather sinister story is attached to the disposal of her remains, according to an account which appeared in *The Times* of June 17, 1824.

From this it appears that Fogell Crachami, the father of the dwarf, applied to the magistrate at Marlborough Street Police Court for a warrant to arrest a person named Gilligan, to whom her body had been entrusted, and who was alleged to have disappeared with it. He had occupied splendid apartments in the house of Mr. Dorlan, a fashionable tailor in Duke Street, St. James's, but he had gone away, leaving behind him nothing but the dwarf's little bed, and the dress the tailor had made for her, in which she was to have been presented to the King.

It transpired that Gilligan had offered the body to Mr. Brooks, of Blenheim Steps, for one hundred guineas, but the sale was not completed.

The father then sought Sir Everard Home, of Sackville Street, through whose influence the dwarf was to have been presented to the King, and from him he learnt, that although Gilligan had offered the body to him, he had refused to purchase it. He agreed, however, to present it to the Royal College of Surgeons, and whatever that body thought proper to vote him, he should receive. To these terms Gilligan agreed, and departed. Sir Everard, to pacify the father, is said to have given him a cheque for ten pounds, on which he left London to join his wife in Ireland.

In striking contrast, her diminutive skeleton now stands side by side with that of Charles Byrne, the Irish giant, in the Museum of the Royal College of Surgeons of England. Here also are casts of her face, arm, hand and foot, and other pathetic relics of the little dwarf include her shoes, which measure 3½ inches long, her tiny thimble and a ring she always wore on her finger.

The remarkable feats performed by a dwarf called Leach astonished London about 1820. He was known as "The Wonderful Youth", and at the age of eighteen is described as "the shortest person in the world". It was said that he could walk under the arm of the famous dwarf, "Lady Morgan", without touching it by nearly four inches. According to his bill, "he was of a pleasing countenance and possessed of great accomplishments. His feats of agility were astounding. Standing upright on his feet he could touch the floor with his fingers; he could sit on the floor in a way no other person could do; but how that was we do not know. He walked down a flight of stairs on his hands with his feet in the air, faster than any other person could on his feet. He could take a pin out of the wall with his mouth, standing on one hand and his feet upwards.

"He balanced himself on his hands on the top of a chair-back, from which he threw himself and alighted on the ground on his hands, walking off on the same with the greatest ease. He placed a pin on the floor, took it up with one hand and supported his balance on the other, while he put it into his mouth. He laid himself on the floor by the strength of his arms, then raised himself up feet foremost and walked off on his hands. He also walked in a horizontal position on his hands under a common table without touching the table with his feet. Standing on a chair, he threw it backwards from him, alighting on his hands, and in that posture walked round the room.

"He possessed a peculiar and surprising way of running totally different from any other person, and challenged the whole world for one thousand guineas, to produce any other person capable of competing with him."

Such were the extraordinary feats performed by this wonderful dwarf.

CHAPTER XXIX

"GENERAL TOM THUMB" AND HIS CAREER—"ADMIRAL VAN TROMP"

Many will no doubt still remember Charles Stratton, popularly known as "General Tom Thumb", who was perhaps the most famous and best-known dwarf of the last century.

He was born at Bridgeport, Connecticut, United States, on January 11, 1832, and at the time of his birth is said to have weighed over the average weight of a new-born infant.

At the age of five months he measured 25 inches, but after that time ceased to grow, until 1845.

He was first exhibited by Phineas T. Barnum at his American Museum in New York, where he became an immediate success, and in a short time is said to have been visited by 30,000 people.

Entertained and petted by many ladies of wealth and invited out to dine with the leading families, Tom Thumb became immensely popular. After a stay of six weeks, he was then taken on tour through the chief American cities, including Boston, Philadelphia, Baltimore and Charleston, and everywhere excited considerable interest.

Barnum, to whose astute advertising he no doubt owed much of his notoriety, then decided to bring him to Europe, and they sailed from New York in January 1844, after being seen off by a crowd of about 10,000 people.

He first appeared in London at the Princess's Theatre on February 21st, in his impersonation of Napoleon Buonaparte, and dressed in a replica in miniature of the well-known uniform usually worn by the Emperor, with cocked hat complete, he would strut about the stage in a most ludicrous manner, to the amusement of the audience.

In appearance, he was a little man with fair hair and good features, with a vivacious expression and a childish, high-pitched voice, which was heard well in a large room.

GENERAL
TOM THUMB,
The American Man in Miniature.

Under the Patronage of
Her Majesty, H. R. H. Prince Albert, the Queen Dowager, H. R. H. the
Duchess of Kent, the King and Queen of the Belgians, the Dukes of

Cambridge, Wellington, Devonshire, Buckingham, the Nobility generally, and
visited in London by 300,000 PERSONS, in the space of
Four Months.

This extraordinary little Gentleman was born in the United States of America, and
is accompanied hither by his Parents, Guardian, and Preceptor. He is Thirteen Years
old—25 Inches high, and SMALLER THAN ANY INFANT THAT EVER
WALKED ALONE, and

WEIGHS ONLY FIFTEEN POUNDS!

The Nobility, Gentry, and Public, are respectfully informed that the LITTLE
GENERAL will return to London, and hold his Public Levees at the

Suffolk Street Gallery, Pall Mall,

On MONDAY, DECEMBER 23rd, & during the Week,

After which he leaves immediately for PARIS

GENERAL TOM THUMB will relate his History, sing a Variety of Songs, appear
in various Dances, &c. He will also give an Imitation of

Napoleon in full Military Costume,
AND
THE GRECIAN STATUES!

The little GENERAL will likewise appear in the magnificent COURT DRESS
which he had the honour of wearing THREE TIMES before HER MAJESTY at
BUCKINGHAM PALACE, and before the Queen Dowager at Marlborough House;
also in his NEW HIGHLAND DRESS, made and presented by Messrs. MEYER
and MORTIMER, of Edinburgh.

The MAGNIFICENT PRESENTS given him by HER MAJESTY, the
QUEEN DOWAGER, the DUKE of DEVONSHIRE, &c., will be exhibited.
The GENERAL will also dispose of his MEMOIRS (6d. each), and his LIKENESS,
with fac-similes of his Autograph, giving STAMPED RECEIPTS, to LADIES only.

The GENERAL's New and Elegant CARRIAGE, drawn by two of the Smallest Ponies
in the World, with Coachman and Footman, in Splendid Liveries, will pass through the
Streets daily, Weather permitting.

Hours of Exhibition, from 11 to 1; 3 to 5; and 7 to 9.
Doors open Half-an-Hour previous.

Admission, One Shilling, regardless of Age.

Printed by T. Brettell, 40, Rupert Street, Haymarket.

TOM THUMB'S BILL, 1844

His acting mainly consisted in posing himself in the attitudes of some famous Greek statues, which he did with absurd effect.

It was Barnum's great ambition to present the little man to Queen Victoria, so soon after his arrival he made every endeavour to bring this about. At length he received an invitation from Mr. Charles Murray, Master of the Queen's Household, to breakfast with him in company with Tom Thumb.

Barnum thus relates the subsequent proceedings:

"Now, Barnum," said Mr. Murray, "I want her Majesty to see the little general before Louis Philippe does. I will try and bring about the presentation to the Queen as soon as possible."

"Two days afterwards", says Barnum, "I received a command from her Majesty to bring the general to Buckingham Palace the next evening.

"On the presentation of Tom Thumb to the Queen, the old Duke of Wellington was present. He was much interested in the little dwarf and visited his exhibition at the Egyptian Hall in Piccadilly several times, usually riding there on horseback attended by an orderly. The Duke's high-crowned hat with an extremely narrow brim was very peculiar, and that of itself would lead to his recognition, if any feature were needed beyond his enormous nose.

"The first time he came to the exhibition, Tom Thumb was personating Napoleon Buonaparte, dressed in the well-known uniform of the Emperor, marching up and down, apparently taking snuff in deep meditation.

"The Duke asked Tom Thumb the subject of his meditations.

"'I was thinking of the loss of the battle of Waterloo,' was the little man's immediate reply."

On April 2, 1844, Barnum was again commanded to take Tom Thumb to see the Queen, and the party included the Queen of the Belgians, the Prince of Wales, the Princess Royal and Princess Alice. At the conclusion of the entertainment, Queen Victoria presented him with a souvenir of mother-of-pearl set with rubies, bearing the crown and her cipher "V.R."

Barnum further tells us that "Her Majesty had a very small pony not any higher than Tom Thumb himself, who then stood twenty-seven inches. The little man greatly wished to have the little pony, though he dared not say so.

"When we went to Windsor Castle later, the Duke of Wellington and a dozen other dignitaries were just coming out of the dining-room.

"Tom Thumb ran up to them and said: 'Good evening, ladies and gentlemen.' When the Queen came out, he said: 'Good evening, Madame. Got a fine picture gallery here?'

"Presently the Queen asked him whether he could dance.

" 'Oh yes, I can dance', he replied, and then danced before the company.

"He was then asked if he could sing? Oh yes, he could sing.

"What could he sing?

" ' "Yankee Doodle" ', he answered.

"In singing one of the verses", says Barnum, "I noticed that Tom Thumb pointed his finger at the Queen, and when it was over, the little man said to me, 'Did you see me point my finger at the Queen when I was singing?'

" 'Yes, you impudent little fellow, why did you do that?' I asked.

" 'Why, don't you know that it says, "Yankee Doodle, Yankee Doodle riding on a pony"?'

"But her Majesty did not take the hint."

He again saw the Queen, together with Prince Albert and the King and Queen of the Belgians, at Buckingham Palace, when the little man was arrayed in full Court dress, and on leaving was presented with a gold watch and chain and a pencil-case, much to his delight.

By this time his popularity in London was extraordinary, and he was so mobbed in the streets, that Barnum decided to have a special carriage built for him which is thus described:

"The body was twenty inches high and eleven inches

wide and the interior was completely fitted in the richest style. The outside of the carriage was painted a rich blue picked out with white and the wheels were red and blue. On the door panels were emblazoned the general's device, consisting of Britannia and the figure of Liberty supported by the British Lion and the American Eagle, with the motto 'Go ahead'. The coachman's box was furnished with a crimson hammer-cloth and decorated with a silver star and red and green flowers. The carriage was drawn by a pair of diminutive Shetland ponies and two boys were engaged as coachman and footman. They were dressed in liveries of sky blue trimmed with silver lace, with aiguillettes tipped with silver; red breeches, with silver garters and buckles, plated buttons, cocked hats and wigs and the footman carried a cane. The entire equipage is said to have cost about £400."

Tom Thumb left London for Paris in February 1845, taking his little carriage with him, and for four months appeared at the Salle des Concerts in the Rue Vivienne. In the evenings he was to be seen at the Vaudeville Theatre, where he took part in a fairy play called *Le Petit Poucet*, that was written expressly for him and which ran for seventy nights.

He was received by King Louis Philippe and the Queen at the Tuileries several times, and received from them many handsome gifts.

After touring through France and Belgium, he visited Spain, where he appeared before Queen Isabella, the Queen-mother and the Court, then at Pampeluna, and accompanied the Queen in the Royal box at a great bull-fight that took place at the time.

He returned to Paris in November and again saw the King and Queen at Saint-Cloud; then left for London the following month.

On his arrival, he was received with the most extraordinary enthusiasm, and was frequently embraced by the crowds of women who thronged to the Egyptian Hall to see him. It is said that in England alone he was kissed by at least a million females, an ordeal in itself, but Tom Thumb took it all with equanimity.

He now made several additions to his repertoire, posing as Cupid with wings and bow; Samson carrying off the gates of Gaza; the fighting gladiator; the slave whetting the knife; Ajax; Discobulus and Hercules; as well as appearing in his impersonations of Napoleon and Frederick the Great.

In 1846, Albert Smith wrote a play for him called *Hop o' my Thumb*, which was produced first at the Lyceum and afterwards at the City of London Theatre. It proved a great success, and drew crowds of children as well as adults, to see the little man's really funny performance in the title-rôle. He went on tour with the play through the provinces, and then to Scotland and Ireland, and his receipts are said to have amounted to £150,000.

He returned to America in 1847, where he married a dwarf called Miss Warren. In November 1864 he again came to London, accompanied by his wife and two other dwarfs known as Commodore Nutt and his sister-in-law, Miss Minnie Warren. The four appeared at St. James's Hall in Piccadilly, and afterwards toured through the provinces.

Although Tom Thumb had now amassed considerable wealth, Barnum says he had become very miserly, except when spending money on himself.

"In some things he was most extravagant and bought a steam yacht, fast horses and a good deal of jewellery, for which he had little use. He loved to play childish tricks and had a great liking for diamonds and other precious stones which he was fond of handling.

His last visit to England was in 1878, when he had aged considerably. On his return to America he retired into private life, and lived on the large fortune he had acquired mainly on his European tours.

About four years after Tom Thumb's first visit to London, a Dutch dwarf named Jan Hannema, who was popularly known as "Admiral van Tromp", was exhibited at the Cosmorama Rooms in Regent Street.

He was born at Fruneker in Friesland about 1839, and when he came to London was nearly ten years of age. His height was 23½ inches, being 3 inches shorter than Tom Thumb, and his weight 16 pounds. It is said he had not increased in height or weight since he was nine months old. He was of fair complexion, with ruddy cheeks and blue eyes, and is said to have been well-formed, intelligent and vivacious.

The King of Holland had granted him a small pension, and he was shown in London to Queen Victoria, Prince Albert and the Duchess of Kent. His performance was also patronized by the Duke and Duchess of Cambridge, the Princess Mary and the Duchess of Gloucester.

His chief impersonation was that of the famous Admiral van Tromp, and arrayed in naval uniform, with a telescope under his arm, he would march about flourishing a sword, as if commanding a ship. He also represented a Dutch burgomaster, smoked a long pipe, marched, sang and danced. He could fence and play cards, and was very fond of music. He remained in London for nearly two years and attracted crowds of people.

In 1853, two diminutive children called the Aztecs were brought to London and excited a great deal of curiosity. The boy was called Maximo and the girl Bartola, and both were under 34 inches in height. They were said to have been discovered in some mysterious and unknown city in Central America, and were believed to be descendants of the ancient Aztec race.

They were exhibited at the Hanover Square Rooms and the Adelaide Gallery and attracted many visitors, but investigation showed that the story was a fiction and that they were merely children of arrested growth. Professor Owen, who examined them, stated that they were dwarf specimens of some race, probably South American, with a mixture of European blood.

Dr. Carl Scherzer, who investigated the case, declared that "they were twin children of a man called Burgos and Espina his wife, living in the village of Decora in St. Salvador.

They were dwarfish and idiotic at their birth. A Spanish trader had got possession of them and sold them to an American who had brought them to Europe."

In appearance they were certainly extraordinary. They had small but long heads with little or no chins, and their deformity was exaggerated by an enormous bunch of black hair, which they each wore at the back of their heads. They had an utter lack of intelligence and were little better than idiots.

In 1867 it was announced that they had been married to each other at a Registrar's office in London, and the wedding was followed by an elaborate breakfast, which was given in Willis's Rooms.

The last dwarf who held an office at the French Court was named Richebourg, who died in the Rue du Four in Paris in 1858. He is said to have been ninety years of age, and was in the service of the Duchess of Orleans, mother of King Louis Philippe, with the title of butler, although he performed none of the duties of the calling. He was 23½ inches in height, and after the first revolution broke out, it is said that he was employed to convey dispatches abroad disguised as a baby-in-arms, the documents being concealed in his cap. He lived in the Rue du Four the last twenty-five years of his life and never ventured outside the door.

It was stated that the Orleans family allowed him a pension of three thousand francs a year, but he lived in the strictest seclusion and was only seen by his family.

CHAPTER XXX

DWARFS AT BARTHOLOMEW FAIR—A CURIOUS
GATHERING

THE exhibition of abnormal creatures, both human and
animal, at country fairs, goes back to a period of over
three centuries at least, and on such occasions dwarfs always
appear to have formed a great attraction.

Hone, who visited Bartholomew Fair on September 5,
1825, tells us that he saw a considerable number there,
including Lydia Walpole, who was 2 feet 11 inches high;
an Indian dwarf, the "Little old woman of Bagdad", who
was 30 inches high; William Phillips of Denbigh, a Welsh
dwarf in military uniform about 3 feet high; a "Dwarf
Family", the reputed father of which, Thomas Day, was
35 inches high; a dwarf boy of six, who was 27 inches high,
and several others.

Here he also saw that "Wonder of Nature", a girl above
fifteen years of age born in Cheshire, who was not much
above eighteen inches long. "She never had a perfect bone
in any part of her, onely the head, yet she hath all her
senses to admiration and discourses, reads very well, sings
and whistles and all very pleasant to hear."

According to her bill, already mentioned, she was afterwards to be seen at "Mr. Croomes at the signe of the
'Shooe and Slap', neer the Hospital-gate in West Smithfield."

Thus, when Barnum, who was a born showman, gathered
a number of abnormal people into what he called his
Museum in New York about the middle of the last century,
he was but carrying out the old custom of attracting the
curious to his show.

Many will recall the extraordinary gathering of what he
called "freaks", that he brought with him when he trans-
ported his show for the first time to London in 1899. The
name "freaks" thus applied was objected to in this country,
and after their arrival, at two meetings held by them in
protest, they decided on the suggestion of Canon Wilberforce,

of Westminster, that they should in future be called "prodigies".

This curious gathering included Hassan Ali, an Egyptian giant, who was 7 feet 11 inches high. His hand was 12 inches long and his foot 26 inches. He was 23 years of age at the time and was born at Siwah-Amous in Egypt. He was married to a girl of fourteen years of age in Cairo who was 6 feet high. He smoked about seventy cigarettes a day and was said to consume two bottles of whisky in the twelve hours. When travelling, two beds placed together, measuring 9 feet by 5 feet, made him a comfortable resting-place. There was also Khusania, a Hindu dwarf who was born at Amdabad in India, who was 22 inches high and weighed 24 pounds. He was married and had a family of four children. Then there was Laloo the Hindu, to whom the arms, legs and shoulders of a parasitic body were attached, who has already been described. Charles Tripp, a man born without arms of English parentage at Woodstock in Ontario. He was of a mechanical turn of mind and wrote letters with his feet.

Among the prodigies was Annie Jones, a bearded woman, who was born in Virginia and whose hair was 6 feet long. Her beard did not grow below the edge of the jaw but was confined to her face.

There was also Billy Wells, the "hard-headed man", who allowed blocks of granite to be broken on his head by the blows of a sledge-hammer, and who, by the force generated by expanding his lungs, was said to be able to break steel chains and tear leather straps an inch and a quarter wide and three-sixteenths of an inch thick, and many other prodigies that do not concern us.

Among the dwarfs exhibited more recently were "General" and Mrs. Small, who were married at St. Bartholomew's Church and declared to be the smallest married couple in the world. The "General", whose name was Morris, was a Welshman and was 2 feet 11 inches high, while his wife was even smaller. They were still touring the country in 1895.

A company of singers known as the "Lilliputians", all of

whom were dwarfs, and who are said to have been gathered in Germany and Austria, toured through America and Europe towards the end of the last century and attracted large audiences wherever they performed.

Mention should also be made of the little French dwarf known as the Princess Topaze, who was born in Paris in 1879. She was 1 foot 11½ inches in height and weighed 14 pounds. She was perfectly formed, very intelligent and vivacious and attracted considerable attention wherever she was shown.

It is interesting to note, in studying the history of dwarfs, that in many cases nature would seem to have compensated them for their deficiency in stature, by endowing them either with great physical strength, highly intelligent brains or longevity. Many lived beyond the usual span of life, and some, as instanced in Mary Jones, the Shropshire dwarf, who was but 32 inches in height, reached the age of one hundred years.

We have endeavoured to show from existing records, that monsters have been born and lived from time to time, from a period dating back at least four thousand years, and according to traditions, persons of gigantic and diminutive stature have also existed from almost equally remote times. There appears to be no reason why the abnormal should disappear from the ranks of mankind. In any case, a short chronicle of their history from the past to the present, is not without some value and importance to those who are desirous of exploring some of the by-paths in the story of the human race.

BIBLIOGRAPHY

ACKERMANN, J.-F. Infantis androgyni historia et iconographia. Ienae, 1805.

ALDROVANDUS, ULYSSES. Opera omnia. Bononiae. 1599-1668.

ALLEN, THOMSON. Remarks on the Early Condition and Probable Origin of Double Monsters. 1844.

ANCILLON. Traité des Eunuques dans lequel on explique toutes les différentes sortes d'Eunuques, quel rang ils ont tenu, et quel cas on en a fait, etc. 1707.

ANDRY, N. Traité de la génération des vers dans le corps de l'homme. Paris, 1700.

Éclaircissements sur le livre de la Génération des vers dans le corps de l'homme. Paris, 1702.

ARISTOTELIS. Liber de mirabilibus auscultationibus explicatus a I. Beckmann, additis annotationibus varior., subjectis sub finem notulis Heynii, etc. Gottingae, 1786.

BANIER. Dissertation sur les Pygmées, par l'abbé Banier.

BARTHOLINI, T. De unicornu observationes novae. Amsterdam, 1678.

BAUHINUS, GASPARUS. De hermaphroditorum monstrorumque partium natura ex Theologorum, Jureconsultorum, Medicorum, Philosophorum et Rabbinorum sententia. Libri duo. Oppenheimii, typis Hieronymi Galleri, aere Iohan. Theod. de Bry, 1614.

BEAUBLÉ. Garçon et fille hermaphrodites. Paris, 1772.

BÉCHET, J. Essai sur les monstruosités humaines. Paris, 1829.

BÉCLARD, P.-A. Leçons orales sur les monstruosités. Paris, 1822.

BENEKE. Disquisitio de ortu et causis monstrorum. Gottingae, 1846.

BÉRARD, J. Causes de la monstruosité et autres anomalies de l'organisation humaine. Paris, 1835.

BERGER DE XIVREY, JULES. Traditions tératologiques. Paris, 1836.

BESCHRYVINGE. Korte Wonderliche. 1563.

BETBEDER. Mémoire sur un enfant monstrueux ayant deux têtes.

BIANCHI, GIAMB. Storia del monstro di due corpi, che nacque sul Pavese in giugno. 1748.

BLASIUS. Observations.

BOERHAVE, ABR.-K. Historia anatomica infantis cujus pars corporis inferior monstrosa. Petropoli, 1754.

BOIASTUAU ou BOYSTUAU, PIERRE. Histoires prodigieuses extraites de plusieurs fameux auteurs grecs et latins, par Boiastuau. Paris, 1597-98.

BOILLOT, Jos. Nouveaux pourtraitz et figures de termes pour user en l'architecture, composez et enrichiz de diversité d'animaulx representez au vray selon l'antipathie et contrariété naturelle de chacun d'iceux. 1592.

BOREL, P. De monstris.

BROCA. Sur les doctrines de la diplogénèse et discussion sur les monstres doubles. (Bull. Soc. anthr., 2e série, t. IX, 1874.)

BROOM, H., and HADLEY, E. Laws of England. London. 1869.

BROWNE, Sir THOMAS. Enquiries into vulgar and common errors. 1673.

BUFFON. Histoire naturelle générale et particulière. Paris, imprim. royale, 1749–1804.

BULWER, J. Artificial Changeling. 1653.

CAPADOSE, ABR. Dissertatio physiologica, pathologica de foetu intra foetum. Lugd. Bat., 1818.

CASSANIONE, JOAN. De gigantibus. Basileae, 1580.

CAULFIELD, J. Portraits, Memoirs and Chronicles. 1819.

CERUTTI. Descriptis Monstra. 1827.

CHARLIER. Monstre sans cerveau, par Charlier. 1865.

CHARVET. Recherches pour servir à l'histoire générale de la monstruosité. Paris, 1827.

CHIAJE, DELLE. Istoria anatomico-teratologica intorno ad una bombina rinocefala-monocola. Neapoli, 1840.

COYER, L'ABBÉ. Lettre au docteur Mathy sur les géants patagons. Bruxelles (Paris), 1767.

DARESTE, C. Recherches sur les origines de la monstruosité double chez les oiseaux. (Ann. sc. nat., 5e série, t. III.)

Mémoire sur la Tératogénie expérimentale et Communications sur les monstres doubles. (Mém. Soc. anthr., 1873–1874.)

De la Production artificielle des monstruosités, ouvrage couronné par l'Académie des Sciences. Paris, Reinwald, 1878.

DEMANGEON, Dr. J. D. Considérations physiologiques sur le pouvoir de l'imagination naturelle durant la grossesse. Paris, 1807.

DENIS, FERDINAND. Le monde enchanté. Cosmographie et histoire naturelle fantastiques du moyen âge. Paris, 1843.

DOEVEREN, G. VAN. Specimen observationum academicarum, ad monstrorum historiam, anatomen, pathologiam, et artem obstetricam praecipue spectantium. Groningae, 1765.

DORNIER, D. Description d'une miniature humaine ou Tableau historique d'une fille naine, remarquable par la petitesse de sa structure, la régularité des formes, etc., etc. Paris, 1817.

DUBE, P. Histoire de deux enfants monstres, nés dans la paroisse de Sept-Fonds, au duché de S. Fergeau, le 20 juillet 1649; par Paul Dube, docteur en médecine à Montargis. Paris, 1650.

FAUST, B.-C. Anatomische Beschreibung zweier Missgeburten, nebst einer Untersuchung der wahrscheinlichen Entstehung der Missgeburten überhaupt (Description anatomique d'un monstre, avec une dissertation sur l'origine des monstres en général). Gotha, 1780.

FORSTER, A. Die Missbildungen des Menschen systematisch dargestellt (Les monstruosités humaines exposées systématiquement). Iéna, 1861.

FREDERICI, GOTTLIEB. Monstrum humanum rarissimum. . . . Lipsiae, 1737.

GEOFFROY SAINT-HILAIRE, ÉTIENNE. Philosophie anatomique des monstruosités humaines. Paris, 1822.

GEOFFROY SAINT-HILAIRE, ISIDORE. Histoire générale et particulière des anomalies de l'organisation chez l'homme et chez les animaux, Paris, J. B. Baillière, 1832–36.

GERVAIS, HENRI. Le Monstre hétéradelphe de Vervins. Paris, Arthus Bertrand, 1877.

GIMMA, HYACINTHE. Dissertationes academicae et hominibus et animalibus fabulosis et brutorum anima et vita. Neapoli, 1714.

GOULD and PYLE. Anomalies and Curiosities of Medicine, 1897.

GRAFENBERG. Monstrorum historia memorabilis monstrosa humanorum. Francof., Becker, 1609.

GUBERNATIS, ANGELO DE. Mythologie zoologique, ou les légendes animales. Paris, 1874.

HABICOT, NICOLAS. Gygantostéologie ou discours des os d'un géant. Paris, 1613.

HIRST, B. C. Human Monsters. 1892.

HOME, EVERARD. Account of Child with Double Head. 1790.

JACOBI, SAM. Commentatio de monstris, quoad medicum forensem. Halae, 1791.

JOUARD, G., docteur en médecine. Des monstruosités et bizarreries de la nature. Paris, 1806.

JULIA DE FONTENELLE, J.-S.-EUG. Notice sur les deux jumeaux Siamois attachés ventre à ventre et sur Rita-Christina. Paris, 1829.

KAHN, J. The Heteradelpha. 1856.

KNACKSTEDT, C.-E.-H. Anatomische Beschreibung einer Missgeburt welche ohne Gehirn und Hirnschädel lebendig geboren wurde (Description anatomique d'un monstre qui naquit vivant, sans crâne ni cervelle.) Saint-Petersbourg, 1791.

KNOX, J. A. Curious Monster.

LESAUVAGE. Mémoire sur les monstruosités dites par inclusion. Caen, 1829.

LEUCKART, RUD. De monstris eorumque causis et ortu. Gottingae, 1845.

LICETUS, FORTUNIO. De monstrorum natura, causis et differentiis libri II, aeneis iconibus ornati. Patavii, 1634.

LYCOSTHENES. Prodigiorum ac ostentorum chronicon . . . adjectis rerum omnium veris imaginibus, conscriptum per Conradum Lycosthenem Rubeaquensem. Basileae, Henr. Petri, 1557.

MANUSCRIPTS. British Museum, Sloane 5220, 5253, 5246.

MECKEL, J.-F. De duplicitate monstrosâ commentarius. Halae, 1815.

MONRO, A. Description of a Monster, 1792.

OBSEQUENS, JULIUS. Prodigiorum liber, nunc demum per Conr. Lycosthenem integritati suae restitutus; Polydori Vergilii de prodigiis
libri III; Jos. Camerarii de ostentis libri II. Basileae, 1552.

OTTO, ADOLPHE. Mémoire sur six monstres humains. Francfort, 1821.
Coll. Hamy.

PALFYN. Description anatomique des parties de la femme qui servent
à la génération, avec un traité des monstres, de leurs causes, par
Licetus. Additions de monstres nouveaux et rares, tels que le
satyre indien et la *femme cornue,* description de la disposition
surprenante des parties de deux enfants joints ensemble par les
troncs. Leyde, 1708.

PANCIRILLUS, G. History of Memorable Things. 1727.

PARÉ, AMBROISE. Deux livres de chirurgie: 1° de la génération de
l'homme . . .; 2° des monstres tans terrestres que marins avec leurs
portraits, plus un petit traité des plaies faites aux parties nerveuses.
Paris, 1573.

PLANCI, JOAN. De monstris ac monstruosis quibusdam epistola. Venet.,
1749.

POISSONNIER, PIERRE. An ab origine monstra? Paris, 1743.

RIOLAN, JOAN. De monstro nato Lutetiae, anno Domini 1605, disputatio
philosophica. Parisiis, 1605.

RUBENS, J. Description of Anatomical Cyclops. 1824.

SCHENK, J. G. Monstrorum. Wunderbuch. 1610.

SCHMUCK, J. W. Fasculi. 1679.

SERRES, ET.-R.-AUG. Recherches d'anatomie transcendante et pa-
thologique, théorie des formations et des déformations organiques,
appliquées à l'anatomie, et de la Duplicité monstrueuse de Rita-
Christina. Paris, 1832.

SLUPER, J. Omnium fere gentian. 1572.

SOMMERING, S.-TH. Abbildungen und Beschreibungen einiger Missgeburten. (Figures et description de quelques monstres.) Mainz, 1791.

SORBINI, A. Tractatus de monstris. Parisiis, 1570.

SQRAEUWEN, P. Specimen. 1802.

STENGELIUS, G. De monstris et monstrosis quam mirabilis, bonus et
justus in mundo administrando sit Deus monstrantibus. Ingol-
stadii, 1647.

TARDIEU, A., et LAUGIER, M. Contribution à l'histoire des monstruosités. Paris, 1874.

TERATOLOGIA. Vols. I and II.

TORKOS. Observationes anatomico-med. de monstro bicorporeo vir-
gineo, etc., 1787.

VILLENEUVE. Description d'une monstruosité consistant en deux fœtus
humains accolés en sens inverse par le sommet de la tête. Paris, 1831.

Vincent de Beauvais, Speculum quadruplex, naturale, doctrinale, morale, historiale. Argentinae, Joannes Mentelin, 1473–1476.

Weinrich, Martin. De Ortu monstrorum commentarius, in quo essentia, differentiae, causae et affectiones explicantur. Breslae, 1596.

Werther, G.-C. Disputatio medica de monstro hungarico. Lipsiae, 1707.

Windle, B. C. Origin of Monsters.

Wood, E. J. Giants and Dwarfs. 1868.

INDEX

Acromegaly and Giantism, 156
"Admiral van Tromp", 238
Aenotherus, the giant, 132
Alypius of Alexandria, 187
'Ambroise Paré on Monsters, 49
American cozener, 98
Anak, Sons of, 131
Anakims, The, 130
Anthropophagi, 19
Antonius, the giant, 132
Arimaspi, tribe of one-eyed men, 19
Astrologers of Babylon, 25
Auguries from births, 29
Augustus, a Roman dwarf, 187
Aymon, a giant soldier, 142
Aztecs, The, 239

Babylonian monsters, 20, 25
Bamford, Edward, the giant hatter,
    214
Barbara Urselin, 202
Barnum's Museum, 241
Beggar of Anjou, 96
Benlli, the Welsh giant, 140
Bertholde—
    a dwarf Prime Minister, 194
    and the King, 194
    his adventures in Verona, 196
    his will, 197
Biddenden Maids' 33
Biddenden Maids, bequest, 34
Biddenden Maids' cakes, 34
Biffin, Miss Sarah, 75
Big Sam, 176
Bishop fish, 107
"Black Dwarf," The, 227
    and Sir Walter Scott, 228
"Black Prince" and his little Turkey
    horse, 199, 200
Blacker, Henry, English giant, 159
Blair's description of Patrick Cotter,
    172
"Bohemian Twins", 90
"Bold Grimace Spaniard", 204
Bolster, the giant, 139
Boruwlaski, Joseph—
    Polish dwarf, 215
    his career, 216

Boruwlaski, Joseph (*continued*)—
    and Bébé, 216
    described, 217
    falls in love, 217
    his marriage, 218
    in London, 218
    his travels, 218
    his concerts, 219
    and Mathews the comedian, 219
    and King George IV, 219
    and the Irish giant, 219
Boy and girl with distinct heads, 67
Boy with "Deus Meus" in his eyes, 68
Boy without legs, 58
Bradley, William, Yorkshire giant,
    177
Brice, James—
    French giant, 180
    marries an English girl, 181
"Brighton Twins", 91
Brothers Knipe, Irish giants, 171
Buchinger, Matthew, 209
    his accomplishments, 209
    his marriages, 210
    his penmanship, 210
    as a Highlander, 211
Bun-yip of Australian tribes, 18
Byrne, Charles (O'Brien)—
    Irish giant, 164
    as porter at St. James's Palace, 166
    stories of, 167
Byrne and the surgeons, 167
    his skeleton, 167
    his slippers, boots, and gloves, 168

Cajanus, Daniel, Swedish giant, 150,
    159
Caroline Crachami's skeleton, 231
Cat woman, The, 205
Catherine de' Medici and her dwarfs,
    189
Cazotte, Marc (Pepin), 77
"Certaine Secrete wonders of Na-
    ture", 45
Chang and Eng, 79
Chang Woo Gow, Chinese giant,
    181
Charles IX and his dwarfs, 188

Child with a bear growing on his back, 67
Child with a double head, 77
Child with five horns, 51
Child with two faces, 94
Child with two heads in Bavaria, 50
Child with two bodies born in England, A.D. 1552, 47
"Childe of Hale", 141
  at Brasenose College, 141
Children without heads, 41
"Changlings" or "Fairy Children", 206
Chinaman without feet, 98
Chulkhurst, Mary and Eliza, 32
Chung, Chinese dwarf, 182
Classification of monsters, 70
Clift, William, describes "The Mermaid", 112
Coan, John, Norfolk dwarf, 212
  and King George II, 213
  plays at Tunbridge Wells, 214
Colloredo, Lazarus-Joannes Baptista, 55
Conjoined-twins as distinct individuals, 124
Conjoined-twins of Weerted, 60
Conopas, Roman dwarf, 187
Coppernin, German dwarf, 214
Corinaeus, Legend of, 135
Cornish giants, 138
"Corsican Fairy", 224
Cotter, Patrick (O'Brien)—
  Irish giant, 168
  stories of, 169
  in a play at Sadlers' Wells, 171
  and the dwarf, 171
  his marriage, 171
  his night walks, 173
  his hand, 174
  his shoes, 174
  his dread of dissection, 174
  his funeral, 175
  his skeleton, 175
Counterfeiting by rascals, 97
Countess Lodoiska, Polish giantess, 181
Crachami, Caroline, the "Sicilian dwarf", 168, 230
Crafty cozeners, 96

Cyclops, 21
Daniel, giant porter to Oliver Cromwell, 145
Day, Thomas, 241
Definition of word "monster", 123
"Derby Twins", 92
Disasters following birth of monsters, 49
Discornet, 86
Divination, 26, 29
Double-headed monster of Gosmore, 72
Dumas, Blanche, 94
Duplex monsters, 125
Dutch giant in London in 1581, 142
Dwarf family, 241
"Dwarf of the World", 201
Dwarf's body disappears, 230
Dwarfs as waiters, 189
Dwarfs at Bartholomew Fair, 241
Dwarfs in Russia and Sweden, 189
Dwarfs at Viennese Court, 188
Dwarfs in Royal service, 186
Dwarfs in Turkish palaces, 190
Dwarfs kept by Roman dignitaries, 187
Dwarfs painted by great masters, 188
Dwarfs and pigmies—
  early traditions, 185
  Hindu legends, 185
  Saxon legends, 185
  made by the devil, 185

Egyptian deities, 20, 119
"Eighth great wonder of the world", 67
Eleazar, the giant, 132
Elsie and Marie, 92
Emms, The, 130
Evans, William, giant porter to King Charles I, 144
Evelyn visits "The Hairy Woman", 202
  visits the Dutch giantess, 153

Fabulous monsters as gargoyles, 120
"Fairy Child", The, 206
Family of gigantic stature, 184
Farrell, Owen, Irish dwarf, 212
Fény, Nicholas (Bébé), 220
  and the Princess Talmond, 221

Ferragus, the giant, 132
Fingall, the Irish giant, 139
  legend of, 139
Fish-boy, The, 109
"Four-eyed man of Cricklade", 21
Four-legged lady", 94
Fraudulent monstrosities, 96
"Freaks" or prodigies, 241
Freeman—
  American giant, 179
  his skeleton, 180
  plays at the Olympic Theatre, 180
Frenz, Louis, French giant, 177

Gabbaras, the giant, 132
"General Tom Thumb", 233
German giant and his wife, 152
Giant archer of the guards, 142
Giant figures in castles, 137
Giant of the "Golden Vest", 140
Giant porter to Queen Elizabeth, 143
Giant porter to King James I, 143
Giant porter to Oliver Cromwell, 145
Giant porters to King Charles I, 144
Giant of the mountains, 181
Giant on the tight-rope, 160
Giant of Trebiggan, 138
Giants' graves, 133
Giants of Trecrobben, 138
Giants—
  in mythology, 129
  in the Bible, 130
  in pasteboard, 134
  in processions, 134
  in Guildhall, 135
  in Old London, 135
  in pageants, 135
  on London Bridge, 135
  in Chester, 136
  how they were made, 136
  in Italy and Spain, 136
  in the Tower of London, 143
Giants and dwarfs assembled in Austria, 148
"Gibb Sisters", 92
Gibson, Richard, dwarf page to Charles I, 191
  famed as a painter, 191
  his marriage, 191

Gigantes, 129
Gigantic guards, 157
Gigli, Bernarto, Italian giant, 162
Giovanni and Giacomo, 85
Godeau, a French dwarf, 189
Gog and Magog, 134
Goliath, 131
Grana, The Irish giantess, 140
Grand Grenadiers, a regiment of giants, 158
Great sea-monster, 116
Great sea-monster off Greenland, 116
Grimes, John, English dwarf, 201
"Gryphons who guarded gold", 19

Hales, Robert, the Norfolk giant, 183
Hales and his gigantic family, 183
Hannema, Jan, 238
Hassan Ali, 242
Hauptman, 229
Headless people, 19
Hecate as a triple-headed monster, 120
Helen and Judith, 71
Hercules, 129
"Hervio Nono", 87, 180
"Heteradelph", 86
Holiburn of the Cairn, 139
Home, Sir Everard, gives account of double-headed child, 78
Horned women, 62
"Horrible serpent with seven heads", 102
Horton, Miss, 76
Hudson, Jeffrey, dwarf page to Charles I, 192
  his adventures, 193
  his costume, 193
  fights a duel, 193
"Hungarian Sisters", 71

Idusio and Secundilla, 132
Immense figures in Egypt, 130
"Indian King", 152
Irish giant in pantomime, 165
Irish giantess in London, 149
Irish giants, Legends of, 139
Irish giants of the XVIII century, 163-75

Jack the Giant-killer legend, 137
John Hunter and Byrne's body, 167
John Jervis, 191
John Simons of Hagbourne, 44
"Joined-twins born in England",
    1112, 34
Jones, Annie, 242
Jones, Mary, a centenarian dwarf,
    243
Jovianus, Emperor, 132
Joyce, William, a gigantic strong
    man, 154

Khusania, 242
King Arthur and the giant, 138
King of Prussia's gigantic guards, 157
King's porter and dwarf, 145
Kingston, William, 74
Kit, the dwarf, 143
Kleyser, John, 75

"La Dame à quatre jambes", 94
"Lady Morgan", 222
    her indignant letter, 223
Laloo, 93, 242
Law of monsters in England, 126
Law of monsters, Roman, 126
Leach, "The Wonderful Youth", 87,
    231
Legal action over "the mermaid",
    115
"L'homme Tronc", 87
Lilliputians, 242
"Little Farey Woman", 206
"Little man of fifty", 201
"Little old woman of Bagdad", 241
"Little Scotchman ", 201
"Little wild man", 208
"Living Colossus", 150, 160
Lolkes, Wybrand, Dutch dwarf, 226
    at the Amphitheatre, 227
"Long Lawyer", 177
    story of, 178
Lycosthenes, Conrad, 37

M'Donald, Samuel, 176
    porter at Carlton House, 176
    his great strength, 176
    his plays at the Opera House, 177
MacGrath, Cornelius, Irish giant, 163

Madame Térésa, 224
Malformations in antiquity, 28
Malone, Edmond, 151
Man-tiger, 101
Man with head growing from his
    body, 57
Man with parasitic head, 53
Man with second body, 51
Man with two bodies, 73
Man without arms, 54
Marcus Tullius, 187
Marie and Rosa Drouin, 90
Marius Maximus, 187
Martichora, 101
Martin van Buren, American giant,
    182
Mary and Ann, 92
Mary and Margaret, 92
Masks worn by African tribes, 18
Maximilian, Emperor, 132
Megrines, Johanna, 58
Men with six arms, 44
Men with tails, 22
Mermaid brought to London, 111
Mermaid declared to be a fraud, 114
Mermaid in Holland, 109
Mermen seen in the sea, 108
Middleton, John, the Lancashire
    giant, 141
Miller, Maximilian, "The Saxon
    giant", 150
Millie and Christine, 88
Miss Freeman, Scottish giantess, 178
"Miss Marian, the Queen of the
    Amazons", 183
"Miracle of Nature, 151
"Mr. Ramus", 189
Monk fish, 106
Monster brought to Rome, A.D. 1496,
    37
Monster in an egg, 51
"Monster of horrible aspect", 37
Monster of Ravenna, 49
Monster serpent seen from H.M.S.
    Daedalus, 117
Monster taken from the Tiber, 46
Monster with four arms, 43
Monster with head of a horse, 61
Monsters—
    in mythology, 17

Monsters (continued)—
in tradition, 17
as omens, 26
in ancient Rome, 30
in early Greece, 30
at Bartholomew Fair, 63
in art, 119
in Assyrian sculpture, 119
in Greek art, 119
in stone, 119
in early Christian art, 120
in Roman art, 120
represented by wood-carvers, 121
represented on armour, 112
in designs, 121
in marble and stone, 122
in tapestries, 122
of the deep, 106
Monstrous beasts, 101
Monstrous female creature, 204
Monstrous fish like a lion, 107
Monstrous hairy woman, 149
Monstrous heads on totem poles, 119
Monstrous Tartar, 149
Multiple tongues, 23
Murphy, Irish giant, 180
Musical dwarfs, 229

Negro fish, 108
"New species of man", 110

Oannes, the Fish-god, 108
Og, Gog and Magog, 143
Og, King of Bashan, 130
One-eyed people, 21
Origin of monsters, 23
"Orissa Sisters", 91

Paap, Simon, Dutch dwarf, 225
Parents put to death for fraud, 97
Paris, James du Plessis, 56, 149
Parsons, Walter, 143
Patagonian giants, Legends of, 133
Payne, Antony, a gigantic Cornish-
    man, 146
    stories of, 147
Pepys visits the Dutch giant, 153
Pepys visits the giantess, 153
Pepys visits a bearded woman, 203
Persian dwarf, 207

Personality of conjoined-twins, 123
Phillips, William, of Denbigh, 241
Philus of Cos, 187
Pigmies in Africa, 185
"Pimlico Twins", 92
Polyphemus, 129
Poro, James, 56
"Prince Gilolo", 69
Princess Topaze, 243
Prognostications from monsters, 26
Psychology of monsters, 123

Queen Elizabeth's giant porter, 143
Queen Mary's dwarf page, 191

Radica and Doadica, 91
Resemblance in dwarfs, 190
Richebourg, last dwarf at French
    Court, 240
Ritchie, David (the Black Dwarf), 227
Ritta and Christina, 84
Roman dwarfs, 186
Rosa and Josepha Blazek, 89
Rosalina and Maria, 90

St. Augustine and headless people, 32
St. Hilaire, Geoffroy, 79
"Sassari Twins", 84
Satyrs, 21
"Saxon giant", 1, 50, 159
"Scottish Brothers", 39
Sea-monster resembling a horse, 116
Sea-monster seen in 1917, 118
Sea-monster taken in Denmark, 110
Sea-monster with face of a man, 107
Sea-serpent off Scotland, 117
Sea-serpent seen from Royal Yacht,
    118
Sea-serpent tales, 116
Sea-serpents in early times, 115
"Serpent of huge bigness", 115
"Short Janetie", Dutch dwarf, 207
Siamese Twins, 79
    how they were discovered, 79
    visit to England, 80
    death of, 84
"Sicilian dwarf", 230
Sisyphus, a Roman dwarf, 187
Skinner, Robert, and his wife, 221
Small, "General", and Mrs., 242

Soldiers fight the terrible wild monster, 104
Souvray, Anne Thérèse, 221
Spanish giant, 178
Spriggans, 138
Strange case of young man with two faces, 73
Strange monster at Quiers, 51
Strange monster of Almayne, 47
Strange monster seen at Charing Cross, 66
Strange monsters in Italy, 41
Stocker, Nannette, 229
Stratton, Charles ("General Tom Thumb", 233)
Strong men, 153, 155
Strong women, 155
"Suffolk boy with bristles", 204
Swan, Anna, the "Nova Scotia giantess", 183
Swedish giant, 152

Tailed natives, 23
Tall and short men, their characteristics, 156
"Tall Briton", a Welsh giant, 157
"Tall Jacob of Sneek", 207
Tall woman, 152
Tarber, Jim, American giant, 183
"Terrible Child of Craconia", 38
"Terrible monster with human head", 103
"Terrible wild monster killed near Jerusalem", 103
"The Hairy Woman", 202
Theutobochus Rex, 133
Three-headed monsters, 54
Timothy Tuck and Thomas Tiptoe, 223
Titans, 129
"Tocci Brothers", 85
Tom Thumb—
    legend, 186
    in London, 233
    in New York, 233
    his performance, 235
    his carriage, 237

Tom Thumb (continued)—
    his marriage, 238
    plays at the Lyceum Theatre, 238
    received by Queen Victoria, 235
    and the Duke of Wellington, 235
    at Windsor Castle, 236
    his popularity, 236
    in Paris, 237
Topham, Thomas, a strong man, 155
Tripp, Charles, 242
Twins joined at the foreheads, 40, 53
Twins with joined heads of Claems, 95
Two-faced monster, 48
Two-headed man, 42
"Two-headed nightingale", 88
Two-headed woman, 41

Unicorn, "a monster of terror", 102
Ursula Dyan, 203

Valakoff, Russian dwarf, 189
    his marriage, 189
Valerius, John, 58
Violet and Daisy Hilton, 91

Walpole, Lydia, 241
"Wasserlinck Sisters", 70
Wells, Billy, 242
Wild men of the woods, 99
"Windsor Fairy", 222
Wolff, Caspar Friedrich, 70
Woman delivered of eggs, 59
"Woman with two heads, one above the other", 67
"Wonderful child from Austria", 63
"Wonder of Nature", 206, 241
"Wonder of the world", 64
"Wonderful youth", 231
Worrenburg, John, Swiss dwarf, 199
Wrath, the giant, 139

"Young Colossus", 101

Zamzummius, The, 130
"Zep", the dwarf of Tycho Brahe, 190

Slatington Library